William Henry Hadow

Studies in Modern Music

Hector Berlioz, Robert Schumann, Richard Wagner

William Henry Hadow

Studies in Modern Music
Hector Berlioz, Robert Schumann, Richard Wagner

ISBN/EAN: 9783337386238

Printed in Europe, USA, Canada, Australia, Japan

Cover: Foto ©Thomas Meinert / pixelio.de

More available books at **www.hansebooks.com**

STUDIES IN MODERN MUSIC

HECTOR BERLIOZ   ROBERT SCHUMANN

RICHARD WAGNER

BY

W. H. HADOW, M.A.

Fellow of Worcester College, Oxford

With Portraits

NEW YORK

MACMILLAN AND CO.

1893

Dedicated
TO
C. HUBERT H. PARRY

NOTE

THE writer wishes to express his indebtedness to the following works :—

Sir George Grove—'Dictionary of Music and Musicians,' particularly Dr Spitta's article on Schumann, and Mr Dannreuther's on Wagner.

Dr Parry—' Studies of the Great Composers.'

Berlioz—' Mémoires' (including the Voyage Musical) Letters, edited by M. Bernard. 'À Travers Chants,' 'Grotesques de la Musique.' 'Soirées d'Orchestre.'

' Berlioz,' by M. Jullien.

Schumann—'Gesammelte Schriften,' edited by Dr Simon (Weltbibliothek, 3 vols.); ' Letters,' translated by Miss Herbert. ' Music and Musicians ' (selections from the Neue Zeitschrift Essays, translated by Miss Ritter. 2 vols.).

'Schumann, Eine Biographie,' by Herr Wasielewski.

'Schumann.' by Dr Reissmann, translated by Mr Alger, (Bohn).

'Schumann,' by Mr J. A. Fuller-Maitland. (Great Musicians Series).

Wagner—'Gesammelte Schriften' (10 vols. Leipsic 1871-1883)*; 'Letters to Liszt,' translated by Dr Hueffer; 'Letters to Dresden Friends,' translated by Mr J. S. Shedlock.

'Richard Wagner's Leben und Wirken,' by Herr Glasenapp.

'Richard Wagner d'après lui-même,' by M. Noufflard (vol. 1.).

'Wagner,' by M. Jullien.

'Wagner as I knew him,' by Dr Praeger.

'Wagner,' by Herr Muncker, translated by Herr D. Landmann.

'Wagner en Caricatures,' by M. Grand-Carteret

Wagner—'Musiciens, Poètes, et Philosophes,' by M. Camille Benoit.

'Le Wagnerisme hors d'Allemagne,' by M. Evenepoel.

---

* A detailed table of contents will be found in the article on Wagner in Grove's Dictionary. The essays are in process of translation by Mr Ashton Ellis; while those on 'The Music of the Future,' on 'Beethoven,' and on 'Conducting,' have already been translated by Mr Dannreuther.

CONTENTS

MUSIC AND MUSICAL CRITICISM: A DISCOURSE ON METHOD

CHAP.		PAGE
I.—THE CONDITIONS OF THE PROBLEM,	. .	3
II.—PRINCIPLES OF MUSICAL JUDGMENT,	. .	22
III.—PRINCIPLES OF MUSICAL JUDGMENT—*CONTINUED*,		39
IV.— ECURUS JUDICAT ORBIS, . . .	.	55

HECTOR BERLIOZ AND THE FRENCH ROMANTIC MOVEMENT

I. —STUDENT DAYS, . . .	.	71
II.—THE SIEGE OF PARIS, . . .	.	94
III.—ESTIMATES AND APPRECIATIONS, . . .	.	124

ROBERT SCHUMANN AND THE ROMANTIC MOVEMENT IN GERMANY

I.—THE BEGINNINGS OF A CAREER, .	.	149
II.—MARRIED LIFE, ...	.	173
III.—SCHUMANN AS COMPOSER AND CRITIC,	.	199

RICHARD WAGNER AND THE REFORM OF THE OPERA

I.—A STRUGGLE FOR EXISTENCE,	. .	235
II.—ART AND REVOLUTION, . .	.	263
III.—THE IMPORT OF THE MUSIC-DRAMA,		298

INDEX,	.	327

LIST OF ILLUSTRATIONS

	PAGE
HECTOR BERLIOZ, *from a photograph*, . .	*Frontispiece*
HENRIETTA SMITHSON, *from a portrait by* DUBUFE, .	85
CLARA WIECK, *from a lithograph by* F. GIERE, . .	154
ROBERT SCHUMANN, *from a daguerreotype*, . .	174
RICHARD WAGNER, *from a portrait by* C. JÄGER, . .	240

MUSIC AND MUSICAL CRITICISM

A DISCOURSE ON METHOD

Sur les objets dont on se propose l'étude il faut chercher non pas les opinions d'autrui, ou ses propres conjectures, mais ce que l'on peut voir clairement avec évidence, ou déduire avec certitude: car la science ne s'acquiert pas autrement.

DESCARTES : *Règles pour la direction de l'esprit.*

Music and Musical Criticism

A DISCOURSE ON METHOD

I

THE CONDITIONS OF THE PROBLEM

IT has often been observed, in various tones of reproach or protest, that we are all growing into a practice of accepting any statement that we hear frequently or authoritatively repeated. From our systems of government and philosophy down to the advertisements in our daily papers everything bears witness to a policy of reiteration. We are, indeed, inclined to be suspicious of new ideas, especially those of unknown origin or authorship : in dealing with any proposition we like, above all things, to know who framed it, and how many people believe it to be true. But if we are satisfied on these points, if we can see the image and superscription of some recognised potentate, and feel the edges smooth with the usage of many hands, we scruple no longer, but take the assertion for sterling, without examining its reverse side or testing the genuineness of its ring. Hence we are at the mercy of our great men, without even the materials for determining a definition of greatness, and with the risk, if they fail us, of falling into that most hopeless form of poverty which consists in a pocketful of counterfeit coin.

Amid the false currency that has thus been brought into circulation is a belief that perception of the beautiful requires not only special training but certain rare and precious qualities as well. We are always hearing of pictures that are 'not intended for the common gaze,' or of poems which are 'not written with any design of pleasing the public,' until we begin to think that we are outsiders and profane persons who have no right to admire, much less to appraise and criticise. We have been, as Blake puts it, 'connoisseured out of our senses,' browbeaten out of all reliance on our own judgment, and driven at last to the comfortless conclusion that all our ideas of beauty are heretical, and that the only true faith is expressed in the warring voices of our æsthetic cliques.

This doctrine is all the more dangerous because of the half-truth that it contains. No doubt popularity may mean nothing. It may be merely the idle applause of an ignorant mob, ready to burn to-morrow what it adores to-day. But, on the other hand, popularity may mean everything. There is no permanent reputation which has not been built on the suffrages of the people—no lasting Palace of Art which has not national feeling for its corner-stone. The love of beauty, in short, is not the monopoly of a privileged class—it is the universal inheritance of all mankind. And while this is true of every art it is particularly true of Music. The laws by which effects of tone are conditioned have as wide a scope as any principles in human thought, and draw their validity from the most fundamental characteristics of our common nature.

Music and Musical Criticism 5

Evidence lies ready to hand in the whole history and record of national melodies. Mozart himself never wrote a finer tune than 'Ye banks and braes' or 'Dear Kitty'; the Volkslieder of Germany and Russia, of France and Italy, of Hungary and Scandinavia, contain gems of purest lustre and inestimable value; Troubadours and Trouvères were writing delightful songs while the accredited professors of the art were quarrelling over tritones; wherever the voice of the people has found free expression there we have a living spring of beauty, a fountain of melodious waters at which generations have slaked their thirst. Undoubtedly the gradual elaboration of scientific rule has been of conspicuous service in musical training, but it has nothing whatever to do with musical inspiration; undoubtedly a misdirection of popular taste has often made a bad tune fashionable, but it has never made one immortal. Time passes, true feeling reasserts itself and the false art vanishes into oblivion : while the songs of the people remain as fresh as when they were created. Nor, as a rule, have these melodies owed their birth to the genius of some celebrated musician; on the contrary, they have sprung from the very heart of the nations that cherish them. In some cases the Composer was an amateur, like Count Rakócky or Martin Luther; in a far larger number he is absolutely unknown; some peasant-bard who lived and died in obscurity, with no reward of fame for the priceless gift that he was bestowing on mankind.

To advance this contention is, of course, to join direct issue with Berlioz's famous statement that Music is not made for all, and that a large number of men must always remain outside the range of its influence. But if the matter come to a conflict of authorities, there is Wagner to set against Berlioz, and Shakespeare to overtop them both, and the popular side has no lack of advocates. It is of more moment to examine the brief, and consider the arguments on which this democratic theory may be supported.

All Art aims at the presentation of an idea of beauty in accordance with certain formal laws. These formal laws, though they differ somewhat, according to the medium employed, yet rest on a common æsthetic basis, and appeal, through the different senses, to a common action of the æsthetic faculty. Pure beauty of colour affects the eye in much the same way as pure beauty of tone affects the ear, and both together derive the pleasure that they afford from certain psychological conditions which belong to all the Arts alike. But if we have to consider the nature of the idea presented we shall find that there is one fundamental distinction which separates off Music from all the so-called 'Representative Arts' in a body. It may be expressed briefly as follows: Painting, Sculpture, and Poetry, apart from the media which they employ, necessarily involve some reference to Nature—Music does not. The three former Arts are in a sense dependent for their subjects on material phenomena external to the artist, the latter requires only the bare fact of sound which serves as its medium. So far as relates to its subject, Music could exist if there were no world of Nature at all.

The distinction will be made clearer if we take the Arts in detail. Painting, for instance, whether we hold with Schopenhauer that it is ultimately ideal, or with Plato that it is a mere copy of objects in Nature, we cannot regard as possible without the existence of natural phenomena. However abstract the idea which the Painter has conceived, it requires a concrete fact round which to crystallise before it can be presented in the artistic product. The Dresden Madonna may not be a 'copy' of a beautiful woman, but unless there were beautiful women it could never have been painted. Turner saw in landscape truths so magnificent that they blinded his weak-eyed critics, but to phrase them in language that men should understand he required that there should be the sunset, and the sea, and the long golden haze in the valley. Even a painter whose avowed aim is to 'bring about a certain harmony of colour' must found that harmony on a material keynote, and must fashion his exquisite nocturnes round the piers of Battersea Bridge or along the vague shadows of Chelsea Reach. A picture, in short, presupposes a model, and can be estimated in some degree by the fidelity with which the characteristics of that model are reproduced.

Sculpture is more abstract than Painting, since it is more restricted both in subject and in treatment, leaving out the important fact of colour, and trusting for its effect mainly to graciousness of line and pose. But it is obvious that, however much the Sculptor idealises his facts, he cannot dispense with them altogether. The Farnese Hercules would be unintelligible and unmeaning if there were not thews and muscles to be observed in man. The Venus of Praxiteles was not, as we know, a portrait of the goddess, but even as a 'guess' it must have had some data to work upon. Of course the element of abstract beauty is supreme in Sculpture as it is in

Painting, but it is to be found in the representation and treatment of its material subjects, not in their invention or creation. Arts which appeal to the eye may partly improve Nature, as Aristotle says, but there can be no doubt that they partly copy her.

To this rule an exception may perhaps be urged in regard of decorative art : the curves of metal work or the columns and traceries of Architecture. And, indeed, it is true that the art of decoration is only partly representative. Some of its effects are certainly drawn from originals of leaf and tendril, of sloping rock and basalt pillar, and so far it is concrete in subject and bears analogy to Painting and Sculpture. But some are, with equal certainty, expressions of pure beauty in line, and so far it is abstract and bears analogy to Music. Thus, to avoid obscuring the issue, it will be best to omit decoration altogether. The contrast is between Music and the representative Arts : if, then, there be a form of decoration which is presentative and direct, that form lies outside the limits of the question.

The Poet stands on a somewhat different level, since his depiction of his subject makes its direct appeal not to the eye but to the imagination. Yet, in his work also, there is a distinctly material factor. We may not accept the definition which declares Poetry to be a criticism of life, but there is no paradox in inverting the phrase and holding life to be, on one side, a criticism of Poetry. For what we call poetic genius is either the intuition of ideas to which the apprehension of the reader will conform, in which case experience is the test of its truth, or it is a magical power of combination, in which case experience is the test of its possibility. No doubt, as Schopenhauer insists, Shakespeare did not draw his characters from life, but life has to supply us with the facts through which alone we can recognise them as human. Even seers like Shelley or Blake, whose thought is farthest removed from our everyday prosaic world, were yet compelled to weave their imagery from the rainbow, and the storm-cloud, and the leaping flame. Take away from Poetry the material facts of Nature and life and there would be nothing left but melodious nonsense.

In all the representative Arts, then, we may notice two aspects: the formal, through which we are presented with pure beauty of colour and line, or pure melody of verse; and the material, in which those formal laws are directed towards the reproduction or combination of certain facts in the phenomenal universe. But in Music the distinction vanishes altogether. The material side is not subordinated to the formal, but completely absorbed in it: and the whole work of the Art is either the pure presentation of abstract Beauty, as in so-called 'Classical' Music, or the suggestion of Beauty tinged with emotion as in the so-called 'Romantic' school. There have, of course, been attempts to make Music reproduce actual sounds, and even actual sights in Nature—the birds in the *Pastoral Symphony*, or the hailstones of the *Israel in Egypt*—but they are always failures, which at best do not bear the same relation to their originals as a fine picture or poem does to its subject. The song, the fugue, the sonata have absolutely no analogues in the world of Nature. Their basis is psychological, not physical, and in them the artist is in direct touch with his idea, and presents it to us, as it were, at first hand. Given sound as the plastic medium, Music asks nothing more : it creates its subjects by the spontaneous activity of the mind. And thus, as Abt Vogler says, in the noblest words that have ever been uttered in its praise :—

Here is the finger of God, a flash of the will that can,
    Existent behind all laws, that made them, and lo ! they are.
And I know not if, save in this, such gift be allowed to man
    That out of three sounds he frame not a fourth sound but a star.
Consider it well, each tone of our scale in itself is nought,
    It is everywhere in the world, loud, soft, and all is said.
Give it to me to use : I mix it with two in my thought
    And—there ! Ye have heard and seen. Consider and bow the head.

Three results follow from this distinction between Music and the representative Arts. First, that musical criticism is pre-eminently difficult to express with clearness or certainty. Language has been so much framed in relation to external Nature that it finds itself at a loss in dealing with conceptions which have no correlatives in the world of phenomena. Again, there are certain obvious details in which the skill of Painter or Sculptor can be estimated by comparison with the model that he has employed. Everybody knows what is meant by saying that a picture is out of drawing, or that a statue is anatomically incorrect, and though such criticisms attach themselves to the body of the work rather than its soul, yet the body must be sound if the soul is to be perfect. But Music is by its very nature precluded from such judgments of comparison, and must attempt to formulate its laws with no aid from outside, and without even the nomenclature requisite for the purpose. Thus it is compelled to fall back upon technical terms, which the reader passes by as unintelligible, or metaphors of 'curve' and 'rhyme,' which he is apt to resent as an intrusion. No doubt other Arts have their special terminology—it is not, for instance, very serviceable to the plain man to be told that the handling of a picture is tight—but the obscurity which is a sign of weakness in the one case is almost a matter of necessity in the other. Or, worse still, the critic takes refuge in dogmatism, and roundly asserts that such and such a piece of work is 'good' or 'bad,' without giving any reasons at all. The inevitable consequence is that the public grows bewildered, impatient, and finally washes its hands of the whole matter. Something at least would be gained if we would take the trouble to understand those technical names which express simple matters of fact, such as 'inversion,' or 'coda,' or 'diminished seventh,' and if our guides would endeavour to explain the principles in accordance with which their judgments are framed. Only then will musical criticism be preserved from the spectacle, too common at the present day, of an imperious preacher haranguing an inattentive audience.

Secondly, Music is of all Arts the most nearly universal in its appeal. The difficulty of expressing its effects in actual word depends upon the 'patrii sermonis egestas,' and leaves untouched any question of their reality or of the range of their influence. Men may perfectly well agree to find in certain tunes the highest embodiment of melodic form without having a common vocabulary of admiration. And in this case alone does the artist stand face to face with his public. There is no intermediary of material fact, no landscape to be painted, no heroic deed to be described; it is 'simple beauty and nought else' which the one communicates to the other, and beauty, moreover, which depends upon psychological conditions common to both. 'From the heart it has come, and to the heart it shall penetrate,' wrote Beethoven on the Mass in D, and all true Music may take these words for its maxim.

Thirdly, no law of Musical Science is to be taken as final. It has validity for the age that obeys it, but it may always be superseded by some greater law in the age to come. To regard the rules of Harmony and Counterpoint as eternal verities is to miss the most obvious lesson in all musical history and tradition. They are, no doubt, binding on us until we can find something better; they claim our loyal allegiance while their dynasty is on the throne. But Music is full of bloodless revolutions, and will see many more before its close. There was a time when men's ears had not grown accustomed to bear the interval of a major third: now no triad is complete without it. There was a time when the notes F and B might not be heard in succession: Beethoven gets one of the most telling effects in his greatest overture from the use of the forbidden phrase. Monteverde, Gluck, Wagner are heroes now for the very reason which made them criminals to the conservatism of their day. And in all cases it was the untutored public that accepted the innovation, while academic pedantry stood aloof and denounced the pioneer as a traitor to his cause.

This, it may be said, simply reduces the position to chaos. On the one hand we have a doctrine that man is the measure of all things, on the other a statement that musical rules are transitory in their very nature; and yet from the two we are expected to evolve a belief that there is some universal consensus, and that its verdict is conclusive. To build a house on the sand is bad enough, but it becomes hopeless when the materials are as shifting as the foundation.

The answer is not far to seek. The 'scientific' laws of Music are transitory, because they have been tentatively constructed during the gradual development of the musical faculty. No power in man is born at full growth: it begins in germ and progresses according to the particular laws that condition its nature. Hence it requires one kind of treatment at one stage, another at another, both being perfectly right and true in relation to their proper period. But there are behind these special rules certain psychological laws which seem, so far we can understand them, to be coeval with humanity itself: and these form the permanent code by which Music is to be judged. The reason why, in past ages, the critics have been so often and so disastrously at fault is that they have mistaken the transitory for the permanent, the rules of musical science for the laws of musical philosophy, and so have tried to confine the adolescent productions of their age within the restrictions that properly belonged to its predecessor. Beethoven began his first Symphony with a chord 'out of the key.' There is not the smallest reason why he should not have done so; but it was not in keeping with the style of Haydn and Mozart, and so the critics fell foul of him. Almost every Composer of genius has suffered in the same way. He has dared to break tradition and he has found himself judged, not by these fundamental laws to which alone tradition owes its value, but by those very rules which his work has helped to dismiss as obsolete. 'Your new landscape is all very well,' said a visitor to Constable's studio, 'but where are you going to put your brown tree?' There is a great deal of the brown tree in musical criticism.

But there are thousands of people who 'hate Classical Music.' If by 'Classical Music' is meant the work of all the greatest Composers indiscriminately, then there is only one reason why people should hate it, namely, that they have not heard it properly. They have sat in the room where a symphony was being performed with the preconceived notion that they were not going to understand it; they have given it an intermittent and perfunctory hearing; and they have gone away with the perfectly intelligible conviction that they were not pleased. For to listen to Music demands close and accurate attention. A tune does not remain in front of us like a picture; it comes, passes, vanishes, and, unless we have caught the tone and rhythm of its opening, there is little hopes of our following the rest. It is like missing the key word of a sentence addressed to us in some foreign language which we imperfectly understand. We lose the point of the whole: but it would be a rash inference to say that the sentence contained no meaning.

A remarkable instance of this may be quoted. M. Fétis the elder, one of the most famous of musical critics, attended a performance of the *Tannhäuser* overture when that work was new and its Composer an easy mark for invective. 'Beyond a poor, ill-harmonised chorale-tune,' he wrote, 'the object of which is to recall the style of the 13th century, there is not a single spark of melody in the whole production.' Never was a more amazing judgment delivered. The remarks about the 13th century may be set aside, they show nothing worse than a want of historical knowledge, but to have passed over Tannhäuser's song is fatal. There it stands in the middle of the allegro, a complete 32-bar tune, in as clear, perfect, and unmistakable a stanza as 'La ci darem' or 'God save the Queen.' There may be differences of opinion as to its merits. It is not, perhaps, one of those supreme efforts of genius about which no question can arise, though it has a strong, manly swing and vigour which would atone for worse faults than it possessses. But to deny its existence altogether is simply to put oneself out of court on a matter of fact, and we can only infer that M. Fétis was inattentive or preoccupied.

Hence it is that so much of the best music improves on acquaintance. At first hearing we are apt to grow puzzled, to miss the significance of the phrases and their relation to one another, to feel ourselves in a labyrinth of beauty through which we have no certain clue. It is only when the work becomes more familiar that we recognise the landmarks and trace the outlines of the plan. No doubt training will do much, but the most keen and cultivated ear may often find itself baffled by the intricacies of a new sonata or a new symphony, and even though it learns something from a single presentation, will learn more if the presentation be repeated. This is especially true of the Modern Schools of composition. Haydn and Mozart wrote on simpler lines. Their structures are more transparent, more readily intelligible, and they both have a habit of isolating their melodies which arrests the attention at once and keeps it fixed. No one has any doubt about the tunes in a Mozart sonata. They lie clear and separate, like diamonds in a jeweller's case, with just enough cotton-velvet between to show their contour and enhance their sparkle. The tunes in a sonata of Brahms are quite as beautiful, but most of us require to hear the composition two or three times before we can fully ascertain their value. Modern Composers, in short, take greater trouble about the setting of the stones, and thus their work requires more careful examination.

There will always be preferences in Music, for absolute catholicity of taste is an ideal to which very few can attain, and the question is complicated by numberless conditions of personal feeling and personal association. Again, we have no more right to demand complete perfection from any Composer than from any Painter or Poet. We must expect some bad work to be mingled with the good, some faults to qualify the merits, provided we realise that the whole man is on a greater scale than ourselves, and that his imperfections may justify us in transferring our sympathy but not in withholding our admiration. One hearer may be more in touch with the sunny serenity of Handel than with the sombre majesty of Brahms; another may feel his blood stirred by Schumann's 'march-music' and remain comparatively cold to the feminine grace and finish of Mendelssohn, but they are not thereby prevented from admitting that all alike are great artists. The difference between true and false art is the difference between food and poison. We may keep that distinction intact without surrendering our right to choose one dish of food rather than another.

So far, then, the upshot is as follows. The test of good music is to be found not in its subservience to formal or arbitrary rules, but in its capacity for satisfying an almost universal requirement in human nature. Subservience to rule is in many cases a means by which Music can attain this end, but it is not an end in itself. Thus the grounds on which our criticism should rest are psychological. To explain the æsthetic basis of Music by mathematical formulæ is even more hopeless than the attempt to derive our scale from the Harmonic Series : and it therefore remains to determine, as far as possible, the broad general principles which we all implicitly recognise as constituting the artistic code. These principles exist unformulated in the mind of every man who prefers one tune to another ; and the sole cause why bad art has ever attained any vogue or fashion is that insufficient attention has been paid to the shape in which it is expressed. Sometimes a song with a poor or vulgar melody has attained some degree of popularity by reason of its words ; sometimes the personal position or influence of a second-rate Composer has elevated his work for the moment into a higher rank, but these forces are extrinsic and their effects ephemeral. If Music be judged fairly and clearly on its own merits, there is never any fear about the verdict.

The object of these principles is to constitute a kind of *Jus Naturale*, a tribunal to which every style may be brought for equitable judgment. Hence, before attempting to codify them, it will be advisable to say a preliminary word on style, with special reference to its historical conditions, since it is on our view of these that our estimate must in a great degree depend.

All Art, before it reaches maturity, passes through two stages, which may roughly be labelled the Classical and the Romantic.¹ In the first, which belongs to its infancy, the rules of style are to a great extent determined by *a priori* laws and traditions, whether created by some master of commanding genius or evolved by the common action of lesser men. In the second there is something of a revolt against tradition, and each artist becomes a law to himself. After the appearance of Romanticism we may have either a renascence of Classical feeling, much altered and modified by the new conditions, or further developments of Romance, or a combination of the two. No doubt at the line of demarcation the styles run into each other, but to declare the distinction invalidated by this fact would be like denying that blue and green are separate colours in the rainbow. All evolution proceeds by regular gradations, and marks each point of departure by the production of indeterminate physical forms.

Instances are not far to seek. The transition as regards Painting and Sculpture has been analysed once for all in Browning's 'Old Pictures in Florence,' where Greek Art teaches us to submit, and Modern to respect ourselves. In the drama we have the Aristotelean unities to mark the Classical School, and the unrestricted display of human passions to exemplify the Romantic. Even in such details as rhythm and metre the distinction holds good. The stately Alexandrines of the Louis XIV. poets form as strong a contrast to the rush and vigour of Victor Hugo as Pope's Palladian couplets, to the untrammelled luxuriance of Keats and Shelley. Heine,

---

¹ Realism is purposely omitted, for Art, so far as it becomes Realist ceases to be artistic. The modern 'naturalist' school of fiction, fo example, *quâ* naturalist, belongs to the domain of science.

Swinburne, Banville, considered as masters of versification alone, would have been quite impossible a century before their time. Now we have Walt Whitman, and nothing is impossible any more.

So it is with Music. From the 16th century to the latter part of the 18th it was dominated by the Classical traditions of counterpoint, and all Composers, except a few revolutionaries like Gluck and Monteverde, regulated their work more or less by the rigid system of the Church. No doubt they retained their individualities: Handel does not write like Bach, or Scarlatti like Rameau, but the styles, though different in feature, were all dressed in a common garb. Beethoven may be said, in a sense, to mark the point of departure; but Beethoven, like Shakespeare, is outside any system of classification. At any rate in the present century we have a school which

> To cries of 'Greek Art and what more wish you?'
> Replies, 'To become now self-acquainters,
> And paint Man, Man, whatever the issue.'

The ideal remains the same, but, instead of the laws of its expression being referred to certain absolutist maxims of musical science, the individual is allowed an entirely free hand, and may write in what style he chooses, provided he justify it by his success. 'Nothing is wrong in Music,' says Schumann, 'which sounds right.'

This assertion of liberty, which is the watchword of Romanticism, is the necessary condition of musical progress. The great masters of counterpoint have said all that there is to say in their style, and it would therefore be idle to uphold it as a fit means of expression at the present day. It has the same educational value that it has always possessed, but its value is now only educational, unless, indeed, the name be extended to cover all forms of polyphonic writing. 'Free counterpoint' simply means polyphony, and had much better be known by that title; otherwise the student is confronted by two treatises, both professing to deal with the same branch of his art, and one filled with prohibitions which the other teaches him to defy. And further, while polyphony is flexible enough to allow unhampered play of individual character, counterpoint, in the proper sense of the term, is rigid and narrow, confining the artist within restrictions as hard as a mediæval coat of mail. Once the armour was necessitated by the manner of warfare, and there was some merit, too, in wearing it with a grace, and in striking one's blow with the least possible sense of constraint or impediment. Now, like the guardsman at Waterloo, our artists prefer to 'fight in their shirt sleeves,' and there is no doubt that they have chosen wisely. Only, it seems a little unscientific to apply the same title to two systems which are so entirely different in aim and method.

However, whether our part-writing be called contrapuntal or not, there is no doubt about its being free; and the same is true with regard to the development of other musical forms. The sonata is still as Beethoven left it, but that is because its rules are liberal enough to admit of almost infinite possibilities of obedience. If those possibilities are ever exhausted the sonata will become as obsolete as the madrigal. Songs are no longer written of necessity in accordance with a stereotyped pattern; opera is no longer subject to the old conventions, or oratorio to the old limitations; Chopin and Liszt have extended the range of pianoforte music; Berlioz, Schumann, and Dvořák have developed the overture, until we are almost in danger of under-estimating subservience and mistaking the eccentric for the original. And this brings us, at last, to the main point and purpose of the present essay: the attempt to determine those deeper laws which underlie the distinctions of Classical and Romantic, of counterpoint and polyphony; those permanent principles of criticism which may enable us to discriminate good from bad without any reference to 'system' or school, and with as little appeal as possible to the technicalities of the Art. That these principles should appear obvious or commonplace is, of course, their highest praise: for it will merely prove the contention that they are implicitly accepted by all men. Whether they succeed or fail in their object is a matter which the reader must decide for himself. At least this much may be urged, that they are in accord with the general practice of the great masters, and that the chief examples of erroneous judgment in Music have arisen from their neglect.

II

PRINCIPLES OF MUSICAL JUDGMENT

FIRST, and most essential, is the Principle of Vitality. The Composer, in one word, must be the parent of his ideas, not their fabricator. In the truest Art the thought is conceived spontaneously, by a single creative impulse, and though the artist may spend much subsequent labour upon its development or presentation, yet the labour is but the nurture and training of the living thing, not the birth-pang that gives it life. Socrates could learn nothing from the Athenian Poets as to their method of production: 'They seemed,' he says, 'to write by a divine madness and enthusiasm.' Goethe could give no account of his Torquato Tasso except that it was 'bone of his bone and flesh of his flesh.' And if we consider the white heat at which Shelley wrote, or Blake painted, or Schubert composed, we shall realise that there is something unconscious, something almost passive in the attitude of genius towards the idea that it expresses. The creative faculty, in short, is intuitive, not ratiocinative.

This by no means precludes the other factor in the case—the necessity of skill and trouble in the phrasing of the thought, and still more in its extension and treatment. Beethoven, as is well known, often tried three or four versions of a theme before he found the particular shape that suited him; but those versions were simply successive embodiments of an idea that was true and vital from the beginning. Again, in an elaborate and complicated work like a symphony or a sonata, there are many occasions for the use of judgment or selection, or other deliberative faculties, but their function is entirely subordinate to the original intuition, from the results of which alone they obtain their credentials. The Athenian Poets who answered Socrates so ill knew that there were certain laws of form to which their tragedies were subject; and knew also that no analysis of those laws could ever reveal the difference between work that was first-rate and work that was not. No doubt all artists, by long practice in their craft, acquire such facility of expression that they can at any time produce something; no doubt, also, a few yield to the temptation, and vex the world with pot-boilers and *pièces d'occasion*: but in so doing they manifestly offer an unworthy gift, and receive in exchange a transitory reward. 'If poems do not possess life,' as the shades of Landor's critics told Plato, 'it would be but a paradox to accredit them with immortality.'

The distinction, after all, is readily enough admitted in the other Arts. Everyone recognises that there is a difference between poetry and verse, and that the difference resides not in the skill of rhyme or phrase, but in the vitality and depth of thought. It is precisely the same with Music. In a perfect scheme of criticism, compositions could be arranged into two classes, of which the second resembles the first as little as a clockwork automaton resembles a man.

So far this may seem to deal with the matter exclusively from the Composer's point of view. He will know whether he is being carried away under the stress of inspiration, or is 'beating his music out' with no higher object than to make his name, and fill his pockets, but how is the world at large to decide? What is this vitality, and how are we to discover its presence? Life in the physical world implies certain definite characteristics by which it can be determined: if, then, 'life' in the artistic world be anything more than an empty metaphor, it must also have marks or qualities sufficient to ensure its recognition. It would merely insult the reader to make the whole difference between true and false Art depend on a principle of which no account can be given.

Now in the physical world it is impossible to define life. We can tell that it is not expressible in terms of chemistry, for living and dead protoplasm are chemically identical, and we are therefore driven to the conclusion that it is an original simple faculty incapable of analysis. But at the same time we have fairly accurate tests for determining its presence. The distinction between organic and inorganic holds good, and science has little difficulty in observing these broad lines of classification. In other words, though we cannot tell what life is, we know enough about its phenomena to make our distinction of 'living' and 'not living' reasonably secure. Similarly it may be impossible in the artistic world to give a logical definition of vitality, but there is no difficulty in supplying a test by which we can detect it. A work of Art is living if it bears throughout the impress of its maker's personality: it is dead if we can trace its true inspiration to an external source.

Every artist has his own manner of thought, and no two artistic characters are alike. If, then, the work be really part of a man's self it will reproduce his features, it will speak with his voice. 'Originality,' says Ruskin, 'is not newness, it is genuineness.'

Thus the work of a true Composer forms one organic whole which differs essentially from that of his predecessors or his contemporaries. Even in the old contrapuntal days, when men were bound by a common method, the distinctions are real and unmistakable; much more in the freer atmosphere of the present time. Schumann, Wagner, Dvorák have as little in common with each other as Bastien-Lepage with Meissonier, or Keats with Browning. Each learns at first hand a portion of Divine truth, and, according to the measure of his capacity, translates it for our understanding. Each speaks out of the abundance of his heart, and brings us a message which it is his alone to conceive and formulate. No doubt all musicians are influenced at first by the phraseology of the times in which they work, but, except for rare instances of quotation, they employ it solely to express their own thoughts, and discard it as soon as they have reached maturity. In any case a Composer is estimated by what he creates, not by what he borrows.

In like manner the primary test of bad Art is its want of genuineness. It is deliberate, artificial, imitative, the lifeless result of forces wholly external. At best it may show the same skill of workmanship as Ausonius' cento from Virgil or the Empress Eudocia's from Homer: at worst it degenerates into a mere patchwork of incongruous phrases, gathered together without love, without intelligence, and sometimes without even the common honesty of the artisan. The ephemeral ballads and dances, which appear for a season and then vanish to their appropriate limbo, are to be condemned not because they are trivial, for there is room in Music even for triviality, but because they have nothing to say to us which has not been better said before. Our waltz writers draw upon Strauss and Chopin for their rhythms, and give us for melody half-remembered echoes of Schumann or Mendelssohn. Our compilers of ballads would indeed be in evil case if it were not for the Volkslieder and the great treasures of Song. Not that they consciously put the Classics under contribution; but having no inceptive force of imagination, they fall back upon memory as its substitute, and decorate their 'crazy quilt' with the mutilated fragments of a Master's weaving.

Music, then, to be worthy of serious regard, must stand as the outcome of its composer's character, and primarily of his original imaginative power. Now there are four ways in which a composition can recall to us the reminiscence of a previous work, and it is important that they should be classified, because on them our whole appreciation of musical plagiarism and musical vitality may be said to depend.

First, by pure coincidence. There are many phrases and cadences which represent the simplest way of saying an elementary thing, and so form a sort of common stock which Composers may employ without any reference to one another. The final bars of a movement, for instance, exhibit in many cases a form as traditional as are the ornamental epithets of the old ballads. Further, a natural thought may occur to two musicians without any suspicion of transference. The opening theme of the *Eroica* Symphony coincides with a tune from an early Operetta of Mozart, which Beethoven had probably never heard and had certainly no intention of copying. The E-flat variation of Schumann's great duet for two pianofortes contains a passage melodically identical with one in the slow movement of Beethoven's third Rasoum-offsky Quartett. The 'subject' of the chorus, 'And with his stripes,' in the *Messiah* appears also in No. 44 of Bach's *Wohltemperirte Klavier* and in the Kyrie of Mozart's *Requiem*. But all these examples prove nothing except the fact of resemblance. There is no reason for supposing that the one Composer imitated the other, for the thoughts are simple enough to have occurred to both spontaneously, and the similarity does not in any of these cases extend to the treatment. A more curious and subtle form of coincidence is found when two ideas, of a more elaborate or recondite nature, resemble each other in embodiment while differing wholly in spirit and feeling. The song 'Willst du dein Herz mir schenken' (attributed to Bach) is extraordinarily close in outline to the air for variations in Beethoven's Serenade Trio, and yet the two not only are alien from one another in character but belong to separate and distinct periods of musical development. So for a few notes the opening melody of Brahms' second Violin Sonata may recall the Preislied from *Meistersinger*, but they have really no more in common than a Botticelli has with a Tintoret. In such cases the test is to be found in the relation borne by the disputed passage to the style of the Composer who uses it on its second appearance. The tune from the Serenade Trio is pure Beethoven, and could not possibly be ascribed to any other master. The tune from the Violin Sonata is, both in thought and treatment, intensely characteristic of Brahms. In both instances the points of likeness are verbal and superficial, and the true comparison is to enumerate the points of difference.

Secondly, by quotation, that is to say, the borrowing from some previous work of a single passage or melody which is foreign to the style of the borrower. Instances of this are rare in all the imaginative Arts. We occasionally find them in Poetry, and though it may give us something of a shock to read the phrase 'most musical, most melancholy' in verse that is not of Milton, it is hard to see on what principle we should be justified in condemning its adoption by Coleridge. Sometimes, too, the Poet makes the quotation his own, as in Tennyson's exquisite adaptation of Dante in Locksley Hall, and indeed we may hold that the proceeding is always legitimate when the words have to be translated from one language to another and where the obligation can be acknowledged. In Music translation is out of the question, acknowledgment is not always possible, and thus the use of quotation is confined within even stricter limits. Still three varieties may be noticed, of which the third is by far the most important to the musical critic. The first is the employment of an existing melody as a theme on which to write original variations. Spohr in his Octett founds a movement of this nature on a rather imperfect version of Handel's 'Harmonious Blacksmith:' Chopin's famous 'Op. 2' was a set of variations on 'La ci darem:' Beethoven, Schumann, Brahms, and other Composers have similarly drawn upon the work of predecessors or contemporaries.

Here, of course, the character of the artist has abundant opportunity of manifesting itself, especially in these modern days when variations are rather independent studies of the theme than embroideries of its texture. But at the same time we feel that the liberty should not be abused, and that it can only be enjoyed by Composers who have elsewhere shown the possession of a high melodic gift. Next comes the selection of some well-known tune as the subject of a thematic movement, *e.g.*, in Schumann's Overture on the Rheinweinlied, or Brahms' on the Student Songs of Germany. This differs from the first in that it leaves even more room for the individuality of the Composer, since the presentation and influence of the subject occupy so much smaller a part in the work as a whole. It must be remembered that conception and treatment are not absolutely exclusive of one another, and that there is as much opening for originality in the accessory ideas as in the main centre round which they are grouped. Last and most remarkable is the incorporation into a work of a single detached episode which does not belong to the Composer. Examples of this are so infrequent that we may doubt whether it has ever been done consciously by any musician of eminence. It seems unreasonable to suppose that the man who could write Beethoven's first Pianoforte Sonata should deliberately borrow the two or three bars from Mozart which stand out, irreconcilable and uncompromising, in the development section of the last movement; or that Gounod should elaborately recall Mendelssohn's ' Be thou faithful until death ' to adorn the Pentecost number of his *Redemption.* Certainly the resemblances are too detailed to be fortuitous, but the most probable explanation is that men of such wide reading were sometimes led to obscure the line between imagination and memory. Psychology knows how closely the two faculties are connected in everyday life, and though their provinces are more distinct in Music than in any other form of human activity, we may at least allow them a strip of march land. Finally, if these quotations are defects they are only spots in the sun. We do not count it a slur upon Coleridge that he owes to Wordsworth a stanza in the 'Ancient Mariner,' and if we did we have all the rest of the poem to admire.

The third type of resemblance is more serious, consisting, as it does, of the wholesale appropriation of an entire number or movement. Here, of course, the classical example is Handel. In the *Israel in Egypt* alone there are large excerpts from a serenata by Stradella, from Erba's *Magnificat*, and from Urio's *Te Deum*, while, by way of climax, the chorus, 'Egypt was glad,' is transcribed almost note for note from an organ canzona by Kerl. This is beyond the skill of any advocate. Even when a Composer borrows a movement from himself we are a little inclined to resent the economy, much more when he breaks into his neighbour's storehouse instead of his own. It is no palliation to urge 'Je prends mon bien là où je le trouve,' for that maxim would excuse the burglar as well as the conqueror. To urge that nobody would have heard of Kerl if Handel had not immortalised his work is to hold that the owner of the ewe lamb ought to feel himself compensated by the fame of the rich man's banquet. If we are to face the facts without sentiment and without prejudice we must admit that these numbers are blots upon the great oratorio of which they form a part. Possibly Handel was tempted by stress of time, for the whole of *Israel in Egypt* was written in twenty-one days. He was, we know, in the habit of making pasticcios from his own works, notably from the early set of chamber duets, parts of which reappear in *Acis*, in the *Messiah* and in *Judas Maccabæus*, and thus may have acquired the custom of transference without sufficiently considering the nature of the source on which he drew. Of course the *Israel* as a whole needs no defence. There is enough magnificent music in the remaining numbers to place Handel in his acknowledged position of supremacy. But, as George Eliot says, with some pertinence, 'You cannot mend a wrong subtraction by doing your addition right.'

Last, and worst of all, is the adaptation of another Composer's structure or method. This may be done deliberately, as in Schumann's 'Erinnerung' or Keats' 'Stanzas in Imitation of Spenser,' to produce some special effect of attribution or reminiscence, which is legitimate enough. But, as a rule, it is the distinctive mark of the bad Artist, and lies below the line which separates true work from false. Its general practice belongs to the sutlers and camp-followers of Music, men who are so far from leading that they do not even belong to the rank and file. From these come organ voluntaries which copy Mendelssohn's mannerisms without a spark of his genius; from these come overtures which have nothing to say about themselves but a great deal to say about Wagner; from these come drawing-room ballads in which humour is represented by mild flirtation or pathos by the hundredth variant of Hans Andersen's

'Match-girl'; from these come anthems and services, chants and hymn tunes, dances and fantasias, in which there is not one touch of originality or one stroke of real and loving workmanship. They have no style of their own, they change like a chameleon by reflection of whatever is nearest, and their sole value is to give some secondary indication of the composer whose writings happen for the moment to be in vogue.

The principle of vitality affords a basis for criticism so far as relates to the ideas presented by the Composer. If these ideas are spontaneous and genuine they fulfil all that we have a right to demand of them; for Music is an Art so ideal in its conditions that in it the first elements of truth and beauty coincide. Our Novelists, we are told, sometimes feel the truth of an ugly story with such overwhelming force that they are constrained against their will to tell it. But Music pure and simple has no story to tell, and if a composition is ugly it is so of deliberate intent. Hence it would follow in natural order to consider those principles which seem to regulate the treatment and presentation of musical ideas when once conceived.

Of these the most obvious is the Principle of Labour. The composer who stands in any true relation to his idea will spare no pains to present it in its most attractive aspect, and to deck it with the utmost ornament that it can legitimately bear. 'If you wish to touch my heart,' writes Horace to the Poets, 'you must begin by showing me that you have touched your own'; and no thought can ever arouse love and reverence in the audience which has not already aroused love and reverence in its creator. A great deal is written about the vanity of the artist, and no doubt when it becomes introspective and self-conscious it deserves to be satirised. But none the less the parental impulse on which it rests is the one essential condition of all good Art. It was not vanity that called forth Handel's tears over ' He was despised,' or that made him see the Heavens opened above the splendours of his ' Hallelujah.'

In one word, if the artist does not love his work he forfeits his claim to the title ; if he does, he should devote to its expression and elaboration the best skill at his command. Sometimes, though very rarely, we find evidences of hurry or carelessness even in the great musicians. The opening of Berlioz's *King Lear* overture, for example, is imperfectly thought out, and contains an error against symmetry which may roughly be paralleled by a false rhyme in a stanza of verse. Here, no doubt, the fault must be admitted, though it is condoned by the vigour and novelty of the rhythm. So, again, one of the principal reasons why we are losing our taste for the Italian operas of half a century ago is undoubtedly to be found in the laxity and indolence of their Composers. Rossini was a man of unquestionable genius ; ' Vieil Olympien,' as M. Montégut says, in contrast to the heroes who have won their way to apotheosis; but Rossini's very facility constituted a temptation which he had seldom strength to resist. The result is that he constantly gives us the impression of working below his best, of clothing his thoughts in the first cheap accompaniment that came into his head, of using his orchestra, in short, ' like a guitar.' The case is stronger with regard to Donizetti. 'Ah! madame,' he said, when asked which was his favourite work, ' a mother always loves her crippled child the best, and

I have so many.' To which we may answer that a Composer has no right to have 'crippled children,' still less to introduce them to the world as ragged starvelings.

In strong contrast is the custom of the greater Masters. Take any one of Beethoven's sonatas and notice, apart from the magnificence of the thoughts, the consummate skill with which he varies his phrases and develops his figures. Take any song of Schubert or Schumann or Brahms and see how the accompaniment supports and illustrates the melody. Not that there is any appearance of effort, for the artist has not reached maturity until he has assimilated the discipline of toil and made it a part of his organic nature. But none the less effort is presupposed. The ease of true artistic expression is not that of a boat drifting down stream; it cuts the water with the sweep of steady oars that have learned their lesson of mastery by long training. Genius is not, perhaps, adequately defined as the power of taking infinite pains, but it necessarily implies that gift if its results are to be worthy of its character. A man must work with patient and single-hearted devotion if he is to attain to the dash of Tintoret or the unerring rapidity of Velasquez.

It may be urged that this insistence on elaboration would be fatal to the simplicity of artistic conception, and would give us results like Thackeray's portrait of Louis XIV., in which the monarch is so disproportionate to his robes. But the question of simplicity is not touched. Nothing can be simpler than Schubert's *Forelle*, and yet it has room for the little flashing figure that completes its charm. Nothing can be simpler than the ballad in Dr Parry's *Judith*, and yet the accompaniment is a study of the highest artistic value. Handel 'wrought with the primary colours,' but to do so he had to learn everything which the science of his time could teach him. Even in the most elementary Volkslieder there is a right and a wrong way; the few chords which they require may contain the affirmation or denial of some harmonic truth, and occasionally, as in Dr Stanford's *Songs of Ireland* their value may be enhanced by a skilful setting which loses no whit of their original purity and lustre. All, in short, which the present principle implies is that the workmanship shall be as good as possible in its kind, a condition as clearly fulfilled by Papageno's songs in *Zauberflöte* as it is by 'Widmung' or 'Mein Lieb' ist Grün.'

But it is one thing to be simple, another to be mawkish. There is no room in Music for the 'Ambrose Philips' style of composition, and the drawing-room bard who 'prattles like a meer stammerer' is in sore need of a new Martinus Scriblerus. The prettiness of melody to which our fashionable ballads owe their favour is in many cases the pale reflection of some Classical beauty, and the accompaniments are too often thin, perfunctory, loveless, the handiwork of men who write for fame or profit and not for Art. Our amateur Composers who boast that they have never studied, our traffickers in Music who make a market of their garrulous facility, our popular song writers who have just wit enough to 'vamp' the tunes that they have borrowed from better men, these are the real traitors in our camp, the real obstacles to progress and enlightenment. Yet in spite of all progress is ultimately certain. The bad music of to-day is in advance of the bad music of twenty years ago. It is still tricky and artificial, but the tricks are better and the artifices less obvious. And meanwhile it is not the feeling of the public that is at fault but its experience.

Yet, if the musical taste of the nation is sound at heart, why does it tolerate bad work even for a moment? Why does it not instinctively turn from productions that are feeble or insincere and enjoy at once those beauties which it is implicitly capable of recognising? Why, in short, has the history of Music been so often a history of conquest over apparently antagonistic forces?

There are three main causes of this phenomenon. First, fashionable music is by no means the worst that is written. It generally implies some cleverness, it often displays a superficial charm or piquancy which may, for the time, deceive a careless hearer. To gauge its originality requires some knowledge, to estimate its intrinsic value demands some attention, and the public is usually too busy either to inform itself about the conditions or to give any careful inspection to the result Hence we grow suspicious of true craftsmanship, let the great work pass as unintelligible, and fall back upon cheap effect and facile prettiness, which involve no effort of comprehension because they have nothing to say. If we could only take the trouble and responsibility of judging for ourselves we should anticipate the decision of posterity, instead of stultifying ourselves by running counter to it. We have no brief to maintain, we are arbiters, not advocates, and the only thing required of us is that we should not go to sleep upon the bench.

Secondly, there are personal and extraneous reasons. In consequence of an unfortunate royalty system it sometimes happens that a great singer will throw the glamour of his voice and method over an entirely unworthy composition. We hear the performance at a ballad concert, we confuse, because we are too lazy to distinguish them, the interpretation with the thing interpreted, we go home with a sense of enjoyment which we take no trouble to analyse, and the next day everybody has bought the song, only to find that its grace was borrowed and its value factitious. A second extraneous reason is that our libretto writers, most of whom seem devoid of any real lyric gift, have fostered a remarkable taste for narrative songs: 'three verse epitomes of three volume novels,' as a distinguished Professor of Music has called them. These, from the very conditions of the case, must be flimsy and superficial; they have no scope for true feeling of any sort, still less for the intensely personal feeling which lyric poetry implies, and to raise them to an artistic level is a task of almost superhuman difficulty. No wonder, then, that the Composers find their nature subdued to what it works in, and turn out with mechanical regularity products which bear the same relation to Music as the 'sensational shillingsworth' of the bookstall does to literature. They find favour because the British Public will always listen to a love story, however ill told; but it is their subject and not their treatment that wins them acceptance.

The third cause lies in our own inadequacy as performers. A generation ago Englishmen who played the piano were almost non-existent, and Englishwomen ended their education with the 'Battle of Prague.' Even now the amateur level in this country is not very high, and we have as yet little chance of familiarising ourselves with Beethoven and Schubert, of bringing them to our firesides and admitting them to our friendship. This is, of course, the principal reason why good Art is ever neglected. To appreciate the best music we must hear it often : to hear it often we must live with it : to live with it we must be in the company of those by whom it can be played and sung. At present we are like the guest in Juvenal, waiting, crust in hand, till the more generous viands make their appearance. Our appetite is healthy enough, but we cannot get at the dishes. No doubt the great Concerts and Festivals have done and are doing incalculable service ; but these rare banquets lose a part of their efficacy if we only starve at home. The one certain panacea for all diseases of musical judgment is that we should learn to perform the great works adequately, and to listen to them with dispassionate minds.

An indication of this lies ready to hand. The average of performance is gradually improving in England, and the love of so-called 'Classical Music' is growing in exact proportion with it. There is still much room for advance, but we have made a start. Musical education is more serious and more widespread ; our amateur societies are growing more numerous, and more earnest in aim ; the foolish social conventions of a past age are dying out, and the musician is finding his proper place in the artistic world. True, the influence has not yet reached the home, and no great reform can be expected while it remains outside. But meanwhile it is drawing nearer and nearer, and its ultimate establishment among us is only a question of time. We may retard it, if we will, by carelessness or indifference, but we cannot stop it or turn it aside. The love of beauty is an inborn faculty in man, and the laws of its growth are the laws of all human progress and human development.

III

PRINCIPLES OF MUSICAL JUDGMENT—*CONTINUED*

GIVEN vitality in the conception of the ideas, and loving workmanship in their presentation, we have all that there is any right to demand in an artistic product, considered detail by detail. But it is not enough that the separate parts should be beautiful: they must be so combined as to express the highest possible approximation to a general type of organic unity and symmetry. Plato warns us that it is not good Art to concentrate ourselves on any one part of our subject to the exclusion of the rest. The Painter who 'makes the eyes of his portrait purple instead of black' more than counterbalances the effect of the single colour by the want of relation which it bears to the work as a whole.[1] So the object of the true musician is not so much to strike us with a single melody or cadence as to satisfy us with the general impression of the entire number or movement. Hence it is necessary that the different elements should be related to each other in due course and gradation, and even, in most cases, that

[1] Plato, *Republic*, Book iv. p. 420.

they should rise by cumulative effects to a final climax.

We require, then, in the third place, a Principle of Proportion in accordance with which the factors of a composition may be held together, not as isolated units but as members of a single organism. A great work must not be a congeries of unconnected beauties, like those out of which the Greek artist is incredibly said to have constructed his Aphrodite: it must be marked by a sense of propriety and subordination, by wise reticence and provident self-control. 'There is music enough,' says Hullah, 'in any one of Schubert's symphonies to set up a musician, of inferior invention but superior skill, with two or three better ones.' The criticism may or may not be just in regard of the particular Composer with whom it deals; but in either case it contains a general truth of great value.

A few applications of this principle will help to explain its scope and purport. The type of structure which is usually, though inaccurately, known as 'Sonata Form' is based upon two 'subjects,' presented in different keys, and connected by a transitional episode modulating from the one to the other. It would be hazardous Art to make the two subjects of equal importance;—Beethoven never does so;—to make the transition as important as either of them would be simply ruinous. Its office is purely subordinate, and a movement which gave it undue prominence would show almost as little sense of construction as the picture of the Supper at Emmaus, in the Contarini room of the Venetian Academy, where the servants behind the table are more vividly painted than the Guest Himself. Certainly the

Music and Musical Criticism

contrast need not be over-emphasised. We do not want a sonata movement to consist, like a drawing-room fantasia, of 'tunes and padding,' for that equally violates proportion on the other side. But the demands of chiaroscuro do not require that the secondary figures in a picture should be painted out, and it does not follow that, if each part in a drama has its use, all the characters should therefore pose as protagonists. Whatever be the form employed, the artist will know how to place his 'high light,' and how to keep the other elements in exactly adequate repression.

Similarly it would seem to be the rule, in the more serious compositions of the great Masters, that each movement should contain one supreme central idea, to which the other parts are, in their respective degrees, ancillary and subservient. It is hardly necessary to select examples, for their range is almost co-extensive with that of Classical Music; but if illustration be required it may be found in the rondo of Beethoven's Sonata in E-flat, Op. 7, in the adagio of the *Pathétique*, and in the first movement of the *Waldstein*. We may notice, too, how this principle is applied by Composers of less constructive skill if we contrast the opening allegro of Schubert's Sonata in A (No. 3) with that of Chopin's in B-flat minor. In the one case the first subject is of chief importance, and the rest of the exposition follows in its retinue; in the other the principal melodic idea lies in the second, and the office of the first is to heighten our expectation by a brilliant effect of contrast. Not that this method can be ascribed to any deliberate or conscious calculation of results: for the artist sees in a single intuition truths which we have laboriously to piece out by subsequent analysis. But none the less the law of organic unity must prevail in every living work, and it can only be obeyed by a fitting subordination among the constituent elements. Hence to expect equal melodic value in all the phrases of a musical composition is to commit an error of criticism to which no other Art or pursuit would tolerate a parallel. Every factor must have its own interest and its own vitality, as it has its own function to fulfil in the general scheme, but if its place is secondary its import must be secondary too. Eye differs in glory from hand, and head from foot, yet all are members of the same body.

Again, it is of great moment that the treatment of the ideas in a composition should be so arranged as to lead up to some definite and intelligible climax. There are certain melodic and harmonic forms which, from their physical effect upon the nerves of the ear, are specially capable of giving pleasure. These the true artist will keep in reserve, and if he deems it necessary to employ them at all, will do so in the latter part of his work and not at the beginning. For one of the conditions of musical effect is that it follows a fixed line of continuity. We can look at a picture from right to left, or from left to right, upwards or downwards, taking its elements in any order that we please to adopt; but in Music the sequence is irrevocable, and the terms 'beginning' and 'end' are settled for us from outside. If, therefore, the interest is to gather and increase as the movement advances, we must expect the more novel or elaborate effects of style to present themselves gradually, in regular course of development. It is the certain sign of a bad musician to exhaust his

richer harmonies or modulations in the first two
pages, and to give us nothing afterwards but an anti-
climax of commonplace phraseology.

The chorale tune in the middle of Chopin's nocturne
in G minor (No. 11) is a remarkable instance of expressive simplicity. Its opening melody is supported
by the plainest and most elementary chords, until we
begin to wonder whether the tints are not too neutral,
and whether a piece of positive colour would not be
a relief. At last, two bars before the end, Chopin
suddenly varies his harmony. The chords introduced
are not in themselves very striking or recondite, they
may be found in thousands of other phrases, but the
effect which they produce in this context is one of almost incomparable beauty. So again in the Romance
in C from Mozart's *Nachtmusik*, in the adagio of
Beethoven's second Sonata, in Schumann's *Warum*,
are melodies which, however admirable their first
presentation, reach a still higher point of value and
interest later on. Instances, indeed, may be found
in every form of good Art from the ballad to the
symphony. At one end we have 'Barbara Allen,'
with each strain more beautiful than the one before,
till it culminates in the perfect sweetness and pathos
of its final cadence; at the other we have the first
movement of the *Eroica*, which may almost be said
to gain fresh strength and vigour with every successive
bar. No doubt it often happens that the themes do
not themselves undergo any structural alteration.
Sometimes in a sonata movement the requisite effect
is gained by the rearrangement of keys, by a change
of context, by a new device of instrumentation or
expression. But in any case there should be something to keep the attention alive; something to show

that the work is not retrograde but progressive. It is a poor composition that recalls the allegory of Horace's Mermaid.

There is not, of course, here maintained that a piece of music should always lead up to some point of positive excitement. On the contrary, much of the best work lies within a narrow range of tone as subdued as that of Corot. But, however few the degrees, the intensity of emotional effect must rise to some appreciable extent as the movement continues. The principle of Proportion, in short, is equally applicable and equally paramount whether the whole scheme of colour be as quiet as that of Sterndale Bennett or as vivid as that of Wagner.

As a corollary it follows that, if the conditions of a work imply the frequent repetition of a passage in the same or similar phraseology, its expression had better be studiously simple throughout. Examples of this case may be found in the chants, hymns, and kyries of our Church Services, in the ballads (properly so called) of our concert rooms, and perhaps in the more elementary dance forms of our peasantry. Here the whole artistic product is completed in the single presentation of the tune, and is not intended to include its indefinite recurrence. Thus, the melody once heard, there can be no further question of climax, for what we expect is not a development of the initial thought but its exact restatement. Now it is clear that phrases which are plain and simple more easily bear repetition than those which are ornate or elaborate. We grow very weary of an epigram or a catchword after we have heard it a dozen times, and the more unusual its shape the more we resent its reappearances. An intensely agreeable flavour is more likely to pall on us than one to which we are comparatively indifferent; and any pleasurable excitation, if unduly prolonged, will lead to surfeit, if not to actual pain.

The same is true in regard of these recurrent musical phrases. Most of us have been afflicted in our experience of Church Services with a chant or a hymn tune, written by a local celebrity to embody some favourite chord or some ingenious modulation. At first hearing we are inclined to be pleased. The device is, perhaps, not very dignified, but it is striking and clever. It shows, at least, that the Composer has bestowed some little thought on his work. But the second verse is less interesting than the first, and the third than the second, until by the time we reach the doxology we would give anything never to have heard the tune at all. And yet the passage in question may have had a real beauty of its own— a beauty which we should have been glad to welcome had it been presented to us under better auspices and in more appropriate surroundings. For, apart from the truth that nerve-vibration ceases to be pleasurable if it is over-stimulated, we may add that the charm of certain special musical effects largely resides in their unexpectedness. Hence their frequent repetition defeats its own end. The great modulation in the 'Quasi-Trio' of Schumann's first Novellette owes much of its magic to the fact that we only hear it twice in the whole work, and it is less successful on the second occasion.

Music is at once sensuous and spiritual. It makes its direct appeal to the auditory nerve, but it has certain qualities which penetrate beyond and reach an æsthetic faculty that we have every right to attribute to the soul. Some of its effects, notably those of harmonisation, seem to fulfil the greater part of their function in the satisfaction of the ear, and their influences on the spiritual side of our nature is remote and secondary. Of those we tire for exactly the same reason as that we grow cloyed by a sweet taste or surfeited by a brilliant colour. Others, on the contrary, notably beauties of conception and melody, appeal to the æsthetic faculty with less intervention of the sense; and of them we do not tire, because our appreciation of them is similar in kind, though not similar in source, to our intellectual love of truth or our moral love of goodness. Hence a merely sensuous Art would be suicidal, for it would attach itself to the transient elements in our admiration, and disregard those that are permanent and abiding. If Spohr loses his hold upon the world it will be because of his chromatic chords, and his cadences that 'slide by semitones'; if he retains his hold it will be due to the genuine beauty of thought that is encrusted by these devices, like the sea-god Glaucus under his covering of shell and weed.

Here, then, is another example of the Law of Proportion. The sensuous side in Music must have its full recognition, for as long as man remains 'a compound of contrarieties' Art can gain nothing by an attempt to be ascetic. But in all true works the spiritual element must predominate. The duty of the Painter, according to Fra Lippo Lippi, is to

> Make the flesh liker and the soul more like,
> Both in their order;

and similarly it is the duty of the musician not to

flatter the sense with an empty compliment of sound, but to reach through sensation to the mental faculties within. There is no fear of ugliness. Ideal beauty is not an excuse whereby to apologise for physical deformity: it is rather the supreme point of health and perfection. If the thought be true and noble it will always find appropriate embodiment, and to trick it out with deliberate appeals to our lower nature is simply a wanton and useless act of desecration.

Verdi's 'Ah! che la morte,' for instance, has the makings of a beautiful melody. It is, perhaps, somewhat languid and sentimental, but it contains genuine feeling, and, up to the cadence, its expression is the natural outgrowth of its thought. Unfortunately at the cadence there appears a touch of cosmetic, and the whole purity of the tune is gone. No doubt we may here be dealing with a difference between the Latin point of view and our own, but to insist upon this would be to introduce into Art the question of an absolute standard which Kant settled once for all in Morals. And if we once admit that Art appeals to some faculty higher than sensation the doctrine of relativity will fare as ill in æsthetic criticism as it does in ethical. The cadence in 'Ah! che la morte' is wrong, because it introduces an element foreign to the general scheme of the melody for the purpose of securing a single sensuous effect. We may, if we will, find a hundred excuses for the Composer, but we cannot deny the blemish in his work. Verdi, however, makes amends in *Otello:* not so our bad musicians, whose whole skill consists in the application of these external and artificial charms. They are like versifiers who try to conceal the poverty of their thought under a jargon of 'poetic' phraseology, or like those London flower-sellers who heighten the perfume of their roses by sprinkling them with eau-de-Cologne.

Fourth, and last, is the Principle of Fitness. In every Art the style must to some extent be determined by the nature of the form employed. The manner of Paradise Lost is not the manner of 'L'Allegro:' both are pure Milton, and yet there is a clear difference between them. Dante is in one mood when he writes the Inferno, in another when he writes the Vita Nuova, and the Madonnas of Bellini shows a marked distinction of sentiment from his Fors Fortuna. No doubt the method of a great genius maintains a generic similarity throughout; but it is, so to speak, crossed by transverse lines that divide it into the several compartments of Epic and Lyric, Tragedy and Comedy, and the like. The same is true in Music. For example, the rondo of a sonata is as a rule less serious than the first movement: for the historical origin of the rondo implies affinities with the ballad form, while that of the first movement draws on sources not of more sweetness but of more sustained strength and dignity. We could hardly imagine a sonata beginning with the rondo of the *Pathétique* or of the *Waldstein* or of Schubert's Sonata in D. The allegretto of Beethoven's first Sonata in E-flat exhibits much the same technical structure as that of the opening allegro; but to transpose the two would be as great an outrage as to set 'Du bist wie eine Blume' in the same style as 'Ich grolle nicht.' Each musical form, in fact, has its own special manner of treatment, and though the lines of demarcation are sometimes slender they are never unreal.

This is particularly true, in modern times, of the broad distinction between Sacred and Secular. Once, when music was contrapuntal, the two may have started from a common source, for Composers were bound by the uniform method that had been systematised and sanctioned by the Church. Further, it was a characteristic of that period that Music should go its own way, with little or no regard to the significance of its words. Thus in Palestrina's *Lamentations* the introductory phrases, 'Incipit Lamentatio,' or 'De Lamentatione,' as well as the names of the Hebrew initial letters, are set with exactly the same care and skill as the verses that follow. No wonder, then, that the more learned secular Composers wrote on sacred lines, and that Bach could adapt for his *Matthäus-Passion* the melody 'Mein Gemuth ist mir verwirret,' which had originally been composed to solace a disappointed lover. In the present century, however, the case is otherwise. The Romantic movement has brought with it not only the privileges but the responsibilities of freedom; and musicians who repudiate convention can no longer plead it as an excuse. Rossini's famous statement, 'Je ne connais que deux espèces de Musique, la bonne et la mauvaise,' is an anachronism; and the crucial instance against it may be found in his own *Stabat Mater*. The whole work is instinct with life: it would have been admirably suited to a ballet or a Romantic opera, but as an exposition of the sweetest and most pathetic of all Latin hymns it is as much out of place as a caricature in an East window or a jest from Candide in a sermon. Let any reader dispassionately consider the quartett 'Sancta Mater istud agas' and ask himself whether it is anything less than

D

immoral. The burly priests at Noyon, who moved the wonder of Mr Stevenson by 'trolling out the *Miserere* like a tavern-catch,' were not further afield than this.

It is not here contended that all music for the service of the Church should be directly devotional in character. The Bible itself is not confined to the direct expression of religious feeling. It has room for the Song of Solomon and the story of Samson and the dramatic histories of Esther or Elijah. But we may demand that music which is to befit a sacred building should be marked by a dignity and a reticence which we do not require elsewhere. We feel instinctively that apart from the associations of the words the music of *Judas Maccabæus* is suited to a Cathedral, and that the music of *Tannhäuser* is not. Even Weber's *Jubilee Cantata*, which is sometimes given at our provincial festivals, produces an impression of levity and triviality analogous to that which we experience on hearing the Lessons theatrically read or a sermon disfigured with extravagant gesture or humorous colloquialism. And the feeling is perfectly right and lawful. Music is not articulate, but it is suggestive, and its suggestion should always be in keeping with the conditions under which it is intended to be heard. Hence to import into the Church music which is in obvious keeping with the theatre or the ballroom is to outrage composer and audience alike. To write for the one in a style only suited to the other is to stand self-condemned in any court of artistic fitness or propriety.

Yet no law is more often transgressed than this by the inferior Church composers of the present day. The theatrical style is the easiest to acquire, for even

Music and Musical Criticism

cheap and tawdry ornaments will look well enough in the glare of the footlights ; and it apparently needs some wit to see that tinsel crowns and paste jewels are only appropriate to the playhouse. Great dramatic composers, men who have decked their stage with gold and their characters with diamonds, know that even the legitimate splendours of the best operatic Art should be subdued in Psalm and Oratorio. Beethoven's two great masses are written in a different temper from *Fidelio*, Berlioz's *Te Deum* is unlike *Les Troyens* or *Béatrice et Bénédict*. Even those composers whose ideal has been pure melody, like Mozart or Schubert, have recognised and observed this distinction, and although with them the sacred works approximate more nearly in style to the secular, yet we shall always find a line of demarcation which is not overstepped. The neglect of this principle, in short, is one of the surest marks of a bad musician. The fashionable choirmasters who fill our services with

> Light quirks of music, broken and uneven,

need no other accusation : 'tis a star-chamber matter on the first count. True the devices are often intrinsically bad in addition, but that is only to be expected. The very fact of introducing a theatrical tone into worship is proof positive of incapacity for good work.

Parsifal may possibly occur to the reader as an exception, but *Parsifal* is no more theatrical than the Ober-Ammergau Passion Play. Wagner, in spite of his 'unorthodoxy' of belief and his intense dramatic sympathies, was too great an Artist to confuse sacred music with secular. No doubt he alternates them, but that is a very different thing. Only certain portions of the work are intended to be religious, such as the Introduction, the March, and the Charfreitagszauber music, and they entirely fulfil the requisite conditions. It is, perhaps, a dangerous experiment to approximate the theatre and the Church at all, but we may at least plead that in this instance the latter has the ascendency at all the points of contact. *Parsifal*, in short, is not an instance of Church music which is theatrical,—that is the crying sin,—but of stage music which at certain moments is devotional. Thus when we play the Introduction in our cathedrals we are simply restoring to Religion what is her own. We do not prohibit a preacher from quoting the last lines of Karshish on the ground that his congregation would not have been edified by an account of that philosopher's travels.

A similar distinction is observable in works that are originally intended for the neutral ground of the concert room; only a few, and those the highest in majesty or serenity of contemplation, are fitted for Church use, but the others have their gradations of dignity and their relative conditions of impressiveness. A violin sonata is not expected to exhibit the same scale as a sestett: thoughts which would be trivial in a symphony are appropriate in a dance or an impromptu. There is room in Music for every style, provided that the ideas expressed are singlehearted and genuine, and provided also that they are suitable to the form through which they are presented. We can admire Offenbach as readily as we admire Caran d'Ache, but we should no more wish the one to write a concert overture in the manner of *La Belle Hélène* than we should wish the other to fresco our Houses of Parliament with the figures of 'Les Courses d'Antiquité.' The humour of the 'Northern Farmer' is undeniable, but it would not suit the Idylls of the King.

It is not, of course, pretended that the foregoing outline is more than the bare sketch of a critical method. The complete determination of any Art is probably beyond the reach of analysis; and in any case the present writer has no desire to attempt so heroic a task. But it is here maintained that the four principles, if obvious, are true, and if commonplace, have been frequently disregarded. Music has often been judged on grounds of personal predilection. Schools have been set in antagonism, forms of composition praised or condemned, ideals upheld or scouted without the least reference to any general code of Artistic laws. We hear one composer censured for deficiency in counterpoint, but we are not told why he ought to be a contrapuntist. We learn that the melodies of another have failed to please the reviewer who writes about him, but we find no indication of the grounds on which this adverse opinion has been formed. The laws of the plastic Arts have been expounded to us by Lessing and Winckelmann, Literature has its prophets in Sainte-Beuve and Vinet and Matthew Arnold, yet Musical Criticism, which is the most difficult of all has seldom made any effort to advance beyond the bounds of a hazardous dogmatism. No doubt the dogmatism has sometimes hit the mark. In the vast majority of cases it has flown hopelessly wide, and, whatever be the issue, there is a Platonic distinction between opinion and knowledge which should necessarily underlie any system of artistic judgment. It may be possible that with all the method in the world Music will never produce a Lessing or a Sainte-Beuve: it is assuredly only through method that she has any chance of doing so.

IV

SECURUS JUDICAT ORBIS

BERLIOZ, in *A Travers Chants*, divides men of imperfect musical sympathy into two classes. Of the one he says, ' Ils ne sentent pas,' of the other, ' Ils ne savent pas.' The former includes all critics who allow their judgment to be trammelled by formalism or darkened by unreasoning tradition : the latter includes those members of the general public who look upon Music as an unattainable mystery, hidden from profane ears by the sacred language of the initiated. There is no doubt which is the worse error. Pedantry is a finger-post which points, not forward to the road that we seek but backward to that which we have already traversed, and we are indeed in evil case if we trust for guidance to its retrograde indications. Fétis judged Wagner by the system of Mozart, Joseph Rubinstein condemned Schumann because his thought was not that of Beethoven, and both alike hindered the progress of the Art that they professed to teach. When Dvořák's *Requiem* was produced at Birmingham, the papers, almost without exception, fastened upon its weaknesses of structure, and altogether omitted to mention that the thoughts are full of a beauty which no other Composer in the world could have conceived. No doubt it is not a perfect work :

few compositions are, unless they have been signed by Beethoven or Brahms; but it contains passage after passage for which any real lover of Music should have been content to give thanks. It is quite right that errors should be noted, for Art is greater than any artist, but it is a poor method of criticism which contents itself with 'picking out the fifths.' Yet this is precisely the function which pedantry most loves to perform. It pays no heed to the vigour or subtlety of the Composer's thought, it has no gratitude for the gift of a new melody or a new cadence, it shrinks aghast from the boldness that has extended the range of harmony or the limits of form, and if it can open its text books and declare that a fugue answer is 'incorrect,' or a resolution 'unaccountable,' it feels that its duty is accomplished. The fate of Berlioz at the Paris Conservatoire is in store for every Composer of eminence whose works are dragged to the steps of this prejudiced tribunal.

There are and always have been some musical critics who are great enough to be generous, but their number is small and their voice too frequently overpowered in the babel of the judgment-seat. For the rest we must only conclude either that their exclusive study of rule and precept induces a narrow and illiberal temper, or that they write with an inadequate sense of their responsibilities. It is so easy to carp, it is so easy to point an epigram at the immaturities of a new genius; and the newspaper reader is always, for the moment, in sympathy with the attack. But the decision is in constant danger of being reversed on appeal. Keats has been vindicated against the *Quarterly*, Shelley against the *Literary Gazette*, and musical criticism has every reason to take the lesson to heart. It must be growing a little weary of constantly advocating the wrong cause.

All this, to any person unacquainted with the facts of the case, may seem a mere idle diatribe, vindictive in tone and uncertain in direction. It appears advisable, therefore, to illustrate the position by a brief sketch of what English criticism has done during the past seventy years. The limit is chosen, not in order to favour any preconceived hypothesis, but simply because it coincides with the beginnings of musical journalism in this country.

We had in the 'twenties' two musical papers—the *Harmonicon* and the *Quarterly Review and Magazine*. The former published articles upon the later Sonatas and Quartetts of Beethoven, in which it stigmatised the Composer as 'obscure,' eccentric,' and 'unmelodious.' The latter took the opportunity of his death in 1827 to present a review of his style and method which deserves some detailed investigation.

The writer begins by complaining that there are 'few marks of study' in Beethoven's work. In all his compositions 'there is not one example of a fugue regularly conducted,' and 'no Composer of established fame has yet existed who has not distinguished himself by the production of fugues or canons.' The inference is obvious. All great musicians hitherto have written fugues, Beethoven has not written fugues, therefore Beethoven is not a great musician. Indeed our critic rises to the affirmation of an axiom, and declares that 'no composition of any length would be endurable without the application of those principles on which canons and fugues are constructed.' After this it is not surprising to hear that the symphonies are prolix and wearisome, notably the '*Pastoral*' and the 'Funereal March' from the *Eroica*. Indeed Beethoven has 'so dosed his countrymen' that they not only mutilate his works but extend the same treatment to those of Haydn and Mozart. Further, it is a pity that the Composer of the *Waldstein* and the *Appassionata* should so often 'have mistaken noise for grandeur, extravagance for originality,' that he should have 'played such fantastic tricks as makes the critics weep,' and that he should have spoiled his effects with 'much that is turgid and not a little that borders on the ridiculous.' 'Compared with Haydn, and even with Mozart,' he is 'deficient in grace and clearness,' and his fate will be that, while 'some of his compositions will never be forgotten,' his more elaborate works 'will be talked of by professors and suffered to lie at peace in their shelves.' It should be remembered that this curious mixture of bad grammar, bad logic, and bad art was written not when Beethoven's works were new and unknown, but after he had completed a life of steady labour and continuous advance. But the whole thing reads too much like a joke to require any serious answer.

Apart from Berlioz, whose failure in this country will be noticed later on, the next Composer of striking originality whose work visited London was Robert Schumann. By this time the *Quarterly Review and Magazine* had come to an end, and our spokesman was Mr H. F. Chorley of the *Athenæum*. He described the new music as a 'display of unattractive cacophony,' and ventured to predict that 'not many more experiments amongst this Composer's work— bad because generally ugly and essentially meagre— would be ventured in England.' Having demolished Schumann, Mr Chorley went over to Germany and heard *Tannhäuser*. 'I have never,' he writes, 'been so blanked, pained, wearied, *insulted* even (the word is not too strong) by any work of pretensions as by this same *Tannhäuser*. . . . It would seem as if chance had determined the proceedings of a musician more poor in melodic inspiration than any predecessor or contemporary: that when a tune had presented itself he used it without caring for its fitness, that when tunes would not come he forced his way along a recitative as uncouth and tasteless as it is ambitious, and as if his system had come upon him as an after-thought, by way of apology for himself and depreciation of his betters.' The 'betters' are enumerated by Mr Hullah in a similar article, and include the names of Rossini, Meyerbeer, and Verdi. Of course Mr Chorley declares that the only tunes in the work are those presented in the overture, *i.e.*, that there is no tune in the march or the prayer or the song to the Evening-Star; and he winds up, with a courage worthy of a better cause, by asserting that 'the instrumentation is singularly unpleasant,' and the sound 'strident, ill-balanced, and wanting body.' Poor Wagner did not even know how to score.

Time went on, but experience does not seem to have brought wisdom. It is a matter of recent memory that our critics found *Lohengrin* 'dull,' and *Walküre* 'monstrous,' that they could see no beauty in *Siegfried*, and no melody in *Tristan*. Brahms gained a hearing in this country through the generosity of a brother Composer. The critics attacked him from the beginning, and we have at the present day professional directors of public taste who are not ashamed to assail the *Deutsches Requiem* with infelicitous gibes. Even our own greatest musician had to pay the penalty for daring to be original. The account of *Prometheus* in the *Musical Times* of October 1877, the account of *Judith* in the *Musical Standards* of December 1888, are standing examples of the way not to criticise. In the latter case the reviewer fell foul of the libretto, with what success the readers of his article will still remember. It is a little imprudent to select passages as unworthy of the book of Judith unless one has the Apocrypha at hand, so as to make sure that they are not in it.

These are the men in whom we are expected to put our trust. They are not the sharpshooters and skirmishers: they are accredited captains of the host, who claim on some ground of knowledge or experience that we should recognise their supremacy and follow where they lead. At best they are like Lord Galway in the war of the Spanish Succession, and 'think it more honourable to fail according to rule than to succeed by innovation.' At worst they trifle with a careless strategy that accepts defeat after defeat without altering its system or even reconnoitring its field of battle. There is no need to examine their other qualifications. One may be a good judge of music and yet write notes on 'Apollidorus' and Hermes 'Trismegitus'; it is no doubt possible to express some judgment of value in a style that never rises above the lower journalism; and even if a man does review performances that have never taken place he may still do justice to the concerts that he has the leisure to attend. But it is a matter of comment that every new departure should be met by the same barrier of dogmatic denunciation, and that genius should still be assailed with those very charges of obscurity and vagueness to which almost all the great Composers of the present century have been successively subjected.

We of the general public are only too glad to accept the report of any critic who can exhibit his credentials, who can show that he possesses some liberality of temper, and, above all, who can deduce his conclusions from some intelligible system of æsthetic principles. But for once we entirely decline to believe the reiterated assertion that the methods of to-day are wrong because they are not the methods of yesterday. Music is a young Art, and as such is essentially progressive. By the laws of its being, by the laws of the human nature on which it rests, it is irrevocably committed to the discovery of new paths.

If, then, our guides are astray, what course is left to us except that we should 'sit down in a forlorn scepticism'? This at least is possible, that we should take the matter into our own hands and use our own judgment. Let us go honestly and loyally to the works of the great Masters and criticise for ourselves. Let us determine what principles of Art we can, and use them as a compass for directing our steps. If we make mistakes they will not be worse than those that have been made for us already; and we shall at any rate approach the difficulty with our eyes open and our minds unfettered. Let our estimate be fearless, for it is better to love Music than to love any musician—let it be reverent, for the very errors of great men are 'high failures' which

> Overleap the bounds
> Of low successes—

let it be genuine, for only so can it detect the presence of truth. But, above all, let us lay aside this false appeal to outworn tradition or prescriptive usage and confine our axioms to those psychological laws which underlie all the Arts alike. We have a right at the outset to demand of every Composer who claims the first rank that he should be original in thought and honest in workmanship, that he should obey some rules of proportion, that he should regulate his music by some considerations of fitness and propriety. For the rest, let us take his message as he utters it, and if we find any reasons for blame we shall assuredly find more for praise and gratitude. It may possibly appear to us that some of Schubert's instrumental works are long, that some of Dvořák's are weak in structure, that Schumann sometimes for a moment touches the borders of the commonplace. But what does it matter? They have written music which will live as long as the Art endures, and it is truer as well as nobler criticism that we should estimate a man by his best.

But to criticise at all demands some study. We cannot detect a plagiarism unless we know the source from which it borrows. We cannot tell whether an ornament is right or wrong without some acquaintance with those laws on which the validity of ornament depends. And for the present we are in the position of Berlioz's second class, 'ceux qui ne savent pas.' We have been content to remain in ignorance partly because we over-estimate the obscurity of Musical Science and partly because our national diffidence inclines us to accept our judgments at second-hand. Here then is an obvious defect to remedy. The necessary laws of Music are few and

Music and Musical Criticism

simple. We can easily acquire the rudiments of harmony, counterpoint, and form, and when we possess them we shall learn more from hearing the great Composers than from all the lectures and analyses in Christendom. To obtain a mastery over the practical application of these laws involves, no doubt, the work of a lifetime; but this is not what we want. It is appreciation not production that we have in view, and our object demands more of the charity that edifieth than of the knowledge that puffeth up.

When we call a Beethoven sonata 'beautiful' we do not use the term in any sense generically different from that in which it is applied to a ballad. One is complex, the other simple, but both are derived from the same laws and contain the same elements. If, then, we can love a ballad we can love a sonata. We only need to see our way through the more complicated work, to know the reason of its form and the interrelation of its melodies, and for this we have already the capacity, which is waiting to be actualised by study and experience. The distinctions between men are slighter than we think. One cannot understand Beethoven, another can understand Beethoven but not Schumann, another finds the difficulties gather when he approaches Brahms or Wagner; all, if they would confess it, are occasionally puzzled by some deeper utterance of genius. But when that is so the true lover of Music will study the passage patiently and generously, not throw it aside with the arrogant inference that an effect is at fault because it is unfamiliar.

The first and most imperative necessity in the matter is that we should free our minds as far as possible of all cant and fetish worship and prejudice

It is only by clearing away these weeds that we can hope to sow any seed of true appreciation. It is only by taking stock frankly and unreservedly of our present position that we can discover the lines along which advance is desirable. Suppose we find ourselves out of sympathy with some acknowledged masterpiece, some work which has stood the lapse of time and the flux of fashions and generations. We may assume at once that we are in the wrong, and that the cause of our mistake lies either in inadequate performance or in conditions which rendered attention difficult, or, lastly, in our own deficiencies of musical knowledge. In any case it is remediable, and if we remedy it we have clearly added a new item to our sum of pure and noble pleasures. But it is childish to denounce a work which we have never properly comprehended; it is worse than childish to simulate an admiration which we do not really feel. If we demand sincerity in the artist he has an equal right to look for the same quality in us.

What we require in England is a more manly and straightforward attitude towards artistic questions. In Music, apparently, we have allowed generations of foreign influence to obliterate our own national style, with the result that the heart of the people has been left untouched, and that criticism has too often been entrusted to careless or mercenary hands. Music can never flourish as an exotic. If it is to grow into a fair and stately tree it must be planted in a national soil. We owe our best gratitude to Germany for the great works that she has put forward for our education, but in order to appreciate them at all we must have the root of the matter in ourselves. Much more if England is to return to the first rank of European Music, she must work upon her own lines, she must deliver her own message. It is false to say that we are unmusical. No unmusical nation could have produced *Sumer is i-cumen in*, or the *Triumphs of Oriana*, or *King Arthur*, no unmusical nation could have filled its churches with the strength of Tallis or the sweetness of Farrant. At least we have the traditions of a past in which our Composers had no need to borrow from their foreign neighbours.

It was a conspicuous piece of bad fortune that the great monodic movement, which originated in Florence, should have spread northward at a time when England was too much occupied with political disturbances to make full use of the occasion. Then came calamity after calamity. Charles II. overran the country with French influence, George I. invaded it with German, until at last it became a recognised fact that in all the more important branches of the Art England should import her music from abroad. Add to this John Bull's unreasoning contempt for the foreigner, and it is not difficult to understand how the national style waned and degraded into a mere echo. Apart from the small school of Glee writers, whose whole history falls within the lifetime of one man, the last English Composer before the present generation was Henry Purcell. The record of our national Music, once among the most glorious in the world, has been virtually in abeyance for the past two centuries. Even the Composers of that period who most nearly attain to the first rank, such as S. S. Wesley and Sterndale Bennett, are too obviously affected by a foreign system to count as exceptions. The voice of our English song, even if it was not silenced altogether, was yet so faint and intermittent that it had no power to cope with the magnificent outburst of German Art. Once there was no musical form to which England did not contribute her share of development. To the growth of the symphony, the quartett, and the sonata she contributed virtually nothing.

Hence all the false taste and the false criticism of those barren years. Music was no longer the outcome of the national life, it was an external thing to be bought with money and to be estimated in proportion to its price. Our own musicians either threw themselves down 'under the eyes of the groundlings,' or if they were too conscientious for that, borrowed their method from the fashionable style. Pierson, who might have done something under more favourable auspices, was driven to Germany by the apathetic indifference of his own countrymen; other composers and virtuosi bid for success by adopting names of German or Italian sound. The whole system became false, heartless, insincere, fatal alike to true judgment and true production. England was abrogating her position as a workshop of Art, and was becoming instead the bazaar at which it was retailed.

Now, at last, the period of our decadence is ended. There has arisen among us a Composer who is capable of restoring our national Music to its true place in the art of Europe. Under his guidance, and by his example, it is still possible that we may rise to the position which we occupied in the time of Elizabeth, and show ourselves once more the worthy comrade and rival of the great nations oversea. Already there are signs that our land is awakening from its long inactivity. We have a means of musical education which can hold its own against the Conservatoires of Paris, or Leipsic, or Vienna. We have a growing and extending interest in musical science. If only the work can be turned into a right direction, if only it can follow the broad, healthy utterance of our national melodies, instead of diverging to copy the phraseology of an alien tongue, if only it will be true and honest and single-hearted, then there is no reason why it should not recover the glory that it has attained in past days. We do not want overtures that imitate *Parsifal*, or cantatas that pile into an incongruous heap the cadences of Grieg and Dvořák. We want to realise once again that distinctive National Art of which the capacity is still latent in the heart of our country.

There is little presumption in the forecast when we already have such first-fruits as *St Cecilia*, and the *De Profundis*, and the *English Symphony*. Grant that all future Music, our own with the rest, must be to some extent affected by the work of Bach and Beethoven, of Schumann and Brahms, yet there is room for a national use even of the inheritance that has been left us by the great German Composers. We may learn in their school without being overpowered by their methods. Milton was steeped in the Classics, yet no poet is more English than he. Addison knew the Latin writers from Lucretius to Claudian, yet the *Spectator* remains the purest example of our national prose. And in like manner our musicians may treat the great Masters as instructors, not as models, and may be influenced by them only in the sense in which Morley was influenced by Marenzio, or Purcell by Lulli.

It is for us listeners to determine whether we will aid this movement or retard it. We may discourage our true Composers by letting their message fall upon inattentive ears, we may turn away to the last prettiness of the drawing-room or the last vulgarity of the music hall, but in so doing we range ourselves of deliberate choice among the antagonists of progress. The day of England's Music is near at hand. Even now the first blow has been struck, the first victory achieved. Let us shake off the mental indolence which shrinks from the trouble of a decision; let us form our judgment by a study of the great Masters, and apply it to a generous appreciation of the Art of our own day; let us find our pleasure where it is purest and most enduring, and it will be added to our reward that we should share in the winning of a national cause.

HECTOR BERLIOZ AND THE FRENCH ROMANTIC MOVEMENT

He is the imagination of France in the century of trouble which followed her great Revolution—an imagination powerful, ambitious, disordered—a light of the world, though a light as wild as that of volcanic flames blown upon by storm; and he is also that better heart of France, tender and fierce, framed for manifold joy and sorrow, rich in domestic feeling and rich in patriotism, heroic, yet not without a self-consciousness of heroism; that eager, self-betraying, intemperate heart which alternates between a defiant wilfulness and the tyranny of an idea or a passion.

DOWDEN: *The Poetry of Victor Hugo.*

Hector Berlioz
AND THE FRENCH ROMANTIC MOVEMENT.

I

STUDENT DAYS

1830 saw more than one revolution in Paris. The storm that broke in thunder on the July barricades only gave direction and impetus to an electrical force that had been gathering over the whole field of national life. In Art, as in Politics, the days of Legitimism were over. Géricault had defied tradition with his *Radeau de la Méduse;* Hugo had declared war in the preface to *Cromwell*, and had just emerged victorious from the famous 'forty days' of *Hernani;* Alfred de Vigny, the most conservative of conspirators, had struck his blow with *Cinq Mars:* everywhere France had declared for freedom, and Charles X. and his censors were in full flight.

It is interesting to notice the manner in which the different movements converged. In earlier days the artist has usually held aloof from political disturbance, or at most has bidden it 'lift not its spear against the Muses' bower.' But in the present century it is the fashion for genius to be in revolt. Wagner was banished from Saxony, Tourguénieff and Dostoieffsky from Russia, Shelley challenged the Castlereagh Government at his Spezian villa, Byron ended the noblest episode of his life at Missolonghi. So in 1830 some of the Romanticists took the opportunity of a new and picturesque experience. The excited mob that battered down the gates of the Louvre found itself reinforced by a fantastic figure, clad in sixteenth-century armour from a neighbouring museum, and hacking at the palace with the same vigour that had lately 'demolished Racine.' Away beyond the Palais Royal, in the Rue Vivienne, rose the ominous strains of the 'Marseillaise,' led by a gaunt student of the Conservatoire, with a keen aquiline face and a mass of unmanageable red hair. Art and Politics had joined hands and were fighting in the same cause.

Berlioz, indeed, even more than Dumas, found the atmosphere of Revolution congenial. He was always in opposition—first to his parents, then to his teachers, later to Fétis and his critics—and it is appropriate enough that he should have won his first musical victory with a cantata finished while the bullets were rattling round his window and flung aside that he might join the *Sainte Canaille* in the streets. In his extraordinarily complex nature were many of the qualities of a popular leader—restless energy, indomitable courage, unquestioning intolerance of prescriptive right, and, above all, entire confidence in himself and his mission. Against these, no doubt, may be set a keen though rather intermittent sense of humour, a touch of petulance, and a sensitiveness so exquisite that his record of it sounds occasionally morbid and unreal. In short, his character like his career was an alternation of extremes. The turbulent annals of the

Romantic movement can scarcely show a more representative hero than the young musician who on that summer afternoon taught the mob to shout its song of liberty, and fainted from pure pleasure as the great tune came surging and echoing about his ears.

He was born at La Côte St André, near Grenoble, on December 11, 1803. His father, Louis Berlioz, was a country doctor with a wide reputation and a large practice; something of an author, too, and an intelligent, cultivated man, who rather prided himself on having no enthusiasms and no prejudices. Madame Berlioz, on the other hand, seems to have been a typical woman of the mountains, ardent, affectionate, narrow-minded, devout in all religious observance, and intensely suspicious of the great world and its unknown temptations. The one looked upon an artistic career as a risk which no sensible person would think of incurring, the other saw a vision of cabarets and green-rooms, of *billets-doux* on the table and bailiffs at the door, and shrank in horror from the idea of a life so little in accord with the traditions of respectability. Never, perhaps, was there a more unfortunate *milieu* for a man of genius. Handel, who was also a doctor's son, found one staunch supporter at home; Schumann after a long struggle succeeded in conciliating his mother's antagonism; but Berlioz had both battles to fight at the same time. No opportune ally came to carry him off, as Frankh carried off Haydn; no Crown Prince surrounded his early efforts with the splendours of imperial patronage: alone and unaided he had to scale an immovable earthwork of argument under a galling fire of appeal and invective. The very tolerance which Dr Berlioz showed to Music as a pastime only accentuated his opposition to Music as a profession. The very love which Madame Berlioz bore to her son only strengthened her voice to testify against his pursuits. From the moment when the boy was old enough to think for himself he found that his foes were those of his own household.

However, the difficulty did not arise at once, and the early years passed happily enough. We have many pleasant vignettes of the child-life: the sunny slopes of St André, the Isère winding through its 'rich golden fertile plain,' the first Communion in the Convent of the Ursulines, the Virgil lesson where the boy broke into a passion of sobs over Dido's lament, and his father, with a kindly tact, closed the book, saying, 'That will do for to-day, I am tired.' Before he was twelve years old Berlioz had fallen hopelessly in love with a Mdlle. Estelle Gautier, 'a tall, slight girl of eighteen, with splendid shining eyes, a mass of hair that might have waved on the casque of Achilles,' and, above all, 'a pair of pink shoes.' 'I had no idea what was the matter with me,' he continues, 'but I suffered acutely, and spent my nights in sleepless anguish. In the daytime I crept away like a wounded bird and hid myself in the maize fields and the orchards. I suffered agonies when any man approached my idol, and it makes me shudder even now when I recall the ring of my uncle's spurs as he danced with her.' There is a tone of sincerity about this which saves it from being altogether grotesque; and we may add that the impression was never effaced. Forty-nine years after Berlioz made a pilgrimage to see his Estelle, and nearly broke down during the interview.

Meantime Music was beginning to assert itself.

The boy found a flageolet in a neglected drawer, and made such dire noises on it that his father in self-defence taught him to play. To this succeeded the flute, and later on the guitar, after which practical instruction came to a standstill. It is noticeable that the two great Masters of modern orchestration should both have been ignorant of the piano. Wagner, indeed, could play a little, though he was not in any sense a pianist, but Berlioz's attainments never rose higher than 'crashing out a few chords,' and he remained to the end of his life rather out of sympathy with the instrument. During his Russian visit in 1847 this disability was nearly proving serious.[1]

Harmony was learned, after a fashion, from the treatises of Rameau and Catel, and the first result appeared in the composition of a sestett and two quintetts for flute and strings. These were afterwards destroyed by their author, who criticised his own works almost as rigorously as Mendelssohn himself, and the same destiny awaited the next production— a set of songs from Florian's *Estelle*. It must have cost Berlioz something of a pang to burn these scraps of autobiography. However, one of the quintetts furnished him with a theme which he afterwards turned to account in the overture to the *Francs Juges*, and the most lugubrious of the songs is reproduced in the introduction to the *Symphonie Fantastique*. More important still is the fact that he came across some musical biographies and some fragments of Gluck's *Orfeo* in his father's library. The former roused his enthusiasm, the latter carried it to fever heat. He fell upon the music as Cowley fell upon Spenser, or Wagner upon Beethoven. It was the

[1] *Mémoires*, chap. lxxi.

first time that he had ever seen work which combined perfect melody with real dramatic force, and we can well understand that when he compared it with the obscure scintillations of Pleyel's quartetts and Drouet's concerti he must have felt

> Like some watcher of the skies
> When a new planet swims into his ken.

Dr Berlioz observed these symptoms with growing concern. Music was all very well in its way, but where was that interest in medicine which ought to be manifesting itself? Again the time was drawing near for the choice of a profession. Something must be done at once or it would be too late. And so the good doctor, remembering the schoolmaster in Horace, who promises his pupils a cake if they will learn their letters, called Hector into his study, showed him Munro's Anatomy, and said, 'Here is your work. Persevere at it and you shall have a beautiful flute, with all the new keys, from Lyons.' It was, of course, a very short-sighted policy, but for the time it triumphed. Berlioz set himself reluctantly to master the structures of mesentery and œsophagus, and in spite of repeated failures contrived by the time he was nineteen to learn all that his father could teach him.

The situation was natural enough. It is not everyone who can foresee the stateliness of the swan in the awkward movements of the ugly duckling. To piece out 'Marlbrouk' imperfectly on an old flageolet does not necessarily give promise of a *Symphonie Fantastique* or a *Damnation de Faust*. And meanwhile the doctor's gig stands at the door; the doctor's patients are waiting throughout the country-side; there is an old-established practice, a reputable name, a certainty of competence and comfort—what more reasonable than to take the boy away from his playthings and turn him to an occupation where he will make his living and do some good to his neighbour? He need not repress his music altogether. It will be a pleasant relaxation for him when his day's work is done. But business first: let him learn to do something useful and he may spend his leisure moments as he likes.

Accordingly, in 1822, he set out for Paris with his cousin Robert, bound for the Medical School, and feeling, no doubt, rather like a condemned criminal on his way to the galleys. But the first day in the dissecting-room was too much for him. He gave one glance round the accumulated horrors, leapt from the window, and fled home, declaring that he would rather die than return to 'that charnel house.' It a little spoils the story to add that, under considerable pressure from Robert, he ultimately did return; but although he liked some of his lecturers—notably Amusat, Thénaud, and Gay-Lussac—he never felt for medicine itself anything more cordial than a 'cold disgust.' However, as he says, he went on stoically, and might have added another to the long list of bad doctors if he had not paid a visit to the Académie de Musique.

Ibi omnis effusus labor. They were playing Salieri's *Danaïdes*, an opera written under Gluck's direct supervision, and it struck home. Back came all the reminiscences of *Orfeo;* back came all the old ambitions and enthusiasms; away flew all the prospects of a medical career. After a short struggle, the conclusion of which was foregone from the first, he threw down the scalpel, established himself in the public library of the Conservatoire, and began to devour Gluck's scores with an appetite sharpened by long abstinence. He read and re-read them, copied them out, learned them by heart, talked about them day and night, and at last wrote off to his father to announce that the die was cast, and that come what may he would be a musician. Dr Berlioz argued, commanded, stormed, all to no purpose. The young scapegrace answered the letters in the intervals of composition, but showed no sign of returning to obedience. The ugly duckling was outside the gate, and not all the clatter of the farmyard could call him back.

It was in the Conservatoire library that he first met Cherubini. The new director had signalised his accession to office by some stringent disciplinary laws, and, among others, had issued an edict that men and women were to enter the building from opposite sides. Berlioz, of course, 'didn't see the notice.' He presented himself at the wrong door, brushed by the servant who tried to stop him, and in a few minutes had drowned all memory of the incident in the depths of *Alceste*. Presently steps approached, and a voice said, 'Here he is.' He looked up. Hottin the porter was standing at his elbow, and beside Hottin was a thin, cadaverous figure, with a pale face, tumbled hair, and fierce gleaming eyes, that glared at the offender as Jeffreys used to glare at his prisoners. The scene that followed has been dramatised once for all in the *Mémoires*. Cherubini began by scolding, continued by forbidding Berlioz the use of the library, which he had no right to do since it was public, and finished by commanding Hottin to seize the rebel and 'carry him off to prison.'

Then, before the eyes of the astonished readers, began a vigorous chase, which only ended when Berlioz reached the door and flung back a Parthian shaft to the effect that he was 'soon coming back to study Gluck again.' It may be presumed that on the next occasion he entered from the Faubourg Poissonière: but one would rather like to know what Hottin said to him when he let him in.

The next thing was to find a master, since it is easier to copy Gluck's scores than to imitate them. So one morning Berlioz presented himself at Lesueur's door armed with a letter of introduction, a cantata, and a canon for three voices—a rather pathetic sacrifice to the gods of counterpoint. He could not have made a better choice. Lesueur, who was then Professor of Composition at the Conservatoire, had been all his life a supporter of the dramatic Ideal in Music, and had even suffered some persecution in the cause. He gave his visitor a kindly reception, read the cantata through, and said, 'There is a good deal of power in your work, but you don't yet know how to write, and your harmony is one mass of blunders. Gerono will teach you the principles of harmony, and when you have mastered them sufficiently to follow me I shall be glad to receive you as a pupil.' In a few weeks Berlioz was ready, and the lessons began in earnest.

Meantime the pupil was working hard on his own account. He set Florian's *Estelle*, dramatised by his friend Gerono, and inspired, no doubt, by a vision of pink shoes. He wrote a 'blustering' bass song on words from Saurin's *Beverley*, and finally he accepted a commission from Masson to compose a mass for St Roch. Here was a chance. He was to have an orchestra of a hundred picked musicians; a still larger choir; Valentino the leader at the Opera to conduct; the work was to be performed on Innocent's day, when the church would be crowded; fame and fortune were sure to come, and La Côte St André would be convinced.

Alas! for the moment La Côte St André triumphed. On the day of the full rehearsal there appeared a chorus of thirty-two, a band consisting of nine violins, a viola, an oboe, a horn, and a bassoon, and a set of copies so full of mistakes that the whole performance broke down. To make matters worse, the next letter from home commented on the 'failure,' and drew some very pointed moral lessons on the subject of self-will and obstinacy. But Berlioz was undaunted. He rewrote the whole work, copied it himself, borrowed 1200 francs from his friend Pons, invaded St Roch once more, and scored a success which his bitterest enemy would allow to be well deserved. The music he describes, with his usual candour, as 'a bad copy of Lesueur's style, with the same casual inequality of colour'; and it is worth adding that when he heard it for the second time, three years later, he incontinently burned it, in company with *Beverley*, *Estelle*, and a Latin oratorio on the Passage of the Red Sea.

Towards the end of 1823 Lesueur got him into the Conservatoire. Fortunately this step did not necessitate a personal interview with the director, and Berlioz was firmly established in his place before he was officially introduced to the dread potentate who had chased him round the library table a year before. They were predestined to antagonism: the one cold, formal, severe, a living model of the *ancien régime* in Music; the other violent, enthusiastic, and as revolutionary as Mirabeau. Cherubini, too, had a touch of malice, a sting which his insubordinate pupil was never tired of irritating; and so the history of the relation between them resolves itself into a rather sordid account of petty tyranny and contemptuous defiance. Even after the Conservatoire days there was never more than a hollow truce between them, and Berlioz is always happiest when he can tell a story at his old master's expense. It may be admitted at once that the whole right did not lie on the younger man's side. Many of the faults which his masters found in his work were real defects—defects which he never entirely erased—and he might undoubtedly have written better if he had not regarded Lesueur's harmony as 'antediluvian' and Reicha's counterpoint as 'barbarous.' At the same time it is difficult to avoid thinking of Beckmesser and Walther von Stoltzing when we read that, on presenting himself for his first Conservatoire examination, he was promptly and ignominiously plucked.

This brought matters to a climax at La Côte St André. Here was an unanswerable argument at last. A musician who failed to answer a few rudimentary questions in the grammar of his own art—why, the thing was preposterous on the face of it, and Dr Berlioz wrote off a peremptory note to say that supplies would be stopped unless the prodigal returned at once. Lesueur—good, easy man—tried to act as mediator, and of course made matters worse. There was nothing for it but that Berlioz should go home and plead his cause in person. His reception was chilling enough, until, after a few days of dumb despair, his father, who was a kind-hearted man with all his sternness, relented at the sight of the boy's misery, and gave him one more chance.

'If after that you fail,' he said, 'you will, I am sure, acknowledge that I have done right, and you will choose some other career. You know what I think of second-rate poets: second-rate artists are no better, and it would be a deep and lasting sorrow to me to see you numbered among the useless members of society.'

Certainly the doctor came well out of this interview; but there was still Madame Berlioz to face. The antagonism which she had always shown to her son's profession was not likely to be mitigated by his ill-success; the voice which she had raised in protest while his chances still hung in the balance grew more vehement now that the scale had apparently turned against him. His utmost entreaties were not strong enough to win over her consent, and at last, after a most painful scene of tears and recriminations, she dismissed him in open anger. When he left his home a few hours afterwards she would not see him to say farewell. He had set his will against hers, and the very love which she bore him only intensified her jealousy towards her rival.

Berlioz went back to Paris with a heavy heart. His allowance of 120 francs a month was none too large, and he owed Pons 1200 francs for the concert expenses at St Roch. But he lived in a garret, he dined off bread and dates, he taught anyone who would learn of him, and in a few months had saved enough to pay off the moiety of his debt. Then came misfortune. His kindly creditor found out his privations, and wrote to tell Dr Berlioz, incidentally mentioning that there were still 600 francs to come, and that his son would certainly starve if he tried to pay them by the same means. It was a remarkable instance of the effect of indiscriminate benevolence. Dr Berlioz paid Pons—and stopped the allowance altogether. He felt, no doubt, rather annoyed that the first result of the hard-given permission should present itself in the form of a dun.

But it is ill trying to expel nature with a fork. Berlioz worked day and night, attended all his classes, took all his pupils, wrote an opera on *Les Francs Juges*, which was immediately refused, and finally, on the brink of starvation, secured a place as chorus singer at the Théâtre de Nouveautés. His competitors were a weaver, a blacksmith, a broken-down actor, and a chorister from St Eustache, so that his victory was not particularly glorious, but it brought him fifty francs a month, and that was something. He found a compatriot as poor as himself, and they set up house together, like a couple of Murger's Bohemians, rich through all their poverty in the two most splendid of human possessions—youth and freedom. About this time he began to study Walter Scott, and wrote an overture to *Waverley*, a fine breezy composition, somewhat open to criticism in its structure, but stronger and simpler than his more famous works, and showing already that marvellous intuition of orchestral effect which has made his name proverbial. There must have been something Irish in his blood. The harmony, counterpoint, and form which he learned from the best teachers in Paris are very frequently defective, while his most indisputable title to immortality lies in the orchestration, for which he had no master at all.

Spring came round again. Berlioz passed his preliminary examination and entered for the Prix de Rome. This admirable institution, the core and centre of the Paris Conservatoire, is a 'travelling fellowship' of £120 for five years, the first two to be spent in the French Academy at Rome, the third in Germany, and the two last in Paris. Unfortunately the conditions were rather academic in 1826. The selected candidates were locked up in separate rooms, with a piano, a pile of music paper, and a 'Classical' poem, and set to write a lyrical scena for one or two voices and orchestra. On the completion of the work, for which twenty-two days were allowed, the compositions were submitted to the professors, and after their ballot to a complete jury of the Académie des Beaux Arts—'painters, sculptors, architects, engravers, etchers, not excluding even the six musicians.' To aid their decision the scena was rapidly played over, but the only accompanying instrument allowed was the piano, and the compositions were criticised according to a *tabulatur* of the most rigorous formal rules. The subject for this year was the death of Orpheus, and it is needless to say that when Berlioz got among the Bacchanals he soon outstripped the meagre resources of the Conservatoire pianist. His work was declared unplayable, and he was excluded from the competition. Nothing in the whole matter seems to have angered him so much as this mutilation of his orchestral effects. 'By destroying them,' as he says, with pardonable exaggeration, 'the piano at once reduces all Composers to the same level, and places the clever, profound, ingenious instrumentalist on the same platform with the ignorant dunce who knows nothing of this branch of his art. The piano is a guillotine, and severs the head of noble or of churl with the same impartial indifference.'

Hector Berlioz 85

French opera was at this time in a most deplorable condition. Rossini had just finished his term of engagement at the Théâtre Italien, and the whole direction was in the hands of his successor Gérard, Kreutzer of the Académie de Musique, and Castil-blaize of the Odéon, three operatic showmen who treated masterpieces 'as gypsies treat stolen children.' Not only did they correct Gluck's instrumentation, like our modern Composers who write additional accompaniments to Handel, and will one day write them to Wagner, but they remodelled and travestied whole works by way of adapting them to the taste of the Parisian populace. *Zauberflöte* appeared as *Les Mystères d'Isis*, by 'Mozart and Laenith,' *Freischütz* was voted too classical for the boulevards, except in the mutilated form of *Robin des Bois*; even Rossini's 'melodious cynicism' and Grétry's delicate humour were hacked and disfigured with the same remorseless cruelty. It is only fair to add that England was not much better. The bills of Covent Garden during the same period are a lasting shame and reproach even to Philistia. Indeed there seems to have been no limit to the presumption of editors and impresarii during the early part of this century. Nägeli 'corrected' one of Beethoven's sonatas. Habeneck and Fétis did the same with his symphonies. Haslinger altered the key of Schubert's so-called *Élégie Impromptu* from G-flat to G. Fancy a picture dealer who should commission his assistants to repaint Titian's 'inappropriate' backgrounds or secularise Angelico's 'monastic' colouring.

Against this vandalism Berlioz waged truceless war. Night after night he took his seat in the pit and avenged 'the wronged great soul of an

Ancient Master' with the most trenchant criticism, delivered in the most stentorian voice. It is a wonder that he was not turned out, as Dumas was on a famous occasion, but somehow he kept his place, and established a reign of terror over performers and audience alike. This, it may be remarked, was not the most politic way of furthering his fortunes. The authorities naturally thought that their pupil would be better occupied in studying counterpoint at home than in preaching insubordination at the opera-house; and they expressed their opinion by rejecting him with ignominy when for the second time he presented himself as a candidate for the Prix de Rome. They were not going to waste good money on an idle scapegrace while there was so much docile mediocrity waiting to be rewarded.

In September 1827 an English company came over to the Odéon to play Shakespeare. It included Liston, Abbott, Charles Kemble, and above all Miss Smithson, an Irish actress of great charm, whose impersonations of Ophelia and Juliet at once took the theatre by storm. Paris was growing a little weary of the trim close-cropped Versailles garden in which, ever since the reaction against Hardy, the French drama had been content to move. 'Le froid petit Racine' had for the moment lost his hold on the hearts of his countrymen, and England and English freedom were in vogue. Letourneur's translation was in everybody's hands: plays had been adapted out of *Othello* and *Macbeth*, the *Débats* had published article after article in praise of 'le grand Shakespeare,' and at last came the chance of seeing in their original form dramas that stood to *Le Cid* and *Athalie* as the ocean to a lake or the open heath to a square-cut lawn.

Hector Berlioz

Berlioz only witnessed two performances; but they were enough. He raved of Shakespeare. He followed Miss Smithson about with gaunt and hungry eyes, until she thought he was mad, and asked her friends for protection. He spent nights of sleepless misery wandering through the streets and faubourgs. He forgot his work, he forgot his ambition, he forgot Cherubini and the Prix de Rome, everything except his hopeless passion and his 'most beautified Ophelia.' At last he roused himself to the resolve that he would give a concert of his own works, in the sole hope that she might hear of it. 'I will show her,' he said, 'that I too am an artist.'

There was something heroic about it all. He worked sixteen hours a day to copy his parts; he half-starved himself to save the money for his chorus; he bearded Larochefoucault, the Secretary of Fine Arts, and obtained his consent .... and then Cherubini put his foot down. The only available concert hall could not be used without his leave, and this he absolutely and peremptorily refused to give. And when Berlioz, armed with a new injunction from the Minister, rode over the director's opposition, Bloc turned out to be an entirely inadequate conductor, the *Mort d'Orphée* broke down at rehearsal and had to be left out of the programme, and, as acme of misfortune, Miss Smithson never heard of the concert at all. Thus does the most fickle god in Olympus reward his faithful votaries.

Fortunately a distraction was at hand. Beethoven's symphonies, which Paris had hitherto known only in mutilated fragments, began to make their appearance at the concerts of the Conservatoire. Like Corneille's play, they were 'condemned by the magistrates, acquitted by the people.' Berton, Paër, Kreutzer, Cherubini[1] held obstinately aloof, while the public listened with the same bewildered enthusiasm which it had lately shown towards the creator of Romeo and Hamlet. Berlioz was on fire at once. He even dragged out Lesueur to hear the *C minor*, and narrates with a pleasure that is wholly free from malice the effect produced on his old master by that greatest of all instrumental works. About the same time Humbert Ferrand, who had written him the libretto of the *Francs Juges*, gave him a place on the staff of the *Révue Européenne*, and thus enabled him to eke out his scanty income by an occasional article on musical subjects. So in spite of all his troubles he contrived to live, and even to nerve himself for a third attempt at the coveted Prix de Rome.

The subject for 1828 was taken from Tasso's *Jerusalem*, the story where Herminia escapes in disguise from the beleaguered city and goes to cure Tancred of his wound. Berlioz, as usual, followed his own judgment, wrote a song *andante* which the programme said should be *agitato*, and consequently missed the prize by two votes, one of them being the director's. He obtained the second prize, a laurel wreath, a gold medal, and a free pass to the opera-house. It seems, somehow, to accentuate the irony.

1829 was in many ways an eventful year. In the first place, he came across Goethe's Faust in a French translation, devoured it with his accustomed voracity, and immediately set eight of the lyrics, and published them at his own expense. This work, which he

[1] 'Ça me fait éternuer' was Cherubini's criticism of Beethoven's later works.

soon afterwards recalled and destroyed,[1] brought him a kind letter of encouragement from Marx of Berlin, and afforded some material which he used in *Le Damnation de Faust* seventeen years after. A more important result of his admiration for Goethe was the composition of the *Symphonie Fantastique*, which he at once offered to the Théâtre de Nouveautés. This time the performance broke down because there were not enough desks for the orchestra. The directors 'had not known that a symphony necessitated such elaborate preparations. Still, two movements, Le Bal and Le Marche au Supplice, were attempted at rehearsal, and even in their imperfect form created a *furore* among the players. Next came a Fantasie Dramatique on Shakespeare's Tempest, a curious unequal piece of work, for five-part chorus and orchestra, with a rather lame Italian libretto and some very effective scoring. It was composed for Gérard, whence no doubt the choice of language, but the resources of the Théâtre Italien were inadequate to meet Berlioz's extensive demands, and he transferred his music to Lubbert of the Opera, who at once put it into his next programme. This time the blind forces of nature entered into competition. Berlioz's *Tempest* was nothing to the thunderstorm which burst over the streets of Paris on the night of the concert. The Fantasie was performed to an audience of under two hundred, and the most unfortunate of all Composers resigned himself to another defeat.

But the Prix de Rome would have made amends. As winner of the second prize in the preceding year

[1] On the title page of the overture to *Waverley* (Op. 1.) is the note: 'La partition des huit scènes de Faust ayant été détruite par l'auteur il l'a remplacée par celle-ci.' Richault published both.

Berlioz had a sort of lien on success, and he worked away vigorously enough at the 'death of Cleopatra,' which had been chosen as subject of the scena.[1] He spared no pains to conciliate his judges. He prefaced his score with a quotation from *Romeo and Juliet*, and they disapproved of Shakespeare. He based his principal song on a syncopated rhythm, and they liked their music 'soothing.' He employed a harmonic progression which is only to be found in so recondite a work as Mozart's sonatas, and they 'could make nothing of those chords from the other world.' In one word, he did his best, and as Boïeldieu candidly admitted, 'they found his best too good.' So this year the prize was not awarded at all.

There is no defending this piece of extreme injustice. Berlioz was in actual want. He was doing the work of two men on a pittance so small that it is a wonder how he escaped starvation. His exercise was of exceptional merit. On the jury's own showing he distanced all competitors. In repute, in ability, in achievement he was fully entitled to a prize, which would have meant five years' freedom from poverty and its attendant worries. He had kept every condition which officialism could impose, every rule which pedantry could formulate, and he lost his reward, not because his work was open to blame, but because there was not one of his critics who had enough knowledge to understand it.

All this time his passion for 'the fair Ophelia' was steadily burning. He wrote her assiduous letters, which, like her original prototype, she 'did repel;' he

[1] His version reappears in *Lélio* as the Chœur des Ombres. The *Tempest* Fantasie will also be found at the end of the same work.

got one of his overtures performed at a benefit where she was to play, 'that he might see his name beside hers in the programme'; finally, he took lodgings opposite her house, only to find that she was leaving Paris in a few hours. In despair he sought out his friend Hiller, then a boy of eighteen, with a handsome Jewish face and bright eyes, to gain that consolation which disappointed lovers always find in talking of their misfortunes. Hiller listened, sympathised, and told the whole story to an inamorata of his own, Mdlle. Mooke[1] the pianist. Unfortunately he added that 'he was not likely to be jealous,' and his fickle mistress at once undertook to convince him that the unlikely is that which happens. She transferred her affections to the newcomer, rallied, comforted, encouraged, made appointments, and the result may easily be divined. It was like the situation in Heine's ballad, only, as we shall see later, with a different ending.

Next year brought the Revolution, and on its turbid flood Berlioz at last sailed in to victory. The *Mort de Cléopatre* had taught him a lesson. With diplomatic astuteness he wrote his new cantata, *Sardanapalus*, in the stiffest, most academic style of which he was capable, and left out altogether the conflagration scene, on which the artistic value of the work depended. The professors were overjoyed. Kreutzer, red with the blood of Beethoven's symphonies, recognised the hand of a fellow-adapter; Boïeldieu realised, with a sigh of relief, that the harmonies were such as a plain man could understand; Catel left his roses to vote for music as innocent as they; even Cherubini's rigorous patriotism

[1] Better known to the world as Madame Pleyel.

could discover no trace of German influence in the composition. Berlioz won the prize, and immediately completed the cantata to his own satisfaction.

Even now Fortune had one more shot in the locker. The Conservatoire gave a public performance of the successful work on the prize day, and the whole of Paris came to hear. The practices had gone admirably, conflagration scene and all; the audience was on tiptoe with expectation; a few *habitués* who had been admitted to the last rehearsal whispered to their neighbours that 'these early numbers were all very well, but there was something coming which would make you jump.' There was a moment of breathless anticipation—a feeble tremolo from the violins—a wild cry from the conductor—a book went spinning across the desks—and that was all. The horns had miscounted their bars, and the explosion flashed in the pan. But Berlioz remembered St Roch. He was not easily beaten, and he determined that his *Sardanapalus* should get a hearing before he left for Italy. Accordingly he organised another concert at the Conservatoire, with a programme consisting of the prize cantata and the *Symphonie Fantastique*, mended his score, interviewed his horns, and at last secured an adequate interpretation of the two works. The symphony aroused a good deal of criticism, some of which was well deserved, but on the whole the concert may be regarded as the culminating success of Berlioz's student life. It must have been a proud moment when he 'looked through all the roaring and the wreaths' and saw Franz Liszt, not 'patient in his stall,' but applauding with that generous appreciation which the great pianist showed to all his contemporaries.

Having won the Prix de Rome Berlioz characteristically discovered that he did not want to leave Paris, and even petitioned the Minister of the Interior to let him off his Italian journey. This, of course was impossible, so he took an affectionate farewell of Mdlle. Mooke, with many protestations of eternal constancy and frequent correspondence, stopped to receive the congratulations of his parents at La Côte St André, and set out from Marseilles in the appropriate company of a batch of Modenese conspirators. On arrival in Rome he presented himself to Horace Vernet, the director, and took his place in the noisy, light-hearted, idle colony of the Villa Medici. It was an easy time. Beyond the necessity of sending home an occasional piece of music, he was free to do what he liked, to wander in the Borghese gardens, to watch the carriages on the Pincian, to go for long rambles to Frascati or Ostia, and, above all, to compose what he pleased with no fear of academic supervision.

II

THE SIEGE OF PARIS

THE day after his arrival Berlioz was introduced to Mendelssohn, then in his twenty-second year, and already known as one of the first Composers in Europe. In order to understand the curious one-sided relation between them it is necessary to realise that Mendelssohn numbered among his existing compositions the Octett, the *Reformation* Symphony, and the *Midsummer Night's Dream*, that he was keenly sensitive to perfection of form, and that his musical sympathies were as narrow as they were intense. A critic who could speak of Schubert's greatest quartett as 'schlechtes musik' was not likely to have much in common with the author of the *Symphonic Fantastique*. And at the first interview, when Berlioz modestly expressed his dissatisfaction with the opening allegro in *Sardanapalus*, Mendelssohn took him warmly by the hand. 'My dear fellow,' he said, 'I'm so glad. I was afraid you liked it.' Still, in spite of an entire incongruity of aim, the two became good friends, and almost constant companions. The kindliness and geniality of the one robbed his criticisms of their sting, and added warmth to his rare approbation; the boisterous spirits of the other broke out in schoolboy tricks that were never malicious and often amusing. It was not until the publication of Mendelssohn's letters that Berlioz learned how low his abilities were rated by the man whose esteem he valued so cordially.[1]

Meantime news from Paris had been growing more and more intermittent. Berlioz became anxious, impatient, miserable, and at last set out for France, in defiance of all academic rule, to discover the reason of this mysterious silence. At Florence he was detained by an attack of quinsy, and on the first day of convalescence[2] received a curt note from Madame Moske announcing her daughter's marriage. The 'fair comforter' had for a second time found constancy impossible.

But no emergency, however unexpected, can baffle a strong character. Without a moment's hesitation the disappointed lover determined to proceed to Paris and kill everybody concerned. He loaded a double-barrelled pistol which he had with him. He put two phials of poison into his pocket. He went to a dressmaker's on the Lung' Arno and bought the costume of a lady's-maid, in which astonishing disguise he proposed to exhibit himself at Madame Mooke's door. He was so preoccupied with his plan of revenge that he left his dress in the coach and had to get another at Genoa. He looked so desperate that the police, in terror for their country,

---

[1] 'He is a perfect caricature without one spark of talent,' was Mendelssohn's judgment on his friend, as expressed in the letter of March 29. On the other hand, Berlioz speaks in the warmest terms of the *Walpurgis Nacht* and the *Midsummer Night's Dream*.

[2] So the *Mémoires*. A letter written from Nice on May 6 gives a few more days to his stay at Florence.

refused to let him pass Turin, and sent him round
by the Riviera instead. And then came reflection.
After all it was no use burning his ships. The project might fail in spite of all precautions; it was
bad strategy to cut off every chance of retreat. So
he wrote to Vernet[1] asking that his name might be
provisionally retained on the books of the Academy,
and promising to wait at Nice till he got his answer.
As the days passed his scheme looked less inevitable.
He began to realise that the sun was shining, that it
was pleasant to lie all day among the orange trees
and sleep out at night on the slopes of the Villefranche hills. In less than a week he had relented,
and another of his most cherished creations had
'broken down at rehearsal.'

As if to add the finishing touch to this remarkable
story, Berlioz declares that the time he spent at Nice
was 'the happiest in his life.' He completely recovered
his spirits, bathed, rambled, played billiards with the
officers of the garrison, and wrote the overture to
King Lear, one of the freshest and most original of
his compositions. Indeed he might have taken up
permanent quarters at the Villa Cherici had not the
local Dogberry arraigned him on suspicion of sketching the fortifications and sent him back to Rome.

At Rome he fell in with the influenza, and for some
time suffered from the depression which is usually
caused by that most disheartening malady. Indeed,
apart from this, the country was growing more and
more antipathetic to him. He had no sense of tolerance, no feeling for the careless facility of Italian life,
no recognition of the value which even superficial

---

[1] From Diano Marina, April 18. A fragment of the letter is preserved by M. Bernard.

beauty may possess; and his letters during the rest of his stay recall Ovid's complaints from Tomi, or Heine's from England. He tells a characteristic story of his rushing into a musicseller's and demanding some piece of Weber's which he wanted to see.

'Never heard of Weber,' said the shopman, 'but here are *Il Pirata, La Straniera, I Montecchi e Capuletti, La Vest . . .*'

'Basta, basta!' roared Berlioz. 'Non avete dunque vergogna? Corpo di Dio!'

That was his verdict. He was always calling upon Italy to be ashamed of itself; of the rough horseplay of its Carnival, of the Church music, 'only fit for Silenus and his crew'; of the opera, where there was so little sense of dramatic propriety that Romeo was played by a woman, as Figaro sometimes is at the present day. Even the scenery of this 'garden peopled with monkeys' was not to be compared with Dauphiny. The wine was a 'thick oily drug,' and the populace a collection of thieves and vagabonds, who had not even the merit of looking picturesque. Clearly we cannot lay very much stress on judgments delivered in so injudicial a temper.

Of course he did little or no work. By the terms of his prize he was compelled to offer one piece of music per annum to the Conservatoire, so he sent the *Resurrexit* from his old St Roch mass, and narrates with great glee that the professors failed to recognise it, and returned him some academic compliments on the progress that it displayed. Beside this he revised the *Symphonie Fantastique*, wrote its sequel, *Lélio*, which is almost entirely a pasticcio of earlier compositions, and sketched an overture to *Rob*

Roy, which he afterwards completed and destroyed.[1] Among shorter compositions of this time may be noticed a rather dismal hymn, on words translated from Moore, a few choruses, and last, but greatest, a setting of Victor Hugo's 'La Captive,' which he wrote on a walking tour at Subiaco. It is without doubt the finest of his songs, and turns to a nobler use that feeling of melancholy which was steadily embittering his daily life.

The fact was that he had grown home-sick, not for France but for Paris. Musical Italy was entirely given over to 'that little shrimp Bellini,' while at home they were performing Beethoven's *Choral Symphony*, and Paganini was giving concerts, and opera meant something vertebrate. The struggle was of short duration. After eighteen months he could stand it no longer, and petitioned to be let off the rest of his travelling time. The petition was granted, and in May 1832 he started to leave Italy with as light a heart as most people feel on entering it.

The first news that greeted him on his return was the intelligence that Miss Smithson was back in Paris, and that she was going to stay through the winter to fulfil another theatrical engagement. It was an odd coincidence, for Berlioz had returned to produce a work in which direct reference was made to her, and had taken as his lodging the room which she had vacated on the previous day. He accepted the omen. In spite of his inconstancy he had never lost the memory of his old passion, and he now took up the thread at the exact point where the Fates had

[1] It was given once at the Conservatoire in 1834, and burned after the concert.

cut it short two years before. But, with a characteristic division of allegiance, he determined to give his concert before he visited the theatre, of which she was directress, for fear that he might again become unmanned by seeing her. It must be remembered that all this time he had not even made her acquaintance, and that she only knew of him by a report that was not altogether favourable. Further, she was far too busy to think of attending concerts, and Berlioz for his part was most anxious that she should stay away. Never was there a more excellent opportunity for *force majeure*. Berlioz was overpersuaded into sending her a ticket; she was overpersuaded into accepting it; the allusion to Ophelia was too plain to be misunderstood: in a few days she received a wild letter begging for an interview, and by the end of the year they had plighted troth.

As usual the clouds began to gather at once. Dr Berlioz disapproved of the marriage, and Miss Smithson's relations were furious. The former refused his consent, the latter filled the air with unscrupulous reports of madness and epilepsy. Then came the failure of the English Theatre; and as culminating misfortune Miss Smithson broke her leg in stepping from her carriage,[1] and had to give up all thought of her profession. As soon as she recovered Berlioz made the preparations for a civil marriage, only to see the wedding contract torn up before his eyes in the notary's office. At last, in October 1833, they were married by banns, and the stormiest year of all this stormy life passed away into blue sky and sunshine. They were both terribly poor, and there was no hope

[1] March 1, 1833. See Berlioz's letter to Humbert Ferrand, dated March 2.

of assistance from either family ; but 'she was mine,' says Berlioz, 'and I defied the world.'

So the little *ménage* went on happily enough in spite of circumstances. Madame Berlioz was a frank, fearless woman, who loved her husband and cared little for hardships. Berlioz was devoted to his wife, and had an absolute faith in the ultimate success of his work. And somehow or other there was always enough to eat, and a roof to keep out the weather, and Liszt was lodging close by, and would come in late at night to recompense their day's labour with the *Waldstein* or the *Pathétique*. Once Madame Berlioz attempted to make a reappearance at the theatre; but the public had forgotten her, there was a new favourite, and the attempt was not repeated.

Towards the end of December Berlioz gave another concert of his own works, under the direction of Gérard. 'I was afraid to conduct in person,' he says, 'for fear of compromising the performance'—a curious admission from a man whose whole work was orchestral. At the end of the performance the Composer stayed behind to chat with the band as they packed up their instruments, and on turning round to the door found himself confronted by the strangest figure he had ever seen. Imagine a long, lean, bloodless face, with a large nose, little brilliant eyes, and black hair that fell curling and clustering upon the shoulders, a body so thin and gaunt that it seemed literally composed of skin and bone, a hand and arm 'like a white handkerchief on the end of a stick,' and you have Paganini. He came forward, stammering in broken French his admiration for the music that he had just heard, took Berlioz's address, and in a short time called upon him with a commission.

Hector Berlioz

'I have a wonderful viola,' he said, 'a real Stradivarius, and should greatly like to play it in public. Would you write me a solo for it?'

Fortunately the viola was an instrument with which Berlioz was in special sympathy. He nearly always gave it a prominent part in his scores, and one of the wisest of his proposed reforms in the Conservatoire was to rescue it from the broken-down violinists to whom it was usually entrusted.[1] After a little demur (for Paganini was himself a composer, and had to be treated with deference) he accepted the commission and started upon the *Childe Harold* symphony, originally intended as a fantasia in two movements, and afterwards enlarged to the orthodox four. Paganini stayed to see the opening allegro, complained that there were too many bars rest for the solo instrument (a criticism typical of all virtuosi in every age and clime), and then left for Nice under doctor's orders. Thus the first performance of the work (November 23, 1834) took place in the absence of the man for whom it was written. The audience applauded with some cordiality, and even encored the Pilgrims' March, but the critics, led by Fétis (whom Berlioz had directly attacked in one of the monologues of *Lélio*[2]), were fierce in denunciation. There is no doubt a great deal in the work to which exception may justly be taken, but like so many of its Composer's creations it began by being arraigned for its defects, and ended by being condemned for its virtues.

By 1835 the musical arena was pretty full, and all Paris was looking at the spectacle with keen interest.

[1] *Mémoires*, ch. lxviii.
[2] *A propos* of Fétis' corrections of Beethoven's harmony.

Berlioz had joined four papers—the *Rénovateur*, the *Monde Dramatique*, the *Gazette Musicale*, and the *Débats*—from which he hurled invective and defiance at the retrogrades, while Fétis the younger retaliated with abuse. *La Caricature* published a satire on 'Le Musicien Incompris,' and Arnal burlesqued the *Symphonie Fantastique* with his 'Episode de la vie d'un Joueur.' 'From the second repetition of the first allegro,' says the actor gravely, 'I wish you to understand how my hero ties his cravat,' a gibe which, however ill-expressed, contains a very fair parody of Berlioz's interminable programmes. One does get a little tired of being told what a piece of music is intended to express, and 'Sonate, que veux-tu?' is not by any means the criticism of a Philistine.

Unfortunately Berlioz hated *feuilleton* writing, and would readily have let his theories fight their own battle had not the birth of his son Louis brought a new mouth to feed into the little establishment of the Rue Neuve St Marc. But the work was gladly undertaken and abundantly repaid. Nothing in all Berlioz's life is more bright and serene than the continued relation of love and confidence that subsisted between him and his son. Apart from one angry letter—and that written under stress of great mental worry—there was never the shadow of a misunderstanding between them. They were companions almost from the first, and when the boy grew up and entered the navy it is very touching to see how wistfully his father bore the parting, and with what anxiety and pride he watched the successful career to its premature close.

The compositions of the year are neither very numerous nor very important. He set Béranger's lines on the death of Napoleon, began a funeral cantata 'à la mémoire des hommes illustres de la France,' and worked off and on at his opera of *Benvenuto Cellini*, but it is quite clear that journalism was leaving him very little time for other pursuits. 'Once,' he says, 'I remained shut up in my room for three whole days trying to write a *feuilleton* on the Opéra Comique and not able even to begin it. Sometimes I remained with my elbows on the table, holding my head with both hands. Sometimes I strode up and down like a soldier on guard in a frost twenty-five degrees below zero. I went to the window looking out on the neighbouring gardens, the heights of Montmartre, the setting sun . . . . and immediately my thoughts carried me a thousand leagues away from that accursed Opéra Comique. And when on turning round my eye fell on the accursed title inscribed at the head of the accursed sheet of paper, so blank, and so obstinately waiting for the other words with which it was to be covered, I felt simply overcome with despair. There was a guitar standing against the table: with one kick I smashed it in the centre . . . . On my chimney two pistols were looking at me with their round eyes . . . . I watched them for a long time . . . . I went so far as to bang my head with my fist. At last, like a schoolboy who cannot do his lesson, I tore my hair and wept with furious indignation.'[1] This is like the 'drangvollen umstanden' amid which Beethoven sometimes wrote, with the additional misery of an entirely uncongenial occupation. Still, on October 2d, he tells Ferrand that *Cellini* is nearly finished, and on December 16th that it has been accepted

[1] *Mémoires* (translated by R. and E. Holmes), ch. lxiii.

(incomplete) by Duponchel. It was not actually ready for performance till 1837.

Meanwhile the post of director of the Gymnase Musicale fell vacant. Berlioz applied for it, and lost it through the influence of M. Thiers, who apparently preferred King Log to King Stork. As a sort of compensation the Government commissioned the unsuccessful candidate to write a Requiem for the victims of the Fieschi conspiracy. For the work they offered the munificent sum of 4000 francs, but on Berlioz replying that he would require 500 musicians they repented of their generosity and cast about for some diplomatic means to delay the performance. Then followed stormy interviews, fierce visits to Government offices, clerks with their eternal 'Ça n'est pas mon affaire,' a dishevelled applicant thundering and gesticulating in the Minister's sanctum, till, towards the end of 1837, news came that General Damrémont had perished under the walls of Constantine, and Berlioz was told that his Requiem would be wanted after all. Accordingly, the gigantic work was performed in the Church of the Invalides, and nearly broke down owing to the incompetence (or perhaps malevolence) of Habeneck, who had some prescriptive right to conduct. Berlioz himself took up the bâton at the critical moment and saved his forces from rout.

Four thousand francs are soon spent, and, in spite of Liszt's generous partisanship, the public showed some reluctance to purchase compositions which it could neither play nor sing. The Professorship of Harmony at the Conservatoire fell vacant, but Cherubini was still director, and Berlioz soon found that his application was so much waste paper. 'We cannot,' said Cherubini, 'give a post of this nature to a man who is not a pianist,' a reply which is almost impudent in its dishonesty, seeing that the great Master himself only used his piano as an aid to composition, and that Bienaimé, on whom the post was finally bestowed, was no more of a virtuoso than Berlioz.

Trouble followed trouble. *Benvenuto Cellini* had been accepted at the Opera, but there were vexatious delays before it could be taken in hand, and when the rehearsals did begin they were not very satisfactory. Berlioz was not allowed to conduct the work himself, and Habeneck could not be induced to learn the *tempi;* the band grew insubordinate and behaved as it does in the *Soirées d'Orchestre;* the chorus singers took the carnival scene too much in earnest, and supplemented it with some practical jokes of their own ; and, worst of all, Duprez was a failure. In his 'Souvenirs d'un Chanteur' the great tenor expresses his opinion of the *rôle* with some freedom ; in any case he was out of sympathy with the music, and did not sing his best until the sestett in the last act. The result was that the opera met with a fate that is probably unique in the history of dramatic art. The overture was encored, and the rest of the work hissed 'with admirable energy and unanimity.' After three days of it Duprez threw up his part, and the work disappeared from the bills.

So far the story has been tragic enough, for there is no tragedy darker than the continued failure of high aims. No doubt Berlioz's reach often exceeded his grasp ; no doubt there were faults of immaturity and one-sidedness in his productions, but the fact remains that he was the greatest French composer of his time, and that he was being left to starve because he wrote his best. We of these latter days, with all the heritage of the Romantic school behind us, are less likely to condemn ideas because of their novelty, or to restrict our judgment to an unthinking defence of prescriptive tradition. Indeed some of us are inclined to err in the opposite direction, and permit Music to be ugly provided it succeeds in being new. It is the necessary outcome of a lack of scientific principle that criticism should be either invertebrate or ossified, and in both cases the man of genius suffers. But from the failure of *Benvenuto Cellini* opens a new chapter, in which triumph succeeds defeat. Not that Paris relented, for she remained obdurate until the end, but the prophet who was so little honoured in his own country began to find adequate recognition and homage abroad.

It started with Paganini. That eccentric genius heard the *Harold* symphony at a Conservatoire concert, rushed on to the stage at the conclusion of the performance, knelt in public to kiss the Composer's hand, and next morning sent him a complimentary letter and a cheque for 20,000 francs. It is said, on Rossini's authority, that the gift really came from Bertin the editor of the *Débats*, and that Paganini was merely the channel through which it was bestowed. This is so exceedingly improbable that it may possibly be true; in any case it does not touch the main issue of the story or colour the streak of dawn that was beginning to show on the horizon. Of course the episode was the talk of Paris, and equally of course it provided hostility with a new weapon. But Berlioz was too happy to fight. He paid off his debts, threw up his journalist work, and started at once on his so-called *Romeo and Juliet* symphony. To it succeeded the *Symphonie Funèbre et Triomphale* for the *fête* of the July Column, and the brilliant, light-hearted *Carnaval Romain* overture, founded on a saltarello which he had already used in his unfortunate opera. It is needless to say that the first of these works was received by the Parisian press with hooting and derision, so at the end of 1840 Berlioz shook the dust of Paris off his feet and started to try his fortunes elsewhere.

There is in human affairs a strange law of compensation by which if a man have two supreme interests he is almost certain to succeed in the one and fail in the other. For the past seven years Berlioz had found at home the solace which gave him strength to fight his wearisome battles in the world of Music. Now he was on the frontier of his triumph, but in order to enter it he had to step across the grave of his married life. Where the fault lay it is impossible to determine. Madame Berlioz grew jealous and morose, her husband began to give cause for both, and the climax was reached when she absolutely refused to hear of his leaving Paris on his proposed journey. There was no open quarrel, but the breach grew wider and wider, until an amicable separation was inevitable, and towards the end of 1840 it took place. The most characteristic feature in the story is that after the separation they often met on terms of friendship, and that the most touching and genuine of all Berlioz's letters is the one in which he speaks of her death fourteen years later.

After a short preliminary flight to Brussels (where we first hear of Mdlle. Recio, 'une cantatrice assez médiocre,' who afterwards became his wife), Berlioz returned to Paris, organised a colossal concert by way of leave-taking, had the usual disturbance over it, and then set out in good earnest to conquer Germany. He travelled from Cologne to Berlin, from Zurich to Copenhagen, gave concerts in all the musical centres, and established a firm reputation throughout a country which Schumann's *Neue Zeitschrift* articles[1] had already predisposed to give him welcome. Mendelssohn offered him every facility for producing his work at Leipsic, exchanged bâtons with him in token of amity, and even praised the treatment of the double-basses in the Requiem, just as he afterwards told Wagner that 'a canonic answer in the second act of *Tannhäuser* had given him pleasure.' There was always a little touch of Atticus in Mendelssohn's relations to his fellow-composers. Schumann broke out of his usual taciturnity to praise the *Offertorium*, with its chorus on two notes; the King of Prussia regulated his royal engagements so as to hear *Romeo and Juliet* at Potsdam; Stuttgart, Weimar, Frankfort, Dresden, Hamburg, opened their gates in turn, until the campaign became one long triumphal procession. Berlioz himself describes the adventures of his travels in a series of letters written to friends at home—Liszt, Heller, Ernst, Heine, even Habeneck, whom the conqueror seems to have included in a general amnesty. And the burden of all the letters is the same: 'I am successful—let them know it in Paris.' It is rather pathetic to see how constantly his thoughts reverted to the great, brilliant, unsympathetic city that had treated him so ill.

By the middle of 1843 he was back in France and hard at work on a new opera, *La Nonne Sanglante*,

---

[1] One in 1835 on the *Symphonie Fantastique*, one in 1838 on the *Francs Juges*.

which he never finished. To the same period belongs *La Tour de Nice*, a remarkable work, 'interspersed,' as M. Bernard declares, 'with hissing, groans, the hooting of owls, and the clank of chains.' But at the first performance so much of the hissing was provided by the audience that the Composer withdrew the piece and destroyed it. One would like to know whether he really intended it seriously, or whether it belongs to the same category as Rossini's famous practical joke, *I due Bruschini*.

A short time before M. Pillet, director of the Opera, had proposed to give a performance of *Freischütz*, supplemented by recitatives in place of the spoken dialogue, and by the addition of a ballet, without which there would be little hope of any audience. This was better than Castil-Blaize and *Robin des Bois*, but it was profanation enough, and we read with some surprise that Berlioz consented to write the one and to score the 'Invitation à la Valse' for the other. 'If I don't,' he said, with logic as irresistible as that of Cowper's schoolboy, 'someone else will.' It may be admitted that the orchestration of the famous waltz is one of the most admirable pieces of workmanship that have ever been turned out, but none the less the principle of adaptation is a bad one, and no one knew this better than the offender himself.[1] And, oddly enough, Berlioz violated his own principles in an even more flagrant manner at his next concert, by giving the scherzo and finale of Beethoven's C

[1] This of course does not apply in the same degree to pianoforte transcriptions of orchestral work, such as Mendelssohn's arrangement of the *Midsummer Night's Dream* or Brahms' of the Haydn Variations. They are etchings of pictures: an adap'ation for orchestra of a pianoorte composition is a picture enlarged from an etching.

minor symphony without the rest. Worse than all, the two movements were sandwiched in between the prayer from *Masaniello* and that from *Mosè in Egitto*. It almost seemed as though his nature were growing demoralised by continually catering for a Philistine public.

However the summer's work knocked him up, and he was sent off to convalesce in the south of France, remembering, as he says, another convalescence through which he had passed in the same district thirteen years before. He gives in the *Grotesques de la Musique* a delightful account of his holiday. The cabman who drove him about Marseilles is almost worthy to stand beside the immortal Tony Weller, and he is only one of a whole gallery of sketches; the harpist at Lyons, whose part consisted of two notes, and who, to make sure of getting them right, removed the rest of the strings from his instrument; the aggrieved stranger who sent Berlioz an anonymous letter made up of the following aphorisms—

> On peut être un grand artiste et être poli.
> Le moucheron peut quelquefois incommoder le lion.
> Signé UN AMATEUR BLESSÉ;

the autograph collector who stole his hat ('it was such a bad one,' he says modestly, 'that I can't ascribe the theft to any other motive'), and a host of others, all described with the same gaiety and good humour.

Once restored to health Berlioz began to yearn for new conquests, and in 1845 he set out on a tour through Austria. He began with Vienna, where, of all people in the world, Donizetti was Kapellmeister, and it is interesting to reflect on the welcome accorded to the Composer of *Lélio* by the Composer of *La Favorita*. Beside Donizetti there were several musicians of European celebrity; Nicolai, Staudigl, Strauss, and a host of others, among whom Berlioz was very soon at home. His concerts were well attended and cordially received, he was fêted by the artists and applauded by the populace, he even succeeded in getting an introduction to Prince Metternich and talking music to that versatile diplomatist. One of the compliments that he won was characteristic enough. He was standing in the Salle des Redoutes listening to the delicate waltz-rhythms of Strauss' orchestra when a stranger rushed up, seized his left hand, and burst out,—

'Sir, you are French and I am Irish, so there is no national *amour-propre* in my opinion. I beg your permission to grasp the hand that wrote *Romeo*. Ah! sir, you understand Shakespeare!'

'Certainly,' said Berlioz; 'but you are mistaken in the hand. I always write with this one.'

From Vienna he went on to Pesth, suffering a good deal on the way from bad roads and copious inundations. He took with him a new weapon in the shape of the Rakócky March, which he had scored at the suggestion of a Viennese amateur as an appeal to Hungarian nationalism. Politically speaking it was rather a perilous achievement, for Deak was then at the height of his influence, and there was plenty of inflammable material lying ready to hand. Artistically it was one of the greatest successes of the tour, and roused the whole room to a fever of delight and enthusiasm. It is difficult for even a cold-blooded English audience to hear that electrical music unmoved, and we may well imagine what effect it produced upon the emotional, impressionable crowd, with whom its very name was sacred.

After Pesth came Prague, where he was received by Liszt and Ambros, and after Prague Breslau, where he was mistaken for De Beriot and entreated to give violin lessons. All this time he was working at the cantata on which his English reputation chiefly rests, *Le Damnation de Faust*. He made his own libretto, borrowing now and then a hint from Gérard Nerval's translation of Goethe, and set it with even more than his accustomed facility. At Passau he wrote the Introduction, one of the best numbers in the whole work; at Vienna the Elbe scene, Mephistophiles' song, 'Voici des Roses,' the Sylphs' Ballet, and the Rakócky March; at Pesth the Ronde des Paysans; at Prague the main part of Marguerite's Apotheosis; and at Breslau the rather dull Chorus of Students. The rest was completed in Paris, where the first representation was given in November 1846 to a scanty and apathetic audience. It was a cruel disappointment to him. After all his successes abroad he had reason to hope that his countrymen would receive him with some show of cordiality, and he found that they had profited by his absence to forget him altogether. 'Nous avons un grand malheur en France,' says M. Thomas, 'nous sommes réfractaires à l'admiration.'

Once more Berlioz turned his eyes to the frontier. Like Napoleon after Jena he realised that there were only two more powers to subjugate—Russia and England—and accordingly, at the invitation of Romberg and Lwoff, he transferred his forces to St Petersburg, stopping at Berlin on the way to get some letters of introduction from the King of Prussia.

He did not much enjoy the journey, since his courier proved to be a brother artist, who used to delay the carriage at the post-houses in order to jot down some wretched dance tune, which he would at once hand on to his patron to harmonise. It is said that there have been some prosperous composers in England who have adopted similar tactics.

The concerts at St Petersburg were most successful, except for the *Carnaval Romain* overture, which for some reason the Russians did not like; but at Moscow occurred a hitch in the arrangements which very nearly prevented Berlioz from getting a hearing at all. The Nobles' Assembly room was the only available concert hall, and the Grand Marshal's permission was necessary before it could be used. Berlioz called upon him.

'What instrument do you play?' asked the Marshal.

'None,' said Berlioz.

'In that case how do you propose to give a concert?'

'To have my compositions performed and conduct the orchestra.'

'Ha! That is an original idea. I never heard of a concert like that. You are aware that if permission is given the artists who make use of it are obliged in return to perform at one of the private gatherings of the nobility?'

'No,' said Berlioz blankly, 'I didn't know that.'

'If you are unable to fulfil this condition, I regret that I have to refuse you, but I cannot do otherwise.'

Next day Berlioz came back, interviewed the Marshal and the Marshal's wife, offered to play the tambourine at their next at home, if they didn't mind his playing it badly (he was always the most audacious of applicants), and finally got the inexorable rule waived for one occasion. But he could not give a second concert, and had to return to the Capital with the feeling, to which travellers in Russia are not unaccustomed, that he was no match for native officialism.

After a short stay at St Petersburg he returned home through Prussia (dining with the King at Sans Souci), spent a week with his father at La Côte St André, and then went on to Paris, where his friends had so far recollected his existence as to be plotting against him.

Mention has already been made of *La Nonne Sanglante*, an opera which Berlioz had begun in 1843 on a libretto borrowed by Scribe from Monk Lewis. At the present moment Berlioz wanted two things, one to get his opera finished and accepted by Roqueplan, the other to obtain some official post in the opera house. Roqueplan, who owed his position a good deal to Berlioz's influence, played off these two wishes against each other. 'It wouldn't do,' he said, ' for your work to be performed if you are officially connected with the place, so if we are going to appoint you the best thing you can do will be to let us have your libretto, and we'll get someone else to set it. That will leave the coast clear.' The logic is perhaps less clear. In any case Berlioz, in a fit of disgust, allowed himself to be fleeced by this confidence-trick, gave up his opera, and of course heard no more of the appointment. The libretto was offered to Halévy, Verdi, and Grisar, and finally accepted by Gounod.

However there came at the same time (October

1847) an offer which, as he says, with pardonable irony, allowed him to exchange *la belle France* for *la perfide Albion*. Jullien, the potentate of English Music, was in sore need of a new sensation at Drury Lane, and invited Berlioz over to conduct a season of Grand opera. The terms were handsome enough—on paper; 10,000 francs for the conductorship, another 10,000 for the expenses of four concerts, and a commission to write a three act opera for the second season. He accepted with alacrity. 'Art in France is dead,' he writes to his friend Ferrand, 'and one must go where it still lives.' In less than a week he was established in Harley Street and hard at work on his new duties.

The result was a *fiasco* beside which the Parisian disasters were trivial. Jullien, as might be expected from his compositions, had not a very high ideal in Music; and so, while the executive resources of the English Opera were above praise, the *répertoire* was confined to Balfe's *Maid of Honour* and Donizetti's *Lucia di Lammermoor*. Even these failed to pay expenses, and when Berlioz put on Gluck's *Iphigénie en Tauride*, and met with another defeat, the treacherous impresario started off on a foraging expedition in the provinces, and left an unpaid conductor to conciliate an unpaid chorus. Before the spring of 1848 the whole establishment was bankrupt, then came the Chartists and the French Revolution, and by the middle of the summer Berlioz was sitting on the ruins of the Faubourg St Antoine moralising over the instability of human fortunes and the difference between promise and performance. He paid three more visits to this country. In 1851 he came over as a member of the jury at the great Exhibition, and wrote an admirably fair and lucid report on the merits of the competing instruments; in 1852 and 1855 he was engaged as conductor of the new Philharmonic Society, and produced at Exeter Hall his *Romeo* symphony and some selections from his *Faust*. But these short periods of expatriation only intensified his love for Paris. He was never at his ease away from the boulevards, and found even the hospitality of London colder than the neglect of his own countrymen. Still, he was in closer sympathy with our methods than any other great artist of his time, and it is worth noting that one of the clearest and most convincing of his critical essays is devoted almost entirely to a review of English musical institutions.[1]

In July 1848 Dr Berlioz died, to the great grief of his son. Since the birth of Louis the two had been entirely reconciled, and the first halting-place after the Russian journey had been at La Côte St André, where father and son talked over old troubles and new successes with entire sympathy and confidence. It speaks highly for both that the one could admit his mistake and the other find justification for it: the Doctor frankly rejoiced that his prognostics had not been fulfilled; the Composer recognised the affection that had underlain repression and antagonism, and recalled the past without a word of complaint or a thought of bitterness. Indeed in some respects the opposition to his wishes had been of real service to him. Had he been allowed to follow his natural bent from the first he might possibly have paid for the greater ease by some sacrifice of originality. It was the sense of revolt which sharpened his faculties to their utmost, and drove him, in the sheer despair of

[1] *Soirées d'Orchestre*, No 21.

rebellion, to trust to his own resources and develop his own methods. There is little fear of compromise if one knows beforehand that nothing will be accepted short of an unconditional surrender. And, by this time, the days of controversy had long been left behind, and nothing remained but a memory of loving care and kindly companionship.

Among the productions of the year may be mentioned the *Treatise on Instrumentation*, which is, oddly enough, numbered among the compositions as Op. 10,[1] and the *Chœur des Bergers*, afterwards included in the *Enfance du Christ*. The story of the latter is well known, but will bear repeating. One evening there was a card-party at the house of a friend. Berlioz, who felt as far out of his element as Herr Teufelsdröckh at an 'Æsthetic Tea,' was sitting apart, bored and unoccupied, when an idea struck him. He called for pencil and paper, ruled lines, and began to sketch out a simple chorus, rather after the style of a Christmas carol. When it was finished he proposed to put his friend Duc's name at the bottom, was dissuaded, and finally invented a 17th century Maître de Chapelle, by name Pierre Ducré, and had the work performed as his. All Paris fell into the trap. Fétis, who as a historian might have been expected to know better, led the chorus of praise, critic after critic applauded the antique severity of the style, and the public even went so far as to declare that 'M. Berlioz could never write a work like that.' The most curious part of the story is that, although there are some slight traces of Gluck's influence in the harmonies, the composition is entirely modern in

[1] It must have been begun as early as 1843. See Schumann's letters to Härtel during that year.

spirit, and could no more have been written in the 17th century than in the 1st. When the approbation was at its height Berlioz acknowleged the authorship, to the intense disgust of his opponents, and proceeded to extend the work to the *Fuite en Egypte*, and afterwards to the *Sacred Trilogy*, which stands as his one effort at oratorio.[1]

With the death of Dr Berlioz the *Mémoires* (written in 1848) come practically to an end, and the materials for biography during the next twenty years are confined to a few supplementary chapters, a handful of letters, and the records of external incidents. It is probably for this reason alone that the latter part of Berlioz's life seems less eventful than the earlier. He had grown tired of writing a diary which was 'as wearisome as a *feuilleton*,' and he was never a very methodical correspondent. The war still continued, but he found less pleasure in recounting its triumphs or railing at its reverses. His life, too, was growing very lonely. He was separated from his wife, his son was away on foreign service, and his father's death was followed in a short time by that of his favourite sister Nanci. There was only Ferrand left.

His visits to England in 1851-2 seem to have been fairly prosperous, and his concerts at Exeter Hall were well attended by the public and well received by the press. But on his return to Paris the old troubles recommenced. Scudo attacked him, and the other critics followed suit; the concert room of the Conservatoire was closed to him by a ministerial intrigue; news of the success of *Benvenuto Cellini* at Weimar was followed by its total failure at Covent

[1] The whole story will be found in the *Grotesques de la Musique*, p. 169.

Garden ; and it is not surprising that, under all these difficulties, he grew daily more morose and suspicious, and began to find indifference in everyone who was not an enthusiast, and hostility in everyone who was not a partisan.

The death of his wife at the beginning of 1854 roused him for a moment from the sordid troubles of his career. There is something bracing in a great sorrow, at any rate when it supervenes on a number of petty cares; and we can have no doubt that in spite of everthing Berlioz was deeply attached to his Ophelia, and felt her loss keenly. After the separation, which had been mainly forced on him by her manner of life, he had often pinched himself to supply her wants; and he once narrates with pathetic simplicity that he threw aside a symphony on which he was working because she was ill and he could earn more for her by journalism. On the other hand, it is true that for the past fourteen years he had formed some sort of *liaison* with Mdlle. Recio, and that the first use he made of his freedom was to marry her.[1] It is a tangled story, which biographers of the present day may well be content to leave unexplained. Unfortunately the second venture was more disastrous than the first. Mdlle. Recio was a singer of small capacity and high ambition, who frequently imperilled the success of her husband's work by insisting on the prima donna's part in its performance. It was a ready judgment on his infidelity that after closing his home to one of the greatest artists in France he should have opened it to one who was only worthy of figuring in Daudet's collection of *Femmes d'Artistes*.

[1] August 1854. See letter to Ferrand, No. lxxviii.

In 1855 came the Paris Exhibition, and Berlioz was commissioned to write a *Te Deum* for its opening and a cantata, *L'Impériale*, for its close. The latter disappeared into the void the day after its production, but the former, at which he had been working on his own account ever since 1849, may well claim to rank beside the Requiem, than which it is even more colossal in its scale and more exacting in its requirements. Among the subscribers to its publication were the Czar, the Kings of Prussia, Saxony, Hanover, and Belgium, and Queen Victoria. Possibly this blaze of royal patronage did something to clear the myopic vision of the Second Empire, for in the next year Berlioz won the greatest distinction which an artist can obtain in France—a *fauteuil* in the Academy. He had already received the ribbon of the Legion of Honour, and a short time after this his list of public rewards closed with his appointment as Librarian to the Conservatoire. There is no doubt some fitness in his ending his days as the authorised custodian of those very scores from which in the beginning he had been hounded by an irate director.

It appears to be the custom in France, if an institution is unsuccessful or inadequate, not to reform it but to set up a substitute in its place. Consequently the comparative failure of the opera house encouraged the Minister of Fine Arts to establish a new lyric theatre on the banks of the Seine, with M. Carvalho as manager. Berlioz, to whom every event was an opportunity, watched the new erection with anxious eyes, and set about the composition of an opera which he intended should be his masterpiece and its talisman. From earliest boyhood he had been a

Hector Berlioz

passionate admirer of Virgil; he knew much of the *Æneid* by heart, and had often solaced his solitary rambles among the Apennines with its noble pathos and the flow of its matchless verse. Accordingly he chose *Les Troyens* as his subject, wrote a libretto, which was read and approved in the Hôtels Rambouillet of the day, and began with his usual rapid enthusiasm to set it to music. The work was in two parts, one on the fall of Troy, one on the episode at Carthage; and the enormous canvas soon filled with colossal figures of Anchises and Æneas, of Cassandra and Dido. But it is one thing to write an opera and another to get it performed. The score was voted too long; the first part was cut out entire and replaced by the short prologue which now appears at the beginning of *Les Troyens à Carthage;* then followed vexatious delays, hope deferred, suspicions of treachery and intrigue, and all the weary round which Berlioz had trodden so often. At last a culminating blow fell when, in 1861, the theatre, which had declared its resources inadequate to his requirements, put on Wagner's *Tannhäuser* by order of Napoleon.

Tannhäuser failed dismally, owing to the organised opposition of Parisian Chauvinism, and Berlioz was furious enough to triumph over its downfall. 'Ah dieu de ciel; quelle representation!' he wrote next day to Madame Massart, 'Quels éclats de rire! Le Parisien s'est montré hier sous un jour tout nouveau; il a ri du mauvais style musical; il a ri des polissonneries d'une orchestration bouffonne, il a ri des naïvetés d'un hautbois: enfin il comprend donc qu'il y a un style en musique. Quant aux horreurs il les a sifflées splendidement.' 'Ah! je suis cruellement vengé,' he wrote to Louis a week later.

Revenge, however, is a double-edged weapon. When *Les Troyens* did at last come before the public it was treated with as scant ceremony as its rival, and Cham produced a very popular caricature in which *Tannhäuser* is represented as a baby asking to see his little brother. The 'masterpiece' only ran for three weeks, and then disappeared from the theatre, the fortune of which it was intended to secure. Berlioz never recovered the shock of its failure He realised that he had shot his last bolt, and that it had missed its mark. At one of the performances there was a fair house (including Meyerbeer, who attended every time), and his friends tried to cheer him by saying, 'Eh bien! les voilà qui viennent.' 'Oui ils viennent,' said the Composer sadly, 'mais moi je m'en vais.'

Two happier incidents lightened the close of this troubled career. During the delay of *Les Troyens* Berlioz wrote the bright little opera of *Béatrice et Bénédict*, which in 1862 was produced under his direction at Weimar, and met with a great and well deserved success. Again, in 1867, after refusing an offer of 100,000 francs to go to New York, he accepted an Imperial invitation to Russia, and was welcomed with even greater cordiality than had been shown him on his previous visit. But the death of his wife, and still more of his son Louis, severed the last ties that bound him to the world; he was attacked by a severe nervous malady, struggled down to the south of France, and there for the third time found convalescence. It was from life's fitful fever that he was suffering, and there was only one cure possible.

At his own wish they carried him back to die in

Paris. He had loved the splendid city with an intensity which not all its heartlessness could diminish : his only thought had been for its service, his only hope for its applause : every triumph that he had won elsewhere had been to him but one more plea for recognition at home : even his suspicions of cabal and intrigue have something pathetic in them, for he could not believe that his own people were alien from him at heart. He died on March 8, 1869, and was buried in the cemetery at Montmartre, Gounod and Ambroise Thomas being among the pall-bearers. The Academy sent a deputation of honour, on the bier were wreaths from Italy, Hungary, and Russia, and the procession was headed by the band of the National Guard playing the funeral march from the *Symphonie Funèbre et Triomphale.* It is, perhaps, not fantastic to find in that work an epitome of its Composer's life : the tragic power of the first movement, with the flashes of brilliance that only deepen the gloom on either hand; the pause by the grave side, and the solemn words spoken over the dead; and, lastly, the song of triumph, which, in spite of the complaints of a *dilettante* pessimism, is the certain reward of all true Art and all noble service.

III

ESTIMATES AND APPRECIATIONS

IN criticising the works of a great composer there are only two questions which it is of any moment to consider. We may ask what was his power of imagination, we may ask what was his command of technical resource, and there inquiry must stop. Nothing is gained by a comparison of styles, for the critic is bound to accept all; nothing is gained by an expression of sympathy for one ideal rather than another, for there are only two possible ideals in Music, and both are equally worthy of regard. It would be as great an error of judgment to condemn the Romantic school in the light of Classical tradition as to decry the masterpieces of Bach and Palestrina because they lack the passion and fervour which belong to a later development of musical feeling. If, therefore, we wish to estimate Berlioz fairly we must take him on his own ground, find out what it was that he intended to express, and then see how far he was successful in carrying his scheme into effect.

Fortunately we have, in the postscript to the *Mémoires*, a manifesto which puts his case in the clearest possible words. 'Generally speaking,' he says, 'my style is very bold, but it has not the slightest tendency to subvert any of the constituent elements of Art. On the contrary, it is my endeavour to add to their number. I never dreamed of making music without melody as so many in France are found to say .... The value of my melodies, their distinction, novelty, and charm, may of course be disputed. It is not for me to estimate them, but to deny their existence is unfair and absurd.' And again : 'The prevailing characteristics of my music are passionate expression, intense ardour, rhythmical animation, and unexpected effects. When I say passionate expression I mean an expression determined on enforcing the inner meaning of its subject, even when the feeling to be expressed is gentle and tender or even profoundly calm. This is the sort of expression that has been found in the *Enfance du Christ*, in the Ciel scene of the *Damnation de Faust*, and in the *Sanctus* of the Requiem.' Here, then, we can see Berlioz's mission as he himself conceived it—not to establish a new kingdom but to enlarge the boundaries of the old; not to supersede existing forms but to animate them with fresh life; and, above all, to make Music a language for the communication of definite poetical ideas and impressions. No doubt he often used his axe with considerable vigour—'j'aime tant à faire craquer les barrières,' as he said—but the fact remains that he enrolled himself in the army of Gluck and Beethoven, and fought to extend their territory, not to conquer it. And now we may apply the two tests formulated above, the test of inspiration and the test of skill.

There can be no two opinions as to the existence of great imaginative power in his work. The very pace at which he often composed is in itself sufficient evidence. The *Marche au Supplice* was written in one night; the Pilgrims' March in *Harold* improvised in a couple of hours; the *Elégie*, one of the wildest and most complicated songs in existence was created in a single flash, while for the *Lacrymosa* in his Requiem he had to invent a system of shorthand in order to embody the ideas that came too fast for ordinary notation. And it must be remembered that this rapid production is not like the facility of a Hasse or a Gyrowetz, flowing with a diluted repetition of current commonplace; the thought here is absolutely new, and is presented with a fulness of detail which none but a master could have conceived. There may be in the earlier compositions some traces of Beethoven's influence, and even some echoes of Gluck, and perhaps Spontini; but every artist must be the child of his circumstances in the initial stages of his work. Beethoven himself begins under the shadow of Mozart, and nevertheless did he emerge later into the free light and air of an artistic personality. Indeed we may assert roundly that there is not one composer in the history of Music who has more claim to originality than Berlioz, not one who has more right to say with Corneille—

> Je ne dois qu'à moi-même toute ma renommée.

On the other hand we must confess, unwillingly enough, that the purity of his imagination was not on a level with its force, and that he wholly lacked that sense of reticence and repression which should be its necessary complement. His thought is sometimes impaired and degraded by that touch of defilement which pathologists note as a possible symptom of insanity; and he never seems to have reflected

Hector Berlioz 127

that, even in the spiritualised language of Music, there are some things which it is better not to say. Two stories will make this clear. During his stay at Rome he conceived the plan of a grand opera (fortunately never carried out) in which an impious and licentious potentate should organise a burlesque Last Judgment, as a mockery to the prophets who denounced him, and find, as the curtain fell, that his pigmy trumpets were silenced by the four angels who announced the real coming of Christ.[1] Again, during his second visit to London he attended the children's service at St Paul's, was immensely impressed by its beauty, as Haydn had been before him, and on leaving the cathedral fancied that he saw the whole scene travestied in Pandemonium. It is to this unwholesome morbid element in his nature that we owe the orgies in *Harold*, the Chorus of Devils in *Faust*, and worse than either, the horrible Ronde du Sabbat in the *Symphonie Fantastique*. And as an inevitable consequence, he is almost entirely wanting in the real epic touch, the white Alpine sublimity of Beethoven's Mass in D or Brahms' *Schicksalslied*. He can inspire wonder but not awe, terror but not reverence, and much of the work which he intended to be most impressive resolves itself into a series of scenes which sometimes rise to the level of the Inferno, and oftener sink to that of the Musée Wiertz.

One region, then, and that the highest, must be regarded as closed to him. He has left no work which breathes the same serene æther as the *Missa Papæ Marcelli*, or the *Messiah*, or the C minor symphony. He comes near the line in the *Sanctus* of

[1] See letter to Ferrand, No. xl. (January 8, 1832).

his Requiem, and perhaps the final chorus of the *Enfance du Christ*. But as a general rule his attempts to express pure religious emotion are either dull, like the Easter Hymn in *Faust*, or preoccupied, like the Pilgrims' March in *Harold*. Still there is much opportunity for noble achievement in lower fields of poetry, and of this he has made abundant use. Like Ben Jonson, in Mr Swinburne's estimate, if he does not belong to the Gods of melody, at any rate he may be numbered among the Titans.

In the first place he has a complete mastery over the whole gamut of fear and pain. The stupendous crashing force of the *Tuba Mirum*, the *Lacrymosa*, echoing with the agony of a panic-stricken world, the *Judex Crederis* from the *Te Deum*, which reiterates higher and higher the expectation of the Great Judge and the appeal to His mercy, are conceived with a vastness of scale, and carried out with an unerring certainty of effect to which we shall hardly find a parallel. 'Berlioz's music,' says Heine in his *Lutèce*, 'has generally something primitive or primeval about it. It makes me think of vast mammoths or other extinct animals, of fabulous empires filled with fabulous crimes, and other enormous impossibilities. He is a magician, and he calls up Babylon, the hanging gardens of Semiramis, the marvels of Nineveh, and the vast temples of Mizraim.' On a lower level, but not less remarkable in execution, is the ride to the Abyss, where Faust and Mephistopheles gallop through a pestilential air, filled with 'horrid shapes and shrieks and sights unholy,' till the end comes, and the most tragic figure in all dramatic poetry sinks with a despairing cry to meet his doom. To say that these things are not worth portraying is simply to remove the landmarks of artistic expression. Everything is worth portraying which is not essentially foul or obscene, and even a degraded subject may sometimes be ennobled by dignity of treatment. No doubt the story of Faust is intrinsically horrible, and Berlioz has fixed upon its least sympathetic aspect. But it is not until we come to the hideous chorus of gibbering fiends that we feel that the legitimate bound is exceeded and that horror passes into loathing.

A second noticeable point is his treatment of the passion of love. There is, perhaps, no form of inspiration in which the Composers of the Romantic school have more displayed their individuality. Chopin, the Musset of Music, is keen, delicate, sensitive, sometimes marring his thought with the querulousness of an invalid; Schumann is strong and manly, loving so much because he loves honour more; Brahms is a poet, intent on weaving a network of beautiful thoughts around his ideal; and the diapason closes full in the perfect, glorious passion, pure and irresistible as flame, of Wagner's *Tristan*. Among all these Berlioz holds an independent place. Apart from the *Symphonie Fantastique*, to which further allusion will be made later, we have the trio in *Faust* and the exquisite adagio in the *Romeo and Juliet* symphony to sound the note of an emotion which knows that it is true and tries to cheat itself into the belief that it may be happy. For there is always an undercurrent of melancholy in his love-music, a sense of present pain, or an apprehension of coming trouble, till tragedy reaches its limit in the heart-broken *Élégie*, and the vindictive despair of *Les Troyens*.

Pathos and humour are proverbially near akin,

and we need feel no surprise that the Composer of *La Captive* should also have written the fencing scene in *Benvenuto Cellini* and Somarone's delightful 'wedding cantata' in *Béatrice et Bénédict*. There is plenty of rough fun, too, in the Auerbach's Keller episode of *Faust*, and above all in the rollicking *Carnaval Romain* overture. But as a rule Berlioz wrote his music seriously and kept his jokes for his *feuilletons*. He did not, perhaps, altogether realise the opportunities for comedy which can be turned to account in a quaint phrase or an unexpected tone: the happy chances which have given us Papageno and Beckmesser, La Belle Hélène and the Mikado. Indeed, if there is any matter for astonishment at all it is that a man who possessed so keen a sense of the ludicrous should not have given it fuller expression in the art which draws as readily from the springs of laughter as it does from the fount of tears.

There remains to be considered one class of poetical ideas which may be called the Spectacular: those in which the music is intended to call up some scenic display, religious, chivalrous, martial, or what not, which it presents to us in repose, with no direct appeal to emotion and little exhibition of present activity. Such, for instance, is the intermezzo in *Les Troyens*, which represents a forest during a hunting scene; such is the *Hymne à la France*, with its stately chorus, such the strong march movement of the *Menace des Francs*, and the sturdy industrialism of the *Chant des Ouvriers*, and such undoubtedly is the Kyrie in the *Requiem*, which suggests some vague remote picture of a cathedral interior, with dim lights and white-robed priests and a hanging cloud of incense. Under this category may come the concert overtures, where Berlioz for once abandons his programme, and is content to indicate rather than prescribe; and at its extreme verge may be placed the *Symphonie Funèbre et Triomphale*, which brings us back again to the world of actual drama.

So far we have examined Berlioz's imaginative power in the light of his own principle: that Music is a definite language capable of communicating definite ideas. It is in defence of this principle that he prefaces so many of his instrumental works with a scheme or programme describing in set words the emotion which his melodies are expected to arouse, or the scene which they are intended to portray. Even the little violin solo which he wrote for Artôt has one of these elaborate analyses on its title page, and accounts for every phrase and every modulation with the most remorseless assiduity.

This principle is not more than a half-truth. It is true that, in the present century at any rate, Music is something more than a 'concourse of sweet sounds,' that it can rouse genuine emotion in the hearer, that it can, under certain circumstances, aid in completing a picture which he already has before his eyes. But, with very few exceptions, it is not true that any given melody can be tied down to any given meaning, or that Music can by itself convey a pictorial idea with any clearness of outline. It is an inarticulate language, and lacks that purely rational element which all nomenclature implies. There is, for instance, no question about the general landscape effect of Beethoven's *Pastoral* symphony, but who can tell what is meant by the allegretto of the seventh or the opening movement of the ninth? They are equally romantic, but the ideas which they suggest are too subtle for the clumsy embodiment of any descriptive phrase. The hearer may make a picture for himself. He may see the 'Love-tragedy' in Chopin's B-flat minor sonata, or the 'Christian martyr' in Schubert's unfinished symphony, but the effect is purely subjective, and he has no word to answer to his neighbour who 'doesn't see it.' No doubt most dance tunes are merry, and most funeral marches are sad, and a movement entitled 'Storm' may be trusted to tell its own story, but beyond these and a few similar exceptions there is no possibility of a convincing interpretation.

In the theatre it is different. There we have the scene in front of us, and the music acts as an accessory, and brings our emotional nature into harmony with its surroundings. The overture to *Rheingold*, which is absolutely meaningless in a concert room, grows full of significance when we see the glimmer of the green water as it answers to the ripple of the strings. The Schmiedelied in *Siegfried* produces double the effect upon us when we hear the music rising and falling as the flames dance and leap and sink back upon the furnace. But except in opera, and within definite limits in oratorio and song, descriptive music fails of its aim. With the aid of words, and still more of scenery and action, it can sometimes present clear pictorial effects: without them, never.

There are two other reasons why the 'Programme' in instrumental music represents a false ideal. In the first place it leaves nothing to the imagination of the hearer, and thus paralyses the one faculty which it ought most directly to stimulate. 'L'art d'ennuyer c'est tout dire,' and the audience has as much right to resent the composer's interference in this matter as sightseers to cashier an officious guide who bores them with explanations when they want to sit still and admire. In the second place, it is painfully open to burlesque. The scherzo in *Romeo and Juliet* was meant by its Composer to express the delicate flight of Queen Mab and her fairy train : the critics compared it to the 'squeaking of an ill-greased syringe.' The ponderous double-bass chords in the 'King of Thule' ballad were written to emphasise the tragic gloom of the story ; but all thought of tragedy flies when we hear them likened to the 'pushing of a heavy table across the floor.' And such parodies are only the natural outcome of a perfectly legitimate impatience. We do not want to be told what the music means : we prefer to find out for ourselves. Let the Composer write, if he will, with some clear poetical thought in his mind—though it may be doubted whether the greatest Masters have done so —but let him not seek to impose it upon our acquiescence. If he does, we simply turn upon his work and exclaim, with M. Bourget's artist, 'Sois belle et tais-toi.'

This position may fairly be illustrated by an examination of Berlioz's most uncompromising piece of 'Programme Music'—the *Symphonie Fantastique*. In his letter to Ferrand (April 16, 1830) the Composer tells the story which the work is intended to express with a fulness of detail which at least shows that he has the courage of his opinions. The opening adagio presents a young artist, with a lively imagination and a sensitive temperament, plunged in that half-morbid reverie which French writers explain as the 'besoin d'aimer.' In the allegro which follows he meets his fate, 'the woman who realises the ideal of beauty and charm for which his heart has yearned,' and gives himself up to the passion which she inspires. His love is typified by a rather sentimental melody, given in full at the opening of the movement, and repeated in various thematic forms throughout the whole work. The second movement proper is an adagio, in which the artist wanders alone through the fields, listening to the shepherd's pipe and the mutterings of a distant storm, and dreaming of the newborn hope that has come to sweeten his solitude. Next comes a ballroom scene, in which he stands apart, silent and preoccupied, watching the dancers with a listless, careless gaze, and cherishing in his heart the persistent melody. In a fit of despair he poisons himself with opium, but the narcotic instead of killing him produces a horrible vision, in which he imagines that he has killed his mistress and that he is condemned to die. The fourth movement is the march to the scene of execution, a long, grim procession, winding up with the *idée fixe* and the sharp flash of the guillotine. Last comes the 'Pensée d'une tête coupée': a hideous orgy of witches and demons, who dance round the coffin, performs a burlesque 'Dies Iræ' for its funeral rite, and welcome with diabolic glee a brutalised and degraded version of the original subject. And so the symphony ends with an indescribable scene of chaos and fury, of fiendish mockery and insult, a delirium of passion, mad, riotous, and unrestrained.

Not a very noble or exalted romance it may be, but this is not the point at issue. The only question is how far Berlioz has succeeded in expressing it through the medium employed, and, with all recognition of his marvellous ingenuity of workmanship, we must admit that he has failed. It is inconceivable that any hearer should write down the story from the music unless he had already some knowledge of its outline, and even with the programme before us we only feel that a set of vague indeterminate forms are being unduly specialised. The recurrent melody may, no doubt, symbolise 'a white woman's robe,' as Heine said, but it could equally well symbolise a hundred other things. The vigour and rush of the opening allegro no doubt suggests agitation, but it may be any one of its various forms. The ball scene, with its exceedingly beautiful waltz tune, contains no necessary thought of despair—much less such despair as would lead to suicide. The *Marche au Supplice* is fierce and gloomy enough, but it might be a battle-hymn or the funeral march of a warrior, and so with the other movements. They all suggest some generic form under which the particular idea may be classified, but they do not indicate the particular idea itself. And this is not through any inadequacy on the part of the composer, for Berlioz has employed all the resources of a vivid imagination to give shape and colour to his idea ; it is simply because he has tried to make Music perform a task, of which from its very nature it will always be incapable. There is a great deal of fine and noble work in the *Symphonie Fantastique*, notably in the three middle movements, but it pleases in spite of the programme, not in consequence of it.

The same is the case with the *Harold* symphony, where the scenes are as loosely strung together as they are in Montgomery's 'Omnipresence of the Deity,' and still more with the *Rêverie et Caprice* for Violin. It is a short fantasia in two movements, adagio and allegro vivace (the first being repeated entire in the middle of the second), pleasantly and melodiously written, though without anything 'fit in itself for much blame or much praise,' unless one should censure it for some deficiencies in form. Turn to the title page and you find that everything has an inner meaning, that F-sharp minor implies despair, that a semiquaver figure is meant to symbolise doubt or agitation, and that 'voluptés fougueuses' are embodied in a most innocent looking melody. Surely it is not a very far cry from this to Arnal and his travesties at the Bal d'Opéra.

But it is a pleasanter task to turn and consider the second of the two points for discussion—the estimate of Berlioz as a musician pure and simple. After all his belief in Programmes is nothing worse than an aberration of genius, which does not really impair the intrinsic value of the work that it interprets; and the contention has been, not that he is lacking in dramatic power, for he possesses it in a very high degree, but that its action is restricted by the necessary limits of the Art to which it belongs. So far as inspiration is concerned, his claim to immortality is incontestable; and it only remains to examine the ability that he displayed in dealing with the various modes of musical expression.

These may be enumerated under four main heads: Melody, which is roughly analogous to the drawing in a picture; Harmonisation, by which substance and solidity are given to the melodic outline; Form, which so groups the figures on the canvas as to present them in the best possible relation to each other; and finally, 'le coloris de la Musique,' Instrumentation. Under these, again, may be placed certain subdivisions,—symmetry of phrase, rhythm, modulation, contrapuntal skill, all of which fall into one or other of the above-mentioned classes. Melody, for instance, includes symmetry and rhythm as well as the actual 'curve' which is presented by its succession of tones; counterpoint and its descendant polyphony are clearly subordinate to the general principle of harmonisation, and so with the rest Thus it will be seen that the modes of expression are themselves complex, and contain too many constituent elements to be considered from a single point of view.

Now, there can be no question that Berlioz has left us some tunes of very high worth. *La Captive* is a complete and final answer to the critics who have regarded its Composer as unmelodious; the love scene in *Romeo* is as beautiful as an adagio of Schubert; the great septett in *Les Troyens*, the 'Chœur des Bergers' in the *Enfance du Christ*, Hero's song, 'Je vais le voir' in *Béatrice et Bénédict*, the Sanctus in the *Requiem*, are only random instances of work which places him uncontrovertibly in the first rank of musicians. Equally successful, though expressive of a more easily attainab'e ideal, are Mephistopheles' serenade in *Faust*, the ball scene in the *Symphonie Fantastique*, and the 'Aubade' from the *Feuillets d'Album*. The Harold *motif*, too, with its curious reminiscence of the opening allegro in Beethoven's seventh symphony, is full of a noble melancholy, while the famous *idée fixe*, though certainly of less value, has nevertheless a marked expression and character of its own.

But every man, as George Sand said, has the defects of his qualities. Berlioz was one of the greatest masters of rhythm and modulation that the world has ever seen, and he frequently ruins his effects in consequence. He varies his metres till he destroys the homogeneity of his stanza, he changes his key with a forcible wrench that surprises without pleasing, in one word, he is so suspicious of monotony that he often falls into restlessness. The Villanelle in the *Nuits d'Été* begins in A major, and after two or three bars is thrown over the wall into B-flat; the Pilgrims' March in *Harold*, which opens with a magnificent phrase, is similarly spoiled by a cadence at the end of the fourth line; on many occasions a good idea is abandoned where it ought to be developed, simplicity is sacrificed for epigram, directness for ingenuity, until the whole result is as depressing as a jest book. 'This is where so many young composers fail,' writes Haydn in one of his letters; 'they string together a number of fragments, they break off almost as soon as they have begun, and so at the end the listener carries away no definite impression.'

And yet how fine his rhythms are! Look at the opening phrase in the *King Lear* overture, at the accompaniment figure in the *Lacrymosa*, at the fascinating tune of the Sylphs' Ballet in *Faust*, at the whole Carnival scene in *Benvenuto Cellini*, and a hundred others. Modulation is a lesser gift, for anyone can learn how to modulate, but only a genius of the highest order could have devised a metrical system of such variety and extent. And it must be remembered that devices which seem to us familiar, like the persistent figure of the Chœur des Ombres in *Lélio*, or the alteration of *tempo* in the various presentations of the *idée fixe*, were comparatively or entirely new in Berlioz's day. Rhythm was then, as he says, in 'A Travers Chants' the least developed of all modes of musical expression, and we may well forgive him if he sometimes lost control of a pioneer's enthusiasm and treated as an end in itself the power which his predecessors had under-estimated even as a means.

Melody and Harmony are so closely interconnected in modern Music, that it may perhaps seem unnecessary to give the latter any detailed criticism. But, as a matter of fact, every great Composer has his own special manner of harmonisation, by which he can be distinguished almost as readily as by his mastery of form or his power of melodic invention. In this respect Berlioz does not show to such advantage as in some other of the details of his Art. His harmony is rarely rich, except where it is used as the vehicle of a remote or recondite modulation, and it does not often atone for its commonplace character by any real strength or solidity. Like Gluck he is fond of massing the tenor and bass at the bottom of the chord and separating them from the treble and alto by a wide interval, witness the Pilgrims' March in *Harold* and the Shepherds' Chorus in the *Enfance du Christ*, but this device, though often successful on the strings, produces an unequal, 'knotty' effect when used for voices. No doubt he writes his parts with extreme rhythmic independence. Many of his choral works read like operatic ensembles, in which each voice has a character and personality to itself, but even this result can sometimes be compatible with a small minimum of variety in the harmonic progression. A similar weakness is observable in his counterpoint, except of course when he used it for purposes of burlesque. When he attempted it seriously, as in the first chorus of the Te Deum, he usually betrayed a want of mastery, which is intelligible enough if we realise the immense labour and concentration which the method demands and the antagonism which he felt for it throughout. On the other hand, the Amen Chorus in *Faust* is an admirable travesty, and better still is the Wedding Cantata in *Béatrice et Bénédict*, with the unanswerable logic of its text and the angular trills and flourishes of its oboe obbligato.

A more serious defect is his almost invariable looseness of structure. The laws of form are as capable of extension and development as those of melody itself, but if any existing scheme is to be susperseded something better must be put in its place. We cannot suffer a retrograde system of evolution from organic to inorganic, from order to chaos. And, unfortunately, Berlioz seems not to have been aware of this weakness. He protests vigorously in the *Mémoires* against the critics who attacked the construction of the *Symphonic Fantastique*, and declares that in this, as in other things, he was only carrying on legitimate tradition, and 'taking up Music where Beethoven laid it down.' Now the rules of Form are very liberal. It is the easiest thing in the world to satisfy their minimum of requirements, and their rare prohibitions can be obeyed without any sacrifice of dramatic force or poetic expression. Beethoven's 'No. 5' is romantic enough, and it is as strict as an academic exercise; even symphonic poems like Raff's *Lenore* and *Im Walde* keep the general outlines intact though they try certain experiments of detail. But the first movement of the *Symphonic Fantastique* simply breaks the fundamental laws of the art, and that not with the iconoclasm of a reformer, but with the awkwardness of a tyro. Worse still is the opening allegro of the *Harold* symphony, which is nothing more than a fortuitous concourse of phrases, without form and void. The concert overtures are certainly better. The *Francs Juges* is rather free, but may be excused as being essentially operatic in character, while *Waverley*, *King Lear*, and the *Carnaval Romain* keep fairly within the laws, and the *Corsair* strikes out a new form which is perfectly intelligible and highly interesting.[1] Still, even these exceptions must be qualified by the admission that overtures are allowed greater laxity of rule than symphony movements. It is a great pity that so indefatigable a worker did not train himself by practice in chamber music, and thus acquire some of that balance and symmetry which his mercurial character so conspicuously needed.

The last point for consideration is his power of Orchestral effect, in which, perhaps, may be found his most indisputable claim to the admiration of posterity. Indeed, he ranks with Beethoven, Wagner, and Dvořák as one of the four greatest masters of Instrumentation that the world has ever seen. Their styles are curiously different. Beethoven's, strong, pure, pellucid, like the sea in calm weather; Wagner's, rich with deep and changing colour, that satisfies even while it baffles; Dvořák's, bright with a glint of sunshine upon the waves; Berlioz's, rolling with a storm of billows and a flash of scattering spray. He possessed in a high degree every quality which successful scoring implies, a complete knowledge of the strength and weakness of each instrument, great skill in treatment and combination, ready invention,

[1] It may perhaps be regarded as a development of the form in the first movement of Beethoven's P.F. sonata in E., Op. 109. At any rate that is the nearest analogue.

and boundless audacity. Further, he displays in this department of his art that sense of economy and reticence which has been noticed as absent elsewhere. He can be as light-handed as Mozart, witness the Invitation à la Valse, the opening of the Rakócky March, the first number of the *Tempest Fantasie*, and yet when the moment comes to be vigorous or impressive there is no one more strong to wield the thunderbolt and direct the whirlwind. Even the crude violence of his Brigands' Orgy or his Witches' Sabbath becomes almost humanised when we observe the marvellous, matchless skill with which its horrors are presented.

Even in his smaller works he usually writes for an orchestra of more than the normal size, using by preference four bassoons instead of two, and often reinforcing his trumpets with cornets-à-piston, the one piece of doubtful policy in his whole scheme. In the *Requiem* and the *Te Deum* his forces are enormous, the wind doubled, an immense mass of strings (of which he is careful to specify the exact number), and for the Tuba Mirum and Lacrymosa four small bands of brass instruments at the four corners, and eight pairs of kettledrums, in addition to big drums, gongs, and cymbals. The rest of his distinctively orchestral works lie between these two extremes,[1] though it may be noted that in the *Tempest Fantasie* he tries as an experiment his cherished idea of employing the piano, not as a solo instrument but as co-ordinate with strings or wood wind. It would be an endless task to enumerate his triumphs, but we may specify the wonderful viola chords in the Agnus Dei, the use of strings and flutes in the Sanctus—forerunner of

[1] Even his songs (with the exception of the 'Élégie') were originally written for small orchestra and arranged for the piano afterwards.

a similar effect in the prelude to *Lohengrin*—the trombones in the *Francs Juges* and in the magnificent final chorus of the *Te Deum*, and the exquisite wood wind figures, like vanishing soap bubbles, at the end of the Ballet of Sylphs, as conspicuous examples of poetic conception and unerring certainty of touch. His work, in short, marks a new era in instrumentation, and has been directly or indirectly the guide of every composer since his day.

The final verdict, then, would seem to be that Berlioz possessed undoubted genius, in the highest sense of the term, but that he was confined within limits from which he never succeeded in extricating himself. No composer of equal gifts has made so many mistakes: no musician of such little learning has ever attained to similar heights. It is not probable that his name will ever become a household word. The extraordinary difficulty of his compositions is almost as much against them as their gigantic scale, and 'the man who writes for five hundred musicians' is *ceteris paribus* less sure of a hearing than the man who writes for forty. Still, *Faust*, the *Symphonie Fantastique*, and the *Requiem* have already made their mark. *Harold* and *Romeo* have been recently given by Sir Charles Hallé, and in these days of musical festivals and enterprising opera managers there is no reason why we should not hear more of the *Te Deum* and of *Béatrice et Bénédict*. The Concert overtures, too, are well worthy of performance, especially those to *King Lear* and the *Corsair*. It is a pity that we should so rarely admit to our programmes the work of a man who, with all his faults, is the strongest and most original representative of a great artistic nation.

There remains a word to be said on Berlioz's position as critic and *feuilletoniste*. It is, of course, somewhat presumptuous for English readers to express any opinion of his prose, but we may, at least, do justice to his brilliance of description, his wit, and the inexhaustible good humour of his stories. The *Grotesques de la Musique* are full of entertaining things, so is the *Voyage Musical*, so are the *Soirées d'Orchestre;* and they are all written with that delicacy and brightness of touch which make French literature the despair of translators. The very form of them is amusing: scraps of autobiography, anecdotes, epigrams, all thrown down at random, and among them here and there a touch of serious criticism or a suggestion for some practical improvement. Now we have a moment of broad farce, as the account of *Le Phare* in the eighteenth of the *Soirées d'Orchestre*, or the story of the country cousin who was induced to take Lablache for Tom Thumb. Now Berlioz describes his experience of an amateur orchestral society, in which the clarinets had brought the wrong instruments, could not transpose, and would not stop because they 'had paid their subscriptions and so had a right to play.' In another place the whole system of the Claque comes in for some merciless and well-deserved satire. In another we have a very dramatic exposition of the petulance and incapacity which seem fifty years ago to have characterised some of the great public singers. Berlioz, in short, was a keen observer, a born humorist, a thorough partisan, and so possessed the three qualities which are most likely to arouse and retain the attention of his readers.

The criticisms are just what one might expect from a writer of such ardent temperament and such limited range. The man who denied that Palestrina possessed a spark of genius, who spoke of Handel as 'a barrel of pork and beer,' who declared himself unable to make head or tail of the Introduction to *Tristan*, yet gave us an admirable set of studies on Beethoven's symphonies, and analyses of *Freischütz*, *Oberon*, and *Fidelio* which may almost rank as Classics. With Gluck, too, he was always in closest sympathy, and his criticisms of *Orfeo*, *Iphigénie en Tauride*, and *Alceste* are marked by accurate knowledge and sound judgment. But his silences are even more remarkable than his mistakes. An edition of Schubert's best songs was brought out in Paris, yet, except for a casual word about Erlkönig, Berlioz has nothing to say on the subject. Chopin was his friend for many years, yet his one criticism of that Master is that 'he subordinates the orchestra to the piano.' He says a civil word to Schumann about his pianoforte work, but does not seem to know anything about his quartetts or his symphonies. And meantime he can speak of Lwoff and Onslow as great Composers.

But the maxim that 'genius alone understands genius' is probably the least true of all general statements that have ever been made about Music. Genius very rarely understands genius. Handel depreciated Gluck, Rossini hated Weber, Spohr thought the finale of Beethoven's fifth symphony vulgar, and called the great tune in the ninth a 'gassenmelodie,' Mendelssohn regarded Chopin's music as merely dangerous. Apart from contemporary instances, it is only in Schumann that we find a musician who unites the highest creative power with the true breadth and tolerance of a critic. Genius indeed, if it is to be successful, implies an enthusiasm and a concentration which almost inevitably warp the judgment to some extent, and the true guide in matters of taste is the man who just misses the supreme productive intuition and receives a double portion of analytic insight in its place. It may be added that Berlioz's decisions were often marked by a touch of defiance, which explains them even if it does not excuse. But, apart from this, a not unpardonable fault if we remember the constant antagonism against which he had to struggle, we may truly say that in his criticism, as in his composition, he always strove for the highest that he knew, and followed his ideal with consistent and unfaltering heroism. 'S'il fut un grand génie,' wrote Théophile Gautier, 'on peut le discuter encore, le monde est livré aux controverses; mais nul ne penserait à nier qu'il fut un grand caractère.'

ROBERT SCHUMANN AND THE ROMANTIC MOVEMENT IN GERMANY

Love took up the harp of Life, and smote on all the chords
  with might;
Smote the chord of Self, that, trembling, passed in Music out
  of sight.
                    TENNYSON : *Locksley Hall.*

Robert Schumann

AND THE ROMANTIC MOVEMENT IN GERMANY

I

THE BEGINNINGS OF A CAREER

BERLIOZ was the ally of the Romantic movement in literature, Schumann was its child. In France the former took his place amid a small band of explorers who were beginning to forsake the old square-cut Classical road to Parnassus and to strike out across country for themselves. The latter in Germany came into a world where the new paths were already laid, and the new maps already drawn, by the sixty years' work of his literary predecessors. No doubt Schumann was so far an innovator that he embodied in Music the tendencies which German Romanticism had for the most part embodied in words, but none the less the public to which he addressed himself had been previously educated into some sympathy with the methods and objects of Reform. Thus he was never compelled like Berlioz to face his whole nation single-handed, or with only the support of half-a-dozen equally discredited revolutionaries. He was from the outset a member of a recognised party which could count among its leaders some of the greatest poets and essayists of the age. As a natural consequence he is himself the most literary of Composers. Not only did he find in journalism a ready means of expression — very different from the *feuilletons* which Berlioz beat out with such bitter reluctance—but even in his music may be traced the influence of Richter and Heine. It is the outcome of a mind trained in a school of letters.

Such a school was abundantly provided by the bookseller's shop in the market-place at Zwickau, where he made his first appearance in the world on June 8, 1810. His father August Schumann was the senior partner, a man of considerable culture and education, who struck his blow in the national cause by his translations of Scott and Byron, as Schlegel 'conspired against Racine' in his translations of Shakespeare. For the Romantic movement in Germany was not only a reaction against the Classical tradition in general, it was even more a war against France and a revolt against Catholicism. It had its preachers who fulminated like Luther, its diplomatists who plotted like Stein, and, apart from its intellectual interests, it based itself upon some of the strongest national and religious emotions to which a revolution can appeal. Men had long grown weary of 'modelling a clumsy Temple of Art after the be-powdered Olympus of Versailles'; and they were still discussing whether they should raise in its stead the Doric pillars of Voss, or the minarets of the West-Östlicher Divan, or whether they should forsake temples altogether, and, like their Cheruscan ancestry, go to worship in the open forest. So the air was full of controversies and enthusiasms.

Everything which made for freedom was summoned into alliance, and at Weimar, Leipsic, Bayreuth, and a hundred other centres, the new Protestantism issued its manifestoes and directed its campaigns.

Amid these surroundings Schumann grew up to boyhood. His artistic proclivities, fostered by the wise encouragement of his father, began to show themselves early. He was a pianist at six, a composer at seven, and within a very few years we find the child, already famous as an extemporiser, taking part in public performances, where he had to stand up at the piano in order to reach the keys. His first music-master was Kuntzsch, the organist of the Marienkirche at Zwickau, an honest, conscientious teacher of rather limited capacity, who soon declared that his pupil had nothing further to learn from him. The relations between the two seem to have been of the pleasantest nature throughout. As late as 1852 Schumann wrote a cordial letter to congratulate the old Kapellmeister on his fiftieth year of office, and to send him a laurel wreath 'from his grateful and affectionate pupil.' It is only the little men who depreciate their teachers.

Failing Kuntzsch another master had to be found, and August Schumann boldly determined to attack Weber, who had recently entered on his duties at Dresden. Weber listened courteously enough, and promised to undertake the training of the new prodigy; but for some unknown reason the plan fell through. So the boy—a little round-headed, lazy, good-natured boy—was left to his own devices, and went on 'picking out tunes' for himself, or portraying on the piano the characters of his schoolfellows. The only event of his early years is a visit to Carlsbad, where he heard Moscheles and learned for the first time what Music really meant.

Meanwhile the rest of his education was not neglected. After a few years at an elementary school he was entered in the fourth class of the Zwickau Gymnasium, where he immediately organised a small band to perform his compositions. At the same time his literary interests were developing. He ransacked his father's shelves for poets, wrote voluminously both in prose and verse, and in his fifteenth year had so far progressed that he was allowed to contribute to a biographical dictionary which was being published by the firm of Schumann Brothers. It is noticeable that, even at this early period, his favourite authors belonged to the most advanced Romantic party, and that he had already begun to feel the spell of that English singer with whom he remained in closest sympathy throughout his life. Indeed for a year or two his inclinations seem almost to have hung in the balance between Music and Literature: and the two boyish epithalamia preserved by Wasielewski[1] show that his ultimate decision robbed the world of a poet to enrich it with a composer.

In 1826 August Schumann died, at the early age of fifty-three. His loss to the boy was irreparable, for with him went not only the nearest of friends but the most competent and encouraging of guides. To make matters worse, Frau Schumann unhesitatingly declared against an artistic career in any form. Her father had been Rathschirurgus at Zeitz, her elder sons were all settling down to a prosperous burgher life: it was not to be permitted that the youngest boy should go wasting his time over nonsense which

[1] *Biographie*, pp. 309-313.

would never earn enough to keep him in pens and paper. It may seem strange that the prospects of authorship should seem so meagre in the eyes of a publisher's widow; but in any case her view was strongly supported by the boy's guardian, Rudel, and it was decided that, after another year or so at the Gymnasium, Robert should be called upon to choose a profession and sent to Leipsic to study for it. Accordingly, in March 1828, he matriculated as *Studiosus juris*, and began his residence with a hearty contempt for the whole subject, a burning enthusiasm for 'Jean Paul,' and an allowance of twenty-five thalers a month.

It is a little difficult for English readers to understand the full extent and cause of Richter's popularity. To us he is simply a sentimental humorist, a German Sterne in the same sense in which Klopstock is a German Milton. We all know that he called our English summer 'a winter painted green,' and that he invented the delightful dwarf who 'was so short that he only reached up to his own knee, not to speak of other people's.' We all know that he liked to put his preface into the middle of the book, and to interrupt himself at every turn with odd digressions and confidences; but we can hardly realise that in the Augustan period of German literature he had the greatest vogue, that his works outsold those of Goethe and Schiller, and, most surprising of all, that he was accepted as leader and prophet by a large section of his younger contemporaries. The reason seems to be twofold; first, that his sentiment is vital and human, not an affectation assumed as a point of style; secondly, that it managed exactly to chime in with the sympathies and aspirations of the time. 'Goethe's masterpieces,' says Heine, in

one of the finest similes ever written, 'adorn our
Fatherland as beautiful statues adorn a garden.' It
was Richter's 'flower, fruit, and thorn pieces' that
really set the garden ablaze with colour and hung
its trees with the juicy sweetness of autumn.

Schumann did not make the acquaintance of Jean
Paul's writings until some of them had been before
the public for nearly half a century; but when he
once found them out his enthusiasm soon made up
for the lost time. He employed his abundant leisure
in the composition of 'Jean Pauliads'; he inculcated
on everybody the study of his new hero, in the hope,
as he characteristically writes, that mankind might
become 'better and more unhappy'; his own disposition, which had grown more sombre and gloomy
since his father's death, found its natural counterpart
in the pathos of Hesperus and the striving aspirations
of Titan. Throughout his life this influence remained
paramount. Even in his latest years he looked upon
Jean Paul as above criticism.

Meantime the study of law did not advance with
any great success. 'I have not been to a single
lecture,' he writes to his friend Rosen; and again,
more ominously, 'Idealists are like bees: if you
disturb them on their flower they sting.' No doubt
it was more interesting to read Schubert with a few
congenial students, or to pay a visit to Dr Carus', where
there was always good quartett playing and one could
chat between the pieces with Wieck and Marschner.
The former of these was reputed to be one of the
best pianoforte teachers in Germany, and Schumann
at once determined to take lessons from him. It was
a momentous decision. Wieck's favourite pupil was
his daughter Clara, then a child of nine years old,

Clara Wieck

already known in Leipsic as pianist and composer, and destined in after years to carry her fame and that of her husband throughout the length and breadth of Europe. A portrait of her is still extant, taken about this time, and pronounced by Schumann himself to be an excellent likeness. It represents a slender girl, with a bright, simple, intelligent face, seated at one of those queer little square-elbowed pianos which are still to be seen in old houses, and looking round with a smile at the spectator as she touches the keys. Her nature was as winning as Mendelssohn's, frank and sunny, with no taint of petulance or self-consciousness, and it is little wonder that she inspired Schumann from the first with something deeper than admiration.

So passed the winter of 1828. Besides the pianoforte lessons, Schumann worked hard at harmony and counterpoint, of which six months before he had professed himself entirely ignorant,[1] and made a special study of his great musical hero Sebastian Bach. It sounds at first a little odd to hear Bach claimed as the pioneer of the Romantic movement, there seems but little affinity between the old-world sweetness of the *Wohltemperirte Klavier* and the dash and vigour of the *Novelletten*. But on close examination the oddity disappears. The spirit of Bach is far enough removed from Romance, but his form, in many essential respects, anticipates it entirely. He was the most daring harmonist of his century, and it may be said without exaggeration that, among his countrymen at any rate, there is hardly a single 'modern' progression or modulation which cannot be found in his writings. 'Mozart and Haydn,' wrote

[1] Letter to Wiedebein, August 5, 1828.

Schumann in 1840, 'had only a partial and imperfect knowledge of Bach, and we can have no idea how Bach, had they known him in all his greatness, would have affected their creative powers. Mendelssohn, Bennett, Chopin, Hiller, in fact all the so-called Romantic school, approach Bach far more nearly in their music than Mozart ever did: indeed all of them know Bach most thoroughly. I myself confess my sins daily to that mighty one, and endeavour to purify and strengthen myself through him.' In this letter Schumann explains that he is only speaking of German musicians (which makes his inclusion of Bennett and Chopin the more noticeable), and indeed there was one Romantic writer whom he could hardly have cited as evidence. 'When I was at St Petersburg,' says Berlioz, 'they played me a triple concerto of Bach's on three pianos. I do not think that they intended to annoy me.' It would be hardly possible to express more briefly the contrast between the two methods of Romanticism.

All this time Schumann was composing with great industry. He set several of Byron's songs, and wrote a pianoforte quartett and a set of four-handed polonaises, the last in imitation of Schubert, whose death, on November 19th, had affected him very keenly. But as the spring advanced he grew more and more dissatisfied with Leipsic, and at last, following the liberal practice of the German Universities, decided to go and continue his legal studies with his friend Rosen at Heidelberg. He did not say farewell without a pang. 'I found it frightfully hard at the last,' he writes from his brother's house at Schneeberg.' 'A girl's soul,

¹ April 30, 1829.

beautiful, happy, and pure, had enslaved mine. It cost me many struggles, but it is all over now, and here I am quite strong, my tears suppressed, looking forward to a beautiful life at Heidelberg, full of hope and courage.'

There he made some pretence of attending Thibaut's lectures—not so much because Thibaut was an authority on the Pandects as because he had recently published an admirable little treatise on Purity in Musical Art—but even with this bond of union the pupil does not seem to have taken very voluminous notes or to have opened a book outside the lecture-room. Indeed he was far too busy to read law. He practised the piano for seven hours a day, he gave impromptu concerts in the evening, and he started composition in earnest with the *Abegg Variations*, the *Papillons*, and the first sketch of the *Toccata*. Further, he wanted to educate himself by travel. He had already inaugurated his residence at Leipsic by touring about Bavaria, where he met Heine at Munich and Frau Richter at Bayreuth: now he started on a longer flight, and spent the months of September and October in the north of Italy. The diary of his visit reads like a chapter in the Three Musketeers—adventures of love and war at Milan, roguish tradesmen at Venice, and an entire absence of cash everywhere. But, busy or idle, there is not a single word about jurisprudence.

In 1830 the Heidelberg authorities, who had been behaving towards their truant with the most exemplary forbearance, seem to have arrested him for non-payment of university dues. This was a hard blow, for Schumann had just turned virtuous and engaged a private tutor with some vague idea of getting his degree. Perhaps the few days of enforced reflection served to sharpen the edge of his resolve; perhaps, too, he was further stimulated by Paganini's playing, which he had recently heard at Frankfort; at all events he immediately declared open war against Gaius and Justinian, and wrote to Wieck announcing his intention of becoming a pianist, and asking for a plain opinion as to his chances. Wieck sent back a cautious letter pointing out the difficulties of the career, and suggesting obstacles which anyone but an enthusiast would have found insurmountable. Schumann laughed at the difficulties, and, for the obstacles, began at once with the steepest, the opposition of his mother and his guardian.

The terms that he proposed were not unreasonable. 'I wish,' he writes to Rudel, 'to devote myself exclusively to Art for six months under Wieck of Leipsic. If he says that in three years from those six months I can attain the highest walks in Art, then let me go in peace; I shall certainly not perish. But if after the six months Wieck should have the very smallest doubts, I shall have lost nothing as regards jurisprudence, and will gladly go up for my examination in a year.' After a little hesitation the requisite leave was given, and Schumann left Heidelberg with some kindly words of encouragement from Thibaut, who had wit enough to see that it was worth spoiling a bad lawyer to make a great musician. It is noticeable, by the way, that the career was to be that of a virtuoso. Composition was regarded as secondary; and Schumann's warmest expression of hope in this deparment is to be found in the curiously hesitating words which he addresses to his mother: 'Now and then I discover that I have imagination, and perhaps a turn for creating things myself.' But, whether as composer or interpreter, he won his point, and won it, by an odd coincidence, in the same year in which Chopin began his artistic life in Paris and Berlioz emancipated himself from the Conservatoire.

Once back in Leipsic Schumann took up his residence with the Wiecks, and studied the piano in earnest. His progress, though rapid, was too slow for his ambition, and in an evil moment he invented a machine for holding up one finger while the others played exercises. All mechanical devices in Art are bad; this one was fatal. After a few trials he strained the muscles in the third finger of his right hand, and the accident, though slight at first, was made worse by careless treatment. The finger remained practically useless, and the career of a virtuoso was gone for ever. It is fortunate that this calamity did not occur until after the six months of probation were over, otherwise Rudel might have insisted on the terms of the agreement. As it was, the accident only withdrew Schumann from the crowd of great pianists, and led him to the smaller and nobler company of great composers. He treated it, on the whole, light-heartedly enough. The same letter in which he tells his friend Töpken of his crippled hand goes on: 'My prospects are very bright: my reception in the world of Art could not have been more encouraging: Wieck is my oldest friend now, and as for Clara—imagine everything that is perfect and I will endorse it.'

For composition lessons he went to Dorn, the conductor of the Leipsic Opera, who had just brought out as an *entracte* a new and very unsuccessful concert overture by a freshman at the university called Richard Wagner. Dorn's new pupil does not seem to have been very docile, but he worked hard after his own fashion, and, even when he did not follow it, was genuinely grateful for advice. During the winter of 1831 he wrote a symphony in G minor, at Schneeberg, and began a pianoforte concerto which he never finished. The first movement of the symphony was performed in a concert at Zwickau, given in November 1832 by Clara Wieck; the whole work was given once in 1835, and then discarded.

In 1832 the *Abegg Variations* and the *Papillons* received a very favourable notice, written by Grillparzer, in the *Wiener Musickalische Zeitung*. Encouraged by this, Schumann published the first set of '*Caprices after Paganini*,' and followed them up in 1833 with the *Intermezzi* ('Extended Papillons' as he calls them) and the '*Impromptus on a theme of Clara Wieck*.' During the latter year, indeed, he was extremely active. He finished the *Toccata*, wrote a Concert allegro in B minor, completed a second set of Paganini caprices, and began the two great sonatas in G minor and F-sharp minor as well. It is not, perhaps, a full record if one compares it with a year's work of Schubert or Mozart, but it must be remembered that Schumann was still, more or less, in his 'prentice days, and that he had not entirely acquired the facility and certainty of a Master. In many of the early pianoforte works there are alternative readings, sometimes extending over thirty or forty bars, which show that even after he had expressed his thought he was not always satisfied with its form of expression. Of this point more detailed notice will be taken later: it is enough now to indicate that a judgment so anxious and hesitating must of necessity imply some slowness of production. Besides, he was already beginning to revolve in his mind a project which took shape early in 1834: the formation of a musical journal to embody the ideas and aspirations of the new school. The only paper at that time in the field was the *Allgemeine Musikalische Zeitung*, edited by Fink, an amiable periodical which exercised no influence on public opinion, and worse still, did not understand Jean Paul. There was, therefore, abundant opening for a system of criticism which had a national hero to follow and an intelligible cause to support.

Accordingly, on April 3, 1834, appeared the first number of the *Neue Zeitschrift*, a square, four-paged quarto, issued twice a week, and devoted entirely to musical criticism and musical polemics. It was at first edited by a committee consisting of Schumann, Wieck, Schunke the pianist, and Julius Knorr, who was then teaching composition in Leipsic. Before the end of the year, however, Knorr and Wieck both resigned; Schunke died of consumption during the winter, and by the beginning of 1835 Schumann was left sole editor, a position which he occupied for nearly ten years. In 1844 he vacated his chair, and from that time wrote no more, until in 1853 he gave the world his famous article on 'Neue Bahnen.' But, present or absent, he was always the guiding genius of the paper. It was established on his lines, it followed his leadership, it inculcated his principles, and to him in chief it may be said to owe the influence which it still exercises on musical life and thought in Germany.

Never were prophets dressed in a more fantastic garb. The contributors all took their tone from the *Flegeljahre*, and filled their essays with a motley procession of jokes and metaphors, sarcasm jostling sentimentalism, and burlesque treading on the heels of poetry. Now Florestan 'mounts the grand pianoforte' and delivers a Shrovetide speech, which is like Carnival gone mad. Now a packet of dance music is ingeniously reviewed amid the jests and flirtations of a ballroom. Now the editor scatters a handful of sparkling aphorisms, or calls down the lightning of Heaven upon 'the contrapunctilious.' Almost everybody is nick-named. Cramer is 'Old J. B.,' Mendelssohn 'Felix Meritis,' Clara Wieck 'Zilia' or 'Chiarina,' while Schumann himself has a pageful of pseudonyms, some drawn from the Saxon calendar and some from the multiplication table. And yet under all this flood of good spirits there lies solid treasure which well repays the trouble of the diver. Mendelssohn, Chopin, Schubert, Berlioz, Sterndale Bennett, and a host of other Composers, are treated with admirable sympathy and insight. Concerts are criticised, styles compared, even variant readings discussed in a manner which, for all its fantasy, succeeds in saying the last word on almost every topic with which it deals. Indeed the hardest judgment against the *Neue Zeitschrift* is that it sometimes errs through excess of generosity, a fault so rare among musicians that it may pass for once as a virtue. We have nothing like this in England. The nearest approach is perhaps Arbuthnot's well-known 'Trial of M Handel,' and that goes on its way with a solid, bluff

Robert Schumann 163

British directness, very different from the 'nods and becks and wreathed smiles' of these strange creations. France may show a closer parallel in the writings of Berlioz; but Berlioz lets his humour play round the criticisms, Schumann uses his to embody them.

One result of the new journal was the formation of the Davidsbünd. There have, of course, been many instances in history of secret societies gathered together for the propagation of new ideas by the ardour and genius of one man. But there is probably no other example of a brotherhood, existing for many years as a living reality, in which all the members except the founder were fictitious 'It is,' he writes to Dorn, 'a purely abstract and romantic society.' Some musicians were included in a sort of honorary membership, such as Berlioz, who never heard of his election, and Mozart, who had been dead for five-and-fifty years; but the names of the regular Davidsbündler were Florestan and Eusebius, and Raro and Jonathan, and the other children of Schumann's fancy. Yet he treats them as if they were the most concrete of facts. He records their meetings, appraises their works, writes a set of pianoforte pieces to illustrate their struggles, and even composes for them a national anthem without words, in which they are represented as marching against the Philistines and gloriously overcoming Goliath, in the person of the old German *grossvatertanz*.

This curious dual existence had its effect on Schumann's character. He was always indifferent to the meaner objects of ambition, a true idealist, who worked for his cause, not for any personal reward of wealth or reputation. Now he became more dreamy and reserved, more hesitating in the conduct of affairs, more given to long fits of silence and contemplation. Like those strange psychological cases of which we occasionally read, he only began really to live when he could shut his door upon the world and enter into the kingdom of his dreams. Schubert found relaxation after his day's work in the noisy good-fellowship of the *café;* Schumann used to sit apart, with his face to the wall, solitary, oblivious, and preoccupied. Mendelssohn was the life of every company into which he entered: Schumann's favourite form of conversation was what Heine calls 'une conversation Anglaise.' Everybody knows the story of his two hours' silent *tête-à-tête* with his friend Henrietta Voigt, and his departure with a pressure of the hand and the words, 'To-day we have perfectly understood one another.' Indeed, even in these early days may be found evident traces of that mysticism which was afterwards to bring his life to such a tragical termination. The half-humorous, half-pathetic figures which he had created for his companionship were already withdrawing his mind from the realities of earth, and turning it towards that Undiscovered Country on the borders of which he spent his later years.

The compositions of 1834 include the *Carnaval* and the magnificent *Études Symphoniques*, the finest set of variations that had appeared since Beethoven astonished Diabelli with the immortal 33; but in the next year, hampered by the burden of editorial duties, Schumann completed nothing except the F-sharp minor sonata, 'dedicated to Clara by Florestan and Eusebius.' Besides, in 1835, Mendelssohn came to Leipsic as conductor of the Gewandhaus concerts, and everything made way to give him welcome. Since the days when we left him wandering about the Coliseum with Berlioz he had been enjoying a triumphal procession through France, England, and Germany, and had added to his astonishing record of compositions the *Walpurgisnacht*, the *Italian* symphony, the G minor concerto, and the overtures *Hebrides*, *Meeresstille*, and *Melusina*, not to mention a host of minor works. He was then in his twenty-seventh year, handsome, accomplished, popular, and equally famous in every branch of the Art to which he directed his attention. No wonder that Leipsic was on tiptoe at his arrival, and fully expected to become, under his guidance, the most musical city between Königsberg and Cologne.

Schumann first met him at the Wiecks', and the acquaintance there begun soon ripened into a cordial friendship. Nowhere is the *Neue Zeitschrift* more enthusiastic than when it is extolling 'Felix Meritis'; and if the latter did not exactly return the compliment, at least he always spoke most warmly of Schumann, and gave him all the practical assistance in his power. It must, in fact, have been almost impossible for Mendelssohn to admire the work of the Romantic school. The qualities which he valued most in Music were naturally those in which he most excelled—nicety of touch, refinement of thought, perfection of finish—and these are necessarily absent in the stress of a revolutionary movement. He was a great master of style, with an unerring faculty of expression ; and he must have watched with more surprise than pleasure the half-articulate strivings of Romance towards the delivery of a message the full significance of which he never, perhaps, entirely comprehended. To such a man the *Symphonic Fan-*

tastique must have been like *aqua vitæ* to a connoisseur in claret, and even the *Études Symphoniques*, like a rich, full-blooded Burgundy, full of strength and body, but lacking the velvety softness of the true Château Lafite. Or, to borrow a more artistic simile, his attitude towards his contemporaries was that of Andrea del Sarto,—

> I can do with my pencil what I know,
> What I see, what at bottom of my heart
> I wish for, if I ever wish so deep . . .
> I do what many dream of all their lives
> —Dream? Strive to do, and agonise to do,
> And fail in doing.

And yet it may be that in the world of Music, as in the world of Painting, 'failure is progress,' and the stammering phrase contains for the time to come a truth of deeper meaning than the clearly enunciated sentence.

One of the most inexplicable facts in all Schumann's life is his engagement to Ernestine von Fricken, a fellow pupil of his, which took place in the latter part of 1834. It is possible that he had not realised the depth of his feelings for Clara Wieck, though his letters speak of her in terms that can hardly be misunderstood, and he was even then finishing his great sonata for her acceptance. It is possible that he had for the moment given up hope of winning that 'bright particular star,' and so turned elsewhere for solace and comfort. In any case this episode of unfaithfulness was not of very long duration. The engagement lasted but a few months, and then was broken off by mutual consent. By the beginning of 1836 Schumann had determined to put his fate to the touch, and on the 1st of March he could write to tell his Breslau correspondent Kahlert that he had won the highest stake in the whole game of human life. The letter is worth quoting in full, since it sums up as briefly as possible the entire situation.[1]

'MOST HONOURED SIR,—I am not going to give you anything musical to spell out to day, and, without beating about the bush, will come to the point at once. I have a particular favour to ask you. It is this: will you not devote a few moments of your life to act as messenger between two parted souls? At any rate do not betray them. Give me your word that you will not.

'Clara Wieck loves, and is loved in return. You will soon find that out from her gentle, almost supernatural ways and doings. For the present don't ask me the name of the other one. The lovers, however, acted, met, talked, and exchanged their vows without the father's knowledge. He has found them out, wants to take violent measures, and forbids any sort of intercourse on pain of death. Well, it has all happened before, thousands of times. But the worst of it is that they have gone away. The latest news came from Dresden. But we knew nothing for certain, though I suspect, indeed am nearly convinced, that they are at Breslau. Wieck is sure to call upon you at once, and will invite you to come and hear Clara play. Now this is my ardent request, that you should let me know all about Clara as quickly as possible—I mean as to her state of mind, the life she

[1] *Schumann's Letters*, translated by Miss Herbert, Vol. I. p. 79. *Wasielewski*, p. 148.

leads, in fact any news you can obtain directly or indirectly. Please consider all I have told you as a sacred trust, and don't mention this letter either to the old man or to anybody else.

'If Wieck speaks of me it will probably not be in very flattering terms. Don't let that put you out. You will learn to know him. He is a man of honour, in spite of his eccentricities.

'I may further remark that it will be an easy thing for you to obtain Clara's confidence and favour, as I (who am more than well disposed to lovers) have often told her that I corresponded with you. She will be happy to see you on that account.

'Give me your hand, unknown one: I believe your disposition to be so noble that it will not disappoint me. Write soon. A heart, a life depend upon it— my own—it is myself for whom I have been pleading.

'ROBERT SCHUMANN.'

It is not necessary to enter here into the rather miserable story of Wieck's opposition and the measure by which it was finally overcome. For nearly four years Schumann endured all the torments of suspense, sustained to bear them by the unalterable constancy and affection of the noble woman to whom he had entrusted his happiness. Still he was poet enough to teach in song what he learned in suffering. 'My troubles have been productive of much music,' he writes; and again, *à propos* of the *Novelletten*, 'I have never written so thoroughly from the soul as just lately.' Indeed to this period belong some of the most famous of his works: the great *Fantasia* in C, the 'Concerto without Orchestra,' the *Fantasiestücke*, *Novelletten*, and

Kreisleriana, the *Kinderscenen*, the *Arabeske*, *Blumenstück*, and *Humoreske*, all arising, with different accents of triumph or pathos, from the alternating hopes and despairs of a lover's heart.

In 1838 Schumann went to live in Vienna, since, even with Mendelssohn's presence, Leipsic had grown dark to him, and remained in his new quarters for about a year, directing his paper through the medium of his sub-editor, Oswald Lorenz. At Vienna he played a harmless joke on the police authorities which is worth recording, as it shows that his sense of humour was still capable of finding expression. The representatives of law and order were keeping a sharp look out for any symptoms of revolutionary feeling, and as a measure of precaution had absolutely prohibited the performance of the 'Marseillaise.' Schumann, who had been worried by them in regard of the *Neue Zeitschrift*, took his revenge by composing the '*Faschingsschwank aus Wien*,' in which there suddenly dances across the stage a fantastic caricature of the forbidden tune. Nothing could be done, for the prohibition had not been transcended, and there were no police regulations against plagiarism. 'Solvuntur risu tabulæ' was the only possible issue.

The most important result of his visit to Vienna was the discovery of Schubert's C major symphony, which had lain for ten years, neglected and forgotten, at the little house in the Kettenbrücken Gasse. Schumann at once made arrangements for the score to be sent to Leipsic, whither he returned at the beginning of April 1839, just too late to hear its first performance under Mendelssohn's direction. However, he soon made the nearer acquaintance of the work, and in 1840 published on it one of the finest of the *Neue Zeitschrift* articles—an admirable example of the best kind of Romantic criticism. Nothing can be more characteristic than the following passage: 'I shall not attempt to set the symphony in its fitting soil; different ages select different bases for their texts and pictures: where the youth of eighteen finds some famous exploit in a musical work a man only perceives some commonplace event, while the musician probably never thought of either, but simply gave the best music that he happened to feel within him. But everyone must acknowledge that the outer world, bright to-day, gloomy to-morrow, often deeply impresses the inward feeling of the poet or the musician; and all must recognise, while listening to this symphony, that it reveals to us something more than mere fine melody, mere ordinary joy and sorrow, such as music has already expressed in a hundred ways, that it leads us into a region which we have never before explored . . . . Here we find, besides a complete mastery of the technicalities of musical composition, life in every vein, colouring down to the finest grade of possibility, clear expression in detail, meaning throughout, while over the whole is thrown that glow of Romanticism that everywhere accompanies Franz Schubert. And then the heavenly length of the symphony, like one of Jean Paul's romances in four thick volumes, never able to come to an end, for the very best reasons—in order to leave the reader able to go on romancing for himself.'[1] Here we have the whole creed of the party, Richter and all, expressed, as the reader will notice, in a more serious tone than

[1] Schumann, *Music and Musicians*, Vol. I. p. 53.

Schumann usually adopted for his essays. Florestan and Eusebius would have been out of place in dealing with the greatest composition of a dead Master.

In February 1840 Schumann received a doctor's degree from the University of Jena. Ever since 1838 he had been desirous of obtaining some academical distinction, rather as a step towards his marriage than for any more prosaic reason, and he now writes to his friend Keferstein in an amusing state of anxiety about the conditions. 'Shall I have to pass an examination? Will they require a thesis in Latin, or will German do instead? Do you think that they would accept an essay on Shakespeare's relation to Music? Or, better still, would they give me an honorary degree in consideration of the work that I have already done? In what faculty are the honorary degrees granted? Of course I should like Music best'—and so on. After due consideration the university authorities decided to excuse Schumann from the indignity of a test, and sent him a diploma, nominating him Doctor of Philosophy, with all the requisite compliments and superlatives.

Armed with the new honour he set himself resolutely to the accomplishment of his hopes. 'We are young,' he had written to Keferstein, 'we have hands, strength, and some reputation, my own property brings me in an interest of 500 thalers, the paper as much again. My compositions are beginning to command a good price. Now me tell if there can be any cause for apprehension.' So bold a tone is itself a presage of success. Wieck still remained obdurate, but his opposition was overpowered.

After one more hard fight Schumann gained the day, and on September 12th, at the little church of Schönefeld near Leipsic, he was married to Clara Wieck, and began a partnership to which the whole history of Music can furnish no parallel. It is, perhaps, only at Casa Guidi that we can find another instance of genius allied to genius by a bond so close and so divine.

II

MARRIED LIFE

ONE noteworthy result of the change in Schumann's life was the change in his form of production. Hitherto his published works had been exclusively compositions for the pianoforte; now, under the influence of the

Lyric love, half angel and half bird,

he threw himself into song writing, and during the year of his marriage set over one hundred and thirty poems of Heine, Rückert, and others, including the *Myrthen* the *Liebesfrühling* (written in conjunction with his wife), the *Frauenliebe*, the *Dichterliebe*, and many beside. 'I cannot tell you what a delight it is to write for the voice,' he says to a friend; and again, later on, 'I cannot tear myself away from vocal music.' Song, indeed, more than any other musical form, is the natural counterpart of intense emotion, and though it does not always reflect the mood of the Composer, often bears witness to the action of an unusual stimulus from without. Its particular tone may be sad or merry without necessarily implying sadness or merriment in its creator, but to exist at all it requires as condition a higher pitch of excitement than is needed by the more deliberate utterances of the quartett or the sonata. It is therefore only fitting that the year of crisis should also have been the year of 'Schöne Wiege' and 'Er der herrlichste von allen.'

In 1841 he made another new departure and wrote three symphonies, one in B-flat, produced under Mendelssohn's direction on March 31st, the other two in E[1] and D minor, following together, on December 6th. The latter were not very fortunate in their reception, possibly because of their extreme freedom of at structure, possibly because Mendelsshon was away Berlin. In consequence Schumann withdrew them, and indeed did not publish the D minor until ten years after, when it appeared, with considerable alterations and corrections, as No. 4—the C major and the Rhenish symphony having been written in the interim. It is certainly on the first that his reputation as an orchestral writer mainly depends. At the Gewandhaus it gained an enthusiastic welcome, and the only jarring note in the chorus of praise was an ineffectual snarl in the columns of the opposition musical paper. Nothing could have exceeded Mendelssohn's kindness and courtesy. He took the greatest pains with the rehearsals, and even offered to resign his bâton on the night of performance in order that the composer of the 'beautiful symphony' might conduct his work in person. Schumann declined, saying with perfect truth that the score could not be in better hands.

In the same year, beside these symphonic works, there appeared a Fantasia in A minor for pianoforte and orchestra. It is a remarkable composition, partly because it is entirely constructed out of a

---

[1] Published in 1845 as *Overture Scherzo and Finale.*

Robert Schumann 175

single phrase, partly because that phrase is curiously Mendelssohnian in character : not of course near enough for a suspicion of plagiarism, but near enough to show that the hero was beginning in some degree to influence his devoted admirer. The scoring, and still more the structure, are essentially Schumann's own creations; to the latter of which he may be said to have drawn special attention when in 1845 he tacked on two more movements and published the whole as a pianoforte concerto. It is of course no more a strict concerto than the '*Faschingsschwank aus Wien*' is a sonata,[1] but there is fortunately no need to make musical criticism turn on questions of nomenclature. If the wine is to our liking it is sheer ingratitude to pick holes in the label.

1842 was entirely devoted to chamber music. Schumann began by shutting himself up in his study with all Beethoven's quartetts—a very characteristic method of preparing himself for the new form and on emerging, produced in rapid succession the three string quartetts dedicated to Mendelssohn, the pianoforte quintett, the pianoforte quartett, and a short trio which he afterwards published under his favourite title of *Fantasiestücke*. Of these the quintett is as undoubtedly the greatest as it is the most famous. Indeed, for a long time it was the only one of Schumann's works that possessed anything like a European reputation ; and even at the present day it is probably the most popular of all his concerted compositions. It is not so poetical as that of Brahms in F minor, it is not so full of novel effects and piquant surprises as that of Anton Dvořák in A, but it is more simple

[1] See letter to Simonin de Sire, March 15, 1839.

and direct than the one, more solid and workmanlike than the other. It is, in short, a first-rate musical novel, with a good plot, an interesting style, and an abundant display of humour and incident.

In the old student days Schumann had been fond of travelling, but as the years went on he grew more and more disinclined to leave the home where he was perfectly happy and perfectly quiet. However, at the beginning of 1842, he accompanied his wife on a concert tour as far as Hamburg, where the B-flat symphony was performed with great success, and in August, feeling rather overworked, he took a holiday in Bohemia, where he met Prince Metternich at Königswart, and had the honour of a ministerial invitation to Vienna. He did not accept it, partly because nothing could have been less to his taste than the brilliance of an Austrian palace, partly because he wanted to get back to his pleasant, peaceful lodgings in the Inselstrasse, where there was already a little daughter—Mendelssohn's godchild—growing old enough to give him an intelligible welcome. At the same time the Prince's words set him thinking. Vienna, thanks to Beethoven and Schubert, was still one of the most important musical centres in Europe; it had already shown some favour to Schumann's early works; it had afforded him some hospitality during his visit in 1839. Here was a chance of which, after all, it might be worth while taking advantage. So on his return to Leipsic Schumann wrote off to his friend Kossmaly suggesting the plan of a campaign for the conquest of the Viennese.[1] Kossmaly was to write an introductory article in the *Allgemeine Wiener Musik-Zeitung*, and

[1] September 1, 1842.

to get the B-flat symphony performed, after which the Composer was to make his triumphal entry, and to occupy a city which was certain by that time to have capitulated. It is rather pathetic that genius should be compelled to use such arts of strategy; but Schumann had given hostages to fortune, and was compelled to bestir himself for their ransom. 'Formerly,' he writes to the same friend,[1] 'I was perfectly indifferent whether people noticed me or not, but when one has a wife and children everything is different; the future has to be thought of, and one likes to see the fruits of one's labours.' After all the scheme was unnecessary. Schumann did not make his way to Vienna until four years later, and by that time his preliminaries were forgotten, and his works able to command respect on their own merits.

1843 was in many respects an eventful year. At the beginning of January the quintett made its début, with Madame Schumann at the piano and David as first violin. Then came Berlioz flying through Leipsic like a whirlwind, and astonishing all sober folk by his daring, his eccentricity, and his indomitable force. It must have been he who told Schumann that a fugue was a composition in which one voice rushes out before the others, and the listener first of all: a definition on which the *Neue Zeitschrift* hangs a delightful little essay about Mendelssohn's fugues and their relation to Sebastian Bach. On April 2nd was opened the Leipsic Conservatorium, with Mendelssohn as director, Schumann as Professor of Composition,[2] and other great names filling the other

[1] May 5, 1843.
[2] As a matter of fact Schumann took some of the Pianoforte teaching and some of the Composition.

places on the staff. Gade and Moscheles joined it later on, and for many years it remained, as far as Germany was concerned, a 'ministry of all the talents.' Nowadays, when its glory is to some extent obscured by that of Berlin, we are a little too apt to undervalue its greatness, and to underestimate the enormous service that it has rendered for half a century to the cause of musical education. At any rate England has every reason to think highly of an institution to which it owes the training of such men as Mr J. F. Barnett and Sir Arthur Sullivan.

The birth of Schumann's second daughter on April 25th was accompanied by a reconciliation between Madame Schumann and Wieck. 'I am glad of it for Clara's sake,' writes Schumann to Verhulst, though he himself still remained aloof, 'gener invisus inimici soceri.' It would have been hardly possible for him to pardon the injurer at once without a touch of disloyalty towards the injured. However, his was not a nature to resist advances for very long. By the end of the year he had forgiven everything, and the most detailed account of his Russian visit is to be found in a cordial and affectionate letter to his 'dear father' in Leipsic.

During the spring he wrote the set of variations for two pianofortes, which was first performed by his wife and Mendelssohn on August 19th. But the great musical event of the year was *Paradise and the Peri*, 'an oratorio not for the conventicle but for bright happy people,' as he calls it in his letter to Krüger. The score was finished by the middle of June,¹ and the work performed under the Composer's direction on December 4th. Its success was so great

¹ Letter to Verhulst, June 19th.

that it was repeated on December 11th, and given at the Dresden opera house on December 23d. It was indeed 'a new departure for the concert room': not so much in its form, for Handel's *Acis* and Haydn's *Seasons* may be regarded as in some sense its fore-runners, but in the vividness of its expression and the unity of its treatment. Berlioz's *Damnation de Faust*, written two years later, is the work that most nearly resembles it in style, and the two together may be regarded as the parents of that numerous family of dramatic cantatas, among which can be counted such splendid examples as *Rinaldo*, *Prometheus*, and the *Spectre's Bride*. Schumann felt an unusual sense of satisfaction in the youngest-born creation of his Art. Of his quartetts he had written to David, 'I ought to do better'; of *Paradise and the Peri* he said, 'It is my last work, and, I hope, my best. I am full of gratitude to Heaven for having sustained my energies while I wrote it.' We may remember Haydn and the 'Laus Deo' at the end of his scores.

The letters to Breitkopf and Härtel during this year are of special musical interest. On January 4th Schumann discusses the proofs of the three string quartetts, and asks to have them ready by Mendelssohn's birthday, 'the 3d of February, I think.' At the beginning of March he is arranging for the publication of the pianoforte quintett, which is to be a birthday surprise for his wife. 'I suppose,' he adds, with unconscious irony, 'that you will not think twenty Louis d'or too much to give for it.' ... The same letter speaks of the two-piano variations as finished, and, more important still, presses on the firm the claims of Berlioz, whose *Harold* and *Romeo* symphonies Schumann had been hearing at the Gewandhaus. By September 7th he has a new *protégé*, Robert Franz, whose first set of twelve songs (Op. 1) owe their publication to his efforts, and their reception to his encouragement. We may remark in passing that it is not every Composer who is as anxious about the success of other men's work as about that of his own. At the end of the year he made terms for *Paradise and the Peri*— a hundred Louis d'or for the complete work, publication to be taken in hand at once, and the Composer to preserve author's rights for France and England. 'In England especially,' he adds, 'I hope to reap some advantage,' from which we may gather that he did not know Mr Chorley. One curious feature in the agreement is his promise that, if the full score is ready within a year, he will throw in the Fantasia for Pianoforte and Orchestra as a make-weight, a liberal offer of which the firm does not seem to have availed itself. At any rate the Fantasia remained in abeyance until 1845, when it appeared as the first movement of the Pianoforte Concerto.

At the beginning of 1844 Madame Schumann proposed a concert tour in Russia, which was then, for musicians at any rate, the land of El Dorado. Schumann, as usual, was very reluctant to move, and it was only on his wife's threatening to go alone that he at last consented to accompany her.[1] Accordingly they started on January 26th, a little late for complete success, as when they reached St Petersburg the winter season was well advanced and the opera in full swing. So the first two concerts were not very largely attended; but soon Madame

[1] The journey had been in prospect ever since 1840. See Schumann's letter to Keferstein, August 24th of that year.

Schumann's playing made its mark, and the rest of the tour was a series of undisputed victories. It was a new experience for Schumann. 'Here the newspapers can do but little,' he writes; 'everything depends on the court and the *haute volée.*' Before he knew where he was, the shy, reserved, taciturn musician was driving about with Count Wielhorsky, or chatting with the Prince of Oldenburg, or basking in the smiles of the G and Princess Helena herself. Everybody received him with true Russian hospitality. Henselt, the gigantic pianist, repaid some of the debt which he owed to the *Neue Zeitschrift;* Heinrich Romberg, the director of the court concerts, put himself at the disposal of the visitors with the same kindness which he afterwards showed to Berlioz; the Wielhorskys organised a private concert at which the B-flat symphony was performed; even the Emperor and Empress looked down from their Olympian heights and signified their august satisfaction. In the midst of these festivities Schumann heard that an uncle of his, Dr Schnabel, was acting as army surgeon at Tver, and immediately altered his engagements to go and spend the old man's seventieth birthday with him. It is a kindly little touch which rounds off a very agreeable picture.

He was back in Germany by the end of May, picking up the children at Schneeberg and carrying them off to Leipsic, where they were 'received triumphantly by half the Inselstrasse.' The Russian visit had given him so much pleasure that he at once set about the preliminaries for a concert tour in England, and wrote for information to Moscheles, who was at that time resident in London. Moscheles favoured the plan, as also did Mendelssohn, but it ultimately fell through, mainly owing to the impossibility of getting *Paradise and the Peri* published with English words. We did not want Schumann in England. The more serious of our musicians swore by 'the Classics,' and felt that the utmost limit of audacity had been reached by Spohr and Mendelssohn. For the rest we had our own composers: Sir Henry Bishop, who wrote *Mynheer van Dunck*, and Mr Balfe, who wrote the *Bohemian Girl*, and Mr Glover, who was still charming our drawing-rooms with *Jeanette and Jeannot*. We had learned no more about the German Romantic school than we could gather from vague recollections of Canning and the *Anti-Jacobin*: to most of us its language was a sealed book, its method alien, its work incomprehensible. We knew that Italy was the land of Music, because our critics told us so; we knew that Madame Malibran was a great singer, because Mr Alfred Bunn gave her £125 a night; and as long as we could go and hear *Maritana* or *Semiramide* at Drury Lane we were perfectly satisfied. There was no need for us to trouble our heads with a new composer, who wasted his time on 'poetic meanings' and 'inward voices' and other things which we could not understand.

After abandoning his project of a visit to England Schumann settled down to the more congenial work of composition at home. For the past two years he had been thinking and writing much on the subject of German opera. 'It is high time,' says the *Neue Zeitschrift* in September 1842, 'that German composers should give the lie to the reproach that has long lain on them of having been so craven as to leave the field in possession of the Italians and French.' As stated this is rather a strange appeal;

for even if we accept that ingenious system of classification which places Mozart among the Italians, we have still *Fidelio* and *Freischütz, Jessonda* and *Der Vampyr* to show that German Art has not been neglectful of the stage. Schumann, however, rather means that in France and Italy opera was the natural mode of musical expression, while in Germany it was still something of an exotic, grown and cultivated only in the conservatories of a few connoisseurs. Moreover the success of *Paradise and the Peri* had once more turned his thoughts in the direction of dramatic music. During his Russian tour he had been corresponding with his friend Zuccalmaglio about a libretto; on his return to Leipsic he began a regular grand opera on the text of Byron's 'Corsair.' But after two numbers he found the book unsuitable, laid it aside, and started upon the greatest of all his choral works—the incidental music to Goethe's *Faust*.

It is well known that Goethe intended portions of his drama for musical treatment, notably the magnificent finale of the second part. Schumann fastened upon this, and began to set it with the greatest enthusiasm. Its tremendous mysticism, its splendid, soaring verse brought ready inspiration to one who was both a poet and a mystic; and the work was beginning to take definite shape and body when a sudden calamity put a stop to everything. About the beginning of August Schumann was seized with a severe nervous disorder, the first harbinger of that terrible malady which darkened his life until its close. All music had to be given up; the *Neue Zeitschrift* was entrusted to Oswald Lorenz, who had been practically managing it throughout the year, and Schumann moved his residence to Dresden in search of rest and quiet. The winter was almost an entire blank. 'I am not allowed to work at all,' he writes to Krüger, 'and must only rest and go for walks. Sometimes I have not even strength enough for that.' Spring brought some improvement in his condition, and on May 28th he can write to Verhulst: 'I am rather better, and am beginning to work again, which for months has been out of the question.' But another attack in Febuary 1846, and another in the summer of 1847, warned him that it was necessary to be careful, and to husband the resources that he had been expending with such a lavish hand.

The particular shape into which the disease determined was that irregular growth of osseous matter in the brain which doctors recognise as a concomitant symptom of melancholia.[1] It is possible that Schumann inherited the tendency from his mother, who suffered much from headaches and hypochondria in the latter part of her life; in any case he largely developed it by his ceaseless industry and the untiring energy which he threw into all his work.

Even during this period every interval of convalescence was marked by some new sign of productive activity. The year 1845-6 saw the composition of the 'Studies' and 'Sketches' for pedal-piano (of which the former are dedicated to Schumann's old master Kuntzsch of Zwickau), the two sets of Fugues, Op. 60 and Op. 72, and above all, the great Symphony in C, about which Schumann sends a characteristic

---

[1] See Dr Hellbig's diagnosis of the case (*Wasielewski*, p. 230), and compare the results of the *post-mortem* held by Dr Richarz of Endenich (*Wasielewski*, p. 301).

note to Mendelssohn in September 1845. It was produced by Mendelssohn at the Gewandhaus, November 5, 1846.

During his residence at Dresden Schumann made the better acquaintance of Richard Wagner, who had succeeded Weber's old rival Morlacchi as Hofkapellmeister. It was an appropriate time for their meeting, since 1845 is the date of *Tannhäuser*, the first work in which Wagner definitely embodies his theory of dramatic art, and we may well understand the interest with which the score was read by the ardent apostle of German opera. At first, like the rest of the world, Schumann was puzzled by the new departure. 'Wagner has just finished another opera,' he writes to Mendelssohn.[1] 'He is undoubtedly a clever fellow, full of crazy ideas, and bold to a degree. The aristocracy are still raving about *Rienzi*, but I declare that he cannot write four consecutive bars that are melodious or even correct. . . . And now the full score lies beautifully printed before us, fifths and octaves into the bargain, and now he would like to make corrections and erasures. Too late. The music is not a shade better than *Rienzi*, in fact rather weaker and more strained.' Within three weeks Schumann had witnessed a performance of the opera, and with his accustomed honesty wrote off at once to modify his original criticism. 'Perhaps we shall soon have a talk about *Tannhäuser*,' he says. 'I must retract a good deal of what I wrote to you after reading the score. On the stage everything is different. I was quite impressed by some of it.' And his final judgment is expressed in a letter to his old master Heinrich Dorn, dated January 7,

[1] October 22, 1845. Translated by Miss Herbert.

1846. 'I wish you could see *Tannhäuser*: it contains deeper, more original, and altogether a hundredfold better things than his previous operas, though at the same time much that is musically trivial. In short Wagner may become of the highest importance to the stage, at any rate he possesses the requisite courage. The instrumentation I consider excellent, and the whole workmanship far more masterly than it used to be.' We must remember that Schumann was at this time particularly engaged on contrapuntal studies, and so had a special reason for finding *Tannhäuser* uncongenial. Indeed it speaks highly for both musicians that, on so intimate a point of Art, the one should have power to convince and the other generosity to admit conviction.

During the winter of 1846-7 Schumann visited Vienna, Prague, and Berlin, giving concerts and renewing old acquaintanceships. On his return to Dresden he wrote the pianoforte trio in D minor, probably after the quintett the most popular of his chamber works, and then set himself in earnest to carry out his own scheme of operatic composition. After some hesitation he selected as his subject the legend of St Geneviève of Brabant, the story of an innocent wife driven from her home under false charges of infidelity. It had been dramatised by Hebbel from Tieck's poem, and Schumann naturally proposed to use the play as the basis of his libretto. But here a preliminary difficulty occurred. Reinich, who was commissoned to write the book, made a complete failure of it; Hebbel refused to mutilate his child in the interests of an alien cause; finally Schumann was compelled to follow Wagner's lead and construct a text for himself. The work was delayed by another attack of illness, but on recovery Schumann took it in hand at once, and began, with all the vigour of a fresh interest, to call into being his new creations: Siegfried and Genoveva, Drago and Hidulfus, Margaretha the witch and Golo the traitor.

On November 4th all Leipsic was thrown into consternation by the news of Mendelssohn's death. The streets were placarded with official notices, round which men gathered in silent or whispering knots, work was suspended, and the whole city gave itself over to mourning for the premature close of that brilliant career. Schumann felt keenly the loss of his friend and hero. For twelve years he had looked up to Mendelssohn as the embodiment of all that was pure and perfect in contemporary Art; for twelve years he had enjoyed his friendship and profited by his assistance, now 'the king was gone and the kingdom left desolate.' His own wreath for the coffin was the exquisite little elegy called 'Erinnerung,' which, though unmistakably Schumann's in spirit, exactly catches the lilt and melody of the 'Lieder ohne Wörte.' It is a strange coincidence that in the first movement of the pianoforte trio in F, which was written during this year, he inserted, beside the regular subjects, a reminiscence of his song:—
'Dein Bildniss wunderselig hab'ich in Herzens Grund.' He little knew how soon the picture would be draped with black.

In January 1848 a new Philharmonic Society was started in Dresden, with Schumann as conductor. He took great interest in its fortunes, and at once completed for it the scene of 'Faust's Salvation,' which had been lying untouched in his desk for nearly four years. The first performance took place at a semi-private concert on June 25th, and made a great impression. 'Now,' said one of the audience, 'I understand Goethe for the first time,' a criticism which gave Schumann greater pleasure than could have been afforded by any detailed praise of melody or orchestration. Next year the work was given simultaneously at Dresden, Leipsic, and Weimar, on the occasion of the Goethe Centenary, and from that time its renown was assured.

In addition to the scene from *Faust* Schumann completed the music of *Genoveva* between January and August 1848, and composed 'about forty or fifty pianoforte pieces'[1] 'for young people.' Naturally the opera was the work in which he was most interested. 'I think,' he writes, 'that much of it is successful,' and before the end of November he is making arrangements with Rietz to have it brought out at Leipsic. Then, as in the case of Berlioz and *Les Troyens*, came delay and vexation. Rietz promised that the work should be produced at the end of February, but the promise was not followed by any performance. Then came Leipsic fair, an episode which further retarded progress; and as a matter of fact it was not until June 25, 1850, that Schumann's most cherished composition was allowed to make its appearance. Even so it only gained a *succes d'estime*. Spohr, then in his sixty-seventh year, gave it his warm approbation, but the general public let it pass unheeded, and after three representations the opera was withdrawn. Schumann was grievously disappointed. He had borne the deferment of his hopes with singular good temper and patience,

---

[1] Letter to Verhulst, November 4, 1848. The pianoforte pieces are those of the *Weinachts Album*, Op. 68.

refusing at first to believe in any charge of bad faith against Rietz, or of an intrigue against the other Leipsic musicians,[1] and only beginning to doubt their loyalty when, at the beginning of 1850, the performance was indefinitely postponed for the fourth time. But, like all great artists, he did not recognise his own weakness. *Genoveva*, with all its beauties, is not an opera that can possibly hold the stage; it is too serious to be 'pretty,' too heavy to be dramatic, and thus fails in its appeal alike to the cultivated and uncultivated portions of its audience. In the whole list of Schumann's greater compositions it is the least known and the least appreciated.

Despite work and worry Schumann had much improved in health, and the years 1848-9 may be taken as the climax of his career as a Composer. In the latter year alone he wrote nearly thirty works of importance, including the *Manfred* music, which he would have dedicated to Queen Victoria if he had not at the last moment lacked courage to present it, the *Concertstück* for four horns and orchestra, the *Requiem for Mignon*, the *Nachtlied*, the *Spanisches Liederspiel*, full of warm colour and sunny romance; the charming Songs for Children, and the rest of the scenes from *Faust*, with the exception of the midnight scene and the overture. During the same period he began to turn his attention to Sacred Music, and made his first essays in that field with two settings of poems by Rückert, the *Advent Hymn*, and the motet for male voices, 'Verzweifle nicht im Schmerzensthal.' The May

---
[1] Letter to Brendel, Easter 1849. Letter to Rietz, May 20, 1849. Letter to Brendel, September 18, 1849.

Revolution at Dresden does not seem to have affected him in the least. He simply removed his residence to Kreischa, and went on composing as if nothing had happened.

Still the barricades came very near influencing his fortunes indirectly. Herr Hofkapellmeister Richard Wagner took a more intimate part in them than was quite appropriate to his exalted station, and consequently found it prudent to resign his office and betake himself across the border. It seemed only natural that Schumann should be elected to the vacant post. He was director of the two principal choral societies in the place—the Liedertafel and the Philharmonic — he was beyond all question the greatest musician alive, not only in Dresden but in Germany; and he was, moreover, extremely anxious to obtain for his reforms the support and authority of an official position. In 1847 he had discussed with Nottebohm the advisability of applying for the directorship of the Vienna Conservatorium; in 1849 he wrote to Härtel making similar inquiries about Leipsic. Both schemes, however, fell through: the conditions at Vienna were not satisfactory, and at Leipsic the vacancy did not occur, so there was the more reason why Schumann should wish for success in his candidature at Dresden. But it was all in vain. The Saxon Government had a vivid memory of reforming Kapellmeisters, and elected Herr Krebs, an eminent musical conservative, who could show for testimonial twenty-three years of good service at the Hamburg Theatre.

While these negotiations were pending Schumann received a letter from his friend Ferdinand Hiller, who was about to vacate the post of musical director at Düsseldorf in order to accept a similar position at Cologne. Hiller strongly advised him to apply for the former, and urged that his appointment would be almost a foregone conclusion. For some time Schumann hesitated. Düsseldorf was not by any means the same thing as Dresden or Leipsic; Mendelssohn had given bad accounts of its musical capabilities; Rietz had frankly wondered 'how Hiller could persuade himself to go there'; and expatriation was a heavy price to pay for office in a provincial town of no great importance or vitality. True, there were the Niederrheinische Musikfeste, but they only visited Düsseldorf once in three years, and beside them was little or nothing except the winter subscription concerts, which rumour declared to be but languidly supported. Further, it would be impossible to leave Saxony before the middle of 1850, since there were all the rehearsals of *Genoveva* to superintend, and it seemed doubtful whether the electing committee would be able or willing to keep the place open. However, all these difficulties were overcome, the application was made and accepted, and in September 1850 Schumann established himself in his new home and entered on his new duties.

On the whole he was agreeably surprised. He found at his disposal an admirable chorus, and an orchestra trained by Rietz and Hiller to a high degree of efficiency. To secure a good leader he invited over Wasielewski from Leipsic; the greatest pianist in Europe was already at his side; Joachim would sometimes come across from Weimar to play a concerto and exchange memories of Mendelssohn and the old days. Unfortunately it soon appeared that, like many great musicians, Schumann was not a good conductor. His natural hesitation of manner often shrank even from the elementary duty of determining the *tempo;* his shyness and reticence prevented him from criticising the rehearsals in detail; and these defects, serious enough from the beginning, were made more grave by the illness which broke out again in 1851, and, with short periods of intermission, grew steadily worse until the end. It is a strange and ominous fact that one of his reasons against accepting the directorship at Düsseldorf was that there was an asylum in the town, and that he feared the sight of it.

For a while he struggled gallantly against the encroachments of disease. During the month of November 1850 he wrote the fine symphony in E-flat, inspired by a visit to 'Das grosse, heilige Köln'; later in the same winter came the *Bride of Messina* overture, and another to Shakespeare's *Julius Cæsar;* in the summer of 1851 appeared the *King's Son* and the *Pilgrimage of the Rose*, the latter one of the freshest and sweetest of cantatas; during the autumn he revised and published the D minor symphony and wrote the two violin sonatas and the third and last pianoforte trio. At the same time he was corresponding with Richard Pohl, then a student at Leipsic University, about a scheme for a grand oratorio. 'I have been thinking,' he writes on January 19th, 'of Ziska or Luther, but should like a Biblical subject just as well.' By Febuary 14th Luther has been selected, and Schumann sends a long list of conditions. The oratorio must be available for both

Church and concert room; it must not last more than two hours and a half; it must be dramatic rather than narrative, and as full of choruses as the *Israel in Egypt;* half the characters suggested by Pohl are to be cut out; and the whole work is to be studiously simple, 'so that peasant and citizen alike should comprehend it.' Anyone who knows anything of poets will understand that after this the oratorio was given up, though Schumann accepted in its place an arrangement of Uhland's *Sängers Fluch*, ably adapted and enlarged by Pohl for the exigencies of musical treatment. The year's work ended with the appearance, about Christmas time, of the overture to *Hermann and Dorothea*, which was originally intended for a comic opera on the subject of Goethe's poem. But, like Mendelssohn, Schumann was exceedingly fastidious about his libretti, and the project ultimately came to nothing.

His life at Düsseldorf was so quiet and regular that the townspeople might have set their watches by him, as, according to Heine, the citizens of Königsberg did by Kant. Every day at twelve he would walk with Wasielewski in the Hofgarten, every day at six he would accompany the same friend to a neighbouring *café*, where he would take his seat without a word and listen to the conversation round him. The rest of his time was spent in work or in swift silent visits to his more intimate acquaintances. Yet there was nothing moody in his silence. He would follow every word with the most eager interest, and occasionally express his approval with a bright cordial glance towards the speaker: it was more like some form of aphasia than any symptom of apathy or indifference. He was well aware of the peculiarity; but neither jest nor argument had any power to overcome it. His friends grew gradually accustomed to seeing their rooms invaded by a noiseless figure, which entered on tiptoe, sat down at the pianoforte, improvised for a few moments, and then vanished with a nod of farewell.

In March 1852 the Schumanns visited Leipsic, where between the 14th and the 21st several of the more recent compositions were performed. Strangely enough the 'Schumann week' was not an entire success. It is not easy to gauge the musical taste of a public which cannot be moved either by the *Pilgrimage of the Rose* or by the overture to *Manfred*, but Leipsic had treated its old professor with some coldness ever since he resigned his chair, and it now received him with more respect than cordiality. Schumann, for his part, was very little affected by the attitude of his audience. 'I am quite accustomed,' he had told Pohl, 'to find that my deeper and better compositions are not understood at first hearing,' just as Beethoven, when some officious friend told him that his new quartett did not please, simply answered, 'It will please some day.'

Back at Düsseldorf, Schumann completed the *Sängers Fluch*, and wrote in immediate succession the *Mass*, the *Requiem*, and the four choral ballads, 'Vom Pagen und der Königstochter.' Then came six months' complete prostration. The old illness returned in a more serious form, bringing with it not only severe physical pain but the graver symptoms of clouded and distorted imagination. With great reluctance Schumann broke off all work and went to seek recovery with his friend Verhulst at Scheveningen. There the rest and freedom seem to have produced their effect, and by the end of the year he was able to return to his duties, though with much impaired power and much slighter hope of continuance. The few compositions of 1853, the *Luck of Edenhall*, the Festival overture, the Fantasia for Violin and Orchestra, the overture to *Faust*, and one or two smaller works, tell only too plainly the story of an exhausted brain and an ebbing vitality. Even his official work became impossible. When the great Düsseldorf festival took place at Whitsuntide he was only able to conduct it on the first day, and shortly afterwards he was compelled to resign his directorship altogether.

Weary, disappointed, broken in health and fortunes, he might well have found excuse if he had yielded to the stress of circumstances and grown morose like Tasso, or misanthropical like Swift. But through all his long malady there is no recorded word of impatience or bitterness. If he speaks of his trouble, it is simply to apologise for some unfinished composition or some delayed correspondence. As a rule his letters show no change from his former cheerfulness of tone and kindly warmth of manner. There is no mockery at 'the great Aristophanes of Heaven,' no vain lamentation for the loss of pleasant days; even under the shadow of the most terrible disease from which man can suffer his only thoughts are for his friends and for his Art. Younger contemporaries—Tausch, Bargiel, Böhme, Dietrich—received at his hands the same generous help which he had given of old time to Chopin and Berlioz and Sterndale Bennett. His greatest happiness was still the encouragement of all true artistic effort; his chief hope that he might find some worthy successor to carry on the torch in his stead.

All the world knows how that hope was fulfilled. One morning in October there appeared at Schumann's house a boy of twenty, with a letter of introduction from Joachim and an armful of compositions. Schumann read them through with increasing wonder and delight, sent back to Joachim the single sentence, 'Das ist der der kommen musste,' and, after an absence of nine years, returned once more to issue in the *Neue Zeitschrift* a royal proclamation of welcome to the new genius. 'There has come among us,' he said, 'a youth who will give expression to the highest ideals of our time. His thought sweeps forward strong and impetuous as a torrent; yet are the banks bright with painted butterflies and melodious with the song of nightingales. . . . We give him greeting on his entry into the strife. If wounds await him, there are also palms and laurels: whatever the issue, he will bear himself as a valiant warrior.'[1] We may notice that Schumann spoke of the music as showing not only promise but achievement. There will be further advance, he says, but the work already done is that of an undoubted Master. All his letters are full of it: settling terms with publishers, making plans for the *début* at Leipsic, exchanging congratulations with music lovers from Hamburg to Vienna. It is a fitting reward that the voice which had so often been

[1] Adapted from the *Neue Zeitschrift*, October 28, 1853. See also letter to Joachim, October 8th.

raised in commendation of lesser men should devote its last public utterance to the honour of Johannes Brahms.

For a while it seemed as though the new interest had given Schumann a fresh lease of life. His health so far improved that he was able during the winter of 1853 to undertake a very successful concert tour in Holland, and even to make preliminary arrangements for transferring his home to Vienna, since Düsseldorf had no longer any claim on his services. In January 1854 he attended a performance of *Paradise and the Peri* at Hanover, accepted an engagement to conduct his D minor symphony at Frankfort, and then settled down to work with an activity which even for him was unusual. Beside compositions, he was preparing his critical writings for the press, and collecting an anthology of passages relating to Music from all the great poets and philosophers. 'My garden is getting on splendidly,' he writes to Joachim on February 6th. 'In Plato especially I have found some glorious things.'

It was the last flicker of an expiring flame. The excitement of the winter produced an inevitable reaction ; the disease returned in a more malignant form : little by little the overwrought faculties gave way and sank into ruin. Hallucinations grew more persistent and more vivid : first a single musical note, then broken melodic phrases, then articulate voices of menace or warning. Physical pain was intensified by periods of extreme mental distress; memory began to fail; thought became obscure and uncertain; at last the symptoms of insanity declared themselves too plainly to be mistaken. There is no need to continue the story further. Enough that, after an attempt at suicide, Schumann was placed under restraint in a private asylum near Bonn, that he lingered there for two years, with brief periods of respite, and that he died in his wife's arms, July 29, 1856—only forty-six years of age.

III

SCHUMANN AS COMPOSER AND CRITIC

IT is a common matter of accusation against the great Composers that they have not, as a rule, been men of wide culture or varied interests. There is, in fact, a certain insularity about Music. Representative Arts stand to one another as adjoining countries on a continent; the painter often sees his subject in a poem, the poet in a picture, while both alike are in frequent communication with the neutral ground of history and romance. The musician, on the other hand, finds that his special pursuit is isolated from the world of action, that it is independent of the records and achievements of humanity that it stands apart, an autonomous kingdom with no external suzerain or ally. Hence he has less need than his fellow-artists to acquaint himself with the thoughts of any but his own predecessors. It was not by the aid of a general education that Mozart devised his melodies, or Bach his counterpoint, or Beethoven his supreme conception of musical form.

Another reason may be discovered in the fertility of production which the great Composers have almost invariably exhibited. Haydn, with his hundred and twenty symphonies, Schubert, with his six hundred and thirty songs, can have had but little time to explore regions which did not lie directly across their path. Music, indeed, seems to require special concentration of effort; it is more imperious, more absorbing than the other Arts. And thus, while it advances a fuller claim on the service of its votaries, it rewards them with a closer communion and a more frequent vision of the ideal.

But as human nature progresses in complexity the need of general cultivation increases. Men 'who, separate, ignored each other's arts' are replaced by successors who gradually abandon the scheme of self-sufficiency and substitute that of intercourse and exchange. Provinces which were originally parted by a tribal exclusiveness begin to bridge the rivers and clear the mountain passes; at last even the distant island overseas is drawn to some extent into the system, vessels are launched, cables laid, treaties of mutual recognition struck and established. For all culture has its effect on character, and the artist of a highly civilised age must participate in the general development if he is to keep in touch with the public which he addresses. To the musician the need still remains less than to the painter or the poet, but it is no longer inappreciable. In the early days of the Classical ideal a man might be a great composer with the barest minimum of outside knowledge; in the Romantic movement which followed he would be driven to rely less upon *a priori* abstract laws, and more on his own temperament and the general influences by which it was formed.

It may be that this change in the circumstances of composition has not been wholly advantageous.

Music has lost in purity, perhaps in absolute beauty, while it has gained in emotional force and significance. We are far more stirred by Weber than we are by Palestrina—yet Palestrina reaches a height to which neither *Freischütz* nor *Euryanthe* can aspire. There is more dramatic propriety in Liszt than in Haydn, but we would not give up the *Creation* for all the works of the Hungarian Master put together. Music, in short, has grown more sympathetic; it has left its remote Alpine peak and drawn nearer to the tempestuous valleys of our emotional life. It can never cross the great gulf which separates the ideal from the phenomenal, but it stands near enough to the brink for us to see dim outlines and shadowy forms and to occupy ourselves with vain attempts to recognise their features or determine their characteristics.

Schumann's whole life was an endeavour to unite the two ideals. In spirit he is a Romantic of the Romantics, directing his music towards the outside world with a hundred hints and explanations. In form he recognised Bach as his master, and strove to express his ideas in the most elaborate language of the old polyphony. He does not, like Berlioz, splash on his colours principally with an eye to effect. On the contrary, he pays the utmost attention to detail and finish. In a word, his Davidsbund, like our Pre-Raphaelite Brotherhood, was an attempt to adapt ancient methods to modern subjects, with this difference, that whereas our English Pre-Raphaeliteism sometimes lost its hold of the theme in its attention to the treatment, Schumann regards the theme as paramount, and adapts the treatment to it as best he can. Hence the first requisite in estimating his work is to examine the character of his ideas, and especially to explain the contention, already advanced, that in forming them he was much influenced by the Romantic movement in Literature.

Now, as among the musicians of his time, Schumann was exceptionally well read. His Classical attainments was probably allowed to rust during his long life as Composer and journalist; but as late as 1854 he was ransacking Greek authors for passages about Music, and, even if he took Voss's Homer instead of the original, must have gained some acquaintance with the spirit of the *Iliad* and the *Odyssey*. Among our own poets he was a thorough student of Byron and Shakespeare, and knew something at least of Burns and Scott. Of the Italians he certainly read Dante and Petrarch, and possibly others as well; while the Romantic writers of his own country were almost as familiar to him as his own works. He knew his Richter as some Englishmen know Dickens, his Heine as some Frenchmen know Musset. He not only studied Goethe, but interpreted him. Of Rückert, Geibel, Eichendorf, Chamisso, and many other contemporary poets, he was the closest reader and the most valuable commentator. Further, he was himself endowed with some not inconsiderable talent for authorship. It has been already stated that in his earlier days Music and Literature divided his allegiance; at Heidelberg he could astonish his friend Rosen with verse translations of Petrarch's sonnets. During his Russian journey in 1844 he kept an intermittent 'Poetical Diary,' which must at least have implied some facility in metre. His projected romance on the Davidsbund never seems to have come into existence, but in the *Neue Zeitschrift* he treats that society in a manner which shows that he possessed something of the novelist's gift. Florestan, Eusebius, and Raro are distinct living characters, drawn, it may be, from the life, but still 'seen through a temperament,' and contrasted with remarkable skill and consistency. To the last he retained his appreciation of style. The essay on Brahms which closed his career as a journalist is written with the same care as the essay on Chopin which began it. Throughout the whole course he uses his medium like an artist, and endeavours not only to say what he means, but to say it in accordance with the best literary traditions of his time.

Again he acknowledges the debt which his music owed to the study of his favourite author. 'I learned more counterpoint from Jean Paul than from my music-master,' he tells Simonin de Sire; and writing to Henrietta Voigt *à propos* of the Papillons he adds, 'I might tell you a good deal about them had not Jean Paul done it so much better. If you ever have a moment to spare, please read the last chapter of the *Flegeljahre*, where you will find it all in black and white, down to the seven-league boot, in F-sharp minor. (At the end of the *Flegeljahre* I always feel as if the piece was over but the curtain still up.) I may further mention that I have adopted the text to the music and not *vice versa*. Only the last of all, which by a happy chance became an answer to the first, owes its existence to Jean Paul.' It is perhaps difficult for us to see the last number of the Papillons in Wult's departure or Walt's fantastic dream, but the point is that Schumann saw it.[1] The mind that conceived that dainty finale was brought into its particular mood by a literary influence.

Thirdly, in one important point Schumann's method of composition stands in closest relation to the earlier Romantic movement in German poetry. 'The plastic figures in antique Art,' says Heine, 'are identical with the thing represented. The wanderings of the Odyssey mean nothing more than the wanderings of the man called Odysseus, the son of Laertes and the husband of Penelope. It is otherwise in Romantic Art: here the wanderings of the knight have an esoteric signification; they typify, perhaps, the mazes of life in general. The dragon that is vanquished is sin: the almond tree that wafts its fragrance to the hero is the Trinity. . . . Classical Art had to portray only the finite, and its form could be identical with the artist's idea. Romantic Art had to represent, or rather to typify, the infinite and the spiritual, and therefore was compelled to have recourse to a system of traditional or parabolic symbols.' So it is with Music. The tunes in a sonata of Mozart are satisfied to be beautiful melodies and nothing more: no question arises as to their meaning or character. The tunes of Schumann, like the colours of Rossetti, are always trembling on the verge of symbolism. Not, of course, that Music can be tied down to any definite signification: on this point the failure of Berlioz is complete and

[1] Dr Spitta suggests that Schumann meant the last chapter but one—the masked ball at which Wina and Walt are guests. This certainly seems more likely; and in any case the doubt itself is significant.

conclusive. But though it cannot work on the same lines as articulate thought, it may possibly work on parallel lines:—that is to say, it may express some broad generic type of emotion with which the articulate thought may be brought into sympathy. For instance, a great many of Schumann's pianoforte pieces have specific names—Warum, Erster Verlust, Botschaft, and so on. It would be impossible for us to supply the names from hearing the piece; but if we know the names already we shall recognise that the musical treatment is appropriate. This was precisely what Schumann intended. He writes to Dorn, ' I have never come across anything more absurd than Rellstab's criticism of my Kinderscenen. He seems to imagine that I got hold of a crying child and sought for inspiration from its sobs. I don't deny that certain children's faces hovered before my mind while I was composing, but the titles were of course added afterwards, and are, as a matter of fact, merely hints as to the treatment and interpretation.[1] At the same time his indications are curiously detailed. He distinguishes the *Kinderscenen* from the *Weihnachts Album* on the ground that the former are the recollection which a grown man retains of his childhood, while the latter 'consists of imaginings and expectations of young people.'[2] He finds the story of Hero and Leander in the fifth of the *Fantasiestücke:* he accompanies two of the *Davidsbündlertänze* with a running commentary of Florestan and Eusebius; while as climax he declares that in one of Schubert's pianoforte works he and a friend discovered

[1] Compare letter to Moscheles, September 22, 1837.
[2] Letter to Reinecke, October 6, 1848.

exactly the same pageant, 'down to the name of the town in which it was held.' Even his directions for performance show something of the same tendency. In the ordinary indications of *tempo* he is notoriously careless; it is a well-known joke against him that the finale of the 'Concerto without Orchestra' begins, 'So schnell als möglich' and ends 'piu presto,' while there is still a controversy whether the coda of the slow movement in his F major quartett should be marked 'piu mosso' or 'piu lento.' But on the other hand he often suggests the manner of interpretation by such phrases as 'Etwas kokett,' or 'mit humor,' or 'mit innigkeit.' Once he gets as far as 'Etwas hahnbüchen,' a hint which pianists must find some difficulty in taking. The great pianoforte Fantasia in C has a motto from Schlegel, the fourth of the *Waldscenen* has one from Hebbel, and similar texts were appended to the earliest edition of the *Davidsbündlertänze* and of one the *Novelletten*. Everywhere we find the evident intention of establishing a parallelism between Music and some influence from outside. In one word, Schumann did not wish his melodies to tell a definite story or paint a definite picture, but he did wish to bring his hearers into a condition of mind from which they could 'go on romancing for themselves.'

One example of this parallelism deserves a special word of comment, partly from its intrinsic importance, partly because hitherto it has been somewhat underrated. The *Kreisleriana* certainly owe more than their title to Hoffmann's fantastic sketches. Critics who tell us that Schumann 'is expressing his own sorrows, not those of Dr Kreisler,' and that 'he might just as well have called his pieces "Wertheriana," or any other name,' have missed a point which it is of some moment to observe. Among Hoffmann's 'Fantasiestücke in Callot's manier' there are two sets of Kreisleriana, loose, disconnected papers, dealing with Music and musical criticism very much in the style which Schumann afterwards adopted for the *Neue Zeitschrift*. The essay on Beethoven might have been signed 'R. S.,' Florestan and Eusebius might have been members of the Musico-Poetical Club, the Musikfeind was a well-known figure in the editorial sanctum at Leipsic. Even Dr Johannes Kreisler himself—'the little man in a coat the colour of C-sharp minor with an E major coloured collar'—is not far removed in spirit from the party who listened to Chopin's Op. 2, or tried experiments with the 'psychometer.' In short, of all German artists Schumann approaches most nearly to Hoffmann in standpoint. Both deserted Law for Music, both were at the same time composers and journalists, both employed the manner and phraseology of Richter to the advancement of the new school of composition. The differences between them, which no doubt are sufficiently wide, lie mainly outside the domains of the Art: within that domain they fought for the same cause with the same weapons. Hence in calling his pieces 'Kreisleriana' Schumann is expressing a real connection of thought, a real recognition of alliance. They are, in fact, 'Fantasiestücke in Hoffmann's manier,' and bear more intimate relation to the creator of Dr Kreisler than all the copperplates that ever issued from Callot's studio.

The connection is interesting because it illustrates the attempt to relate musical to literary influences under the most favourable of conditions. We have here two men possessed of somewhat similar gifts and united by a common aim. Hoffmann is enough of a composer to have a full understanding of Music; Schumann enough of an author to be closely in touch with Literature. Both desire to reconcile the two, so far as such reconciliation is possible; each sets himself to the work from his own side. Hence in estimating the result of their efforts we shall see once for all the limitations of Musical Romanticism. It is a unique opportunity for determining in what sense effects of tone and effects of word can be held to react upon one another.

Now in the second series of Hoffmann's Kreisleriana is described a meeting of the Musico-Poetical Club, a precursor of the Davidsbund, which assembled in the Kapellmeister's rooms to hear him play, and to profit by his instructions. Unfortunately at the outset there is an accident to the piano, attempts to remedy it only make matters worse, and at last so many of the strings are broken that the instrument becomes practically useless. But the Doctor is equal to the occasion. He seats himself at the keyboard, and striking at intervals such notes as are still available, supplies the place of his fantasia with a long rhapsodical description of its poetic meaning. The performance, in fact, is the exact reverse of a song without words:—it is a pianoforte piece without music. We may notice that Hoffmann is wise enough not to attempt any definiteness of outline. There is no portraiture of hero or heroine, no detailed description of incident, all is left vague, shadowy, indeterminate. Literature has become all but melodic, it is standing on the extreme verge and stretching out its hands over a gulf which it cannot cross. In like manner the Kreisleriana of Schumann are all but articulate. In no other of his pianoforte works is the expression of emotion so clear and so intelligible; the voice is eloquent even though we cannot catch the precise words of its utterance. Here also is no attempt to depict any specific scene or occurrence; the music is suggestive, not descriptive; the end is attained purely and simply by the indication of broad general types of feeling. This, then, would seem to be the conclusion of the whole matter. The most determinate effects of tone produce in the hearer a mental impression analogous to that caused by the least determinate effects of word. As Language becomes more definite, as Music becomes more abstract, so the two recede from one another until they arrive at poles, which have as little in common as a page of Macaulay with a melody of Mozart. At their nearest they can never be brought into contact, for Music is in more senses than one 'a universal language,' and cannot be adequately translated by the concrete particulars of our accustomed speech. But, near or far, their closest points of convergence are the two Kreisleriana.

It may be added that Schumann himself had a clear view of the extent and limits of his position. 'People err,' he says, 'if they think that a Composer puts pen to paper with the predetermination of expressing or depicting some particular fact. Yet we must not estimate outward influences and impressions too lightly . . . . The more elements congenially related to Music which the tone-picture contains within it the more poetic and plastic will be the expression of the composition, and in proportion to the imaginativeness and receptivity of the composer will be the elevating and touching quality of his work.' And again, more boldly: 'The ill-educated man can scarcely believe that Music possesses the power of expressing particular passions, and therefore it is difficult for him to comprehend the more individual Masters. We have learned to express the finer shades of feeling by penetrating more deeply into the mysteries of harmony.' No doubt Schumann is here claiming too much. Music cannot 'express the finer shades of feeling,' it can only suggest the broader types and universals. But in any case we have here the words of a composer who approaches his art from the poetical side, who is as far as possible removed from the abstract, unconscious, unreflective methods of the earlier Masters. Mozart and Haydn were musicians; Schumann was, in the fullest sense of the term, a tone-poet.

So far we have considered the character of Schumann's ideas, and the external or literary influences by which his mind was trained for their conception. It would now follow to complete the account of his education by pointing out the influence exercised upon him by the work of previous Composers. Among these, of course, Bach was paramount. Schumann almost passes over the great triumvirate to whom we owe the sonata, the quartett, and the symphony. Mozart and Haydn hardly affected him at all; Beethoven 'mainly in his later compositions';[1] it is to Bach that he looks

[1] See letter to Krüger, June 14, 1839.

as the second fountain-head of his inspiration. 'Bach and Jean Paul had the greatest influence upon me in former days,' he writes to Kossmaly, and as late as 1851 he makes the same acknowledgment. 'There are three to whom I always go for advice: the simple Gluck, the more intricate Handel, and the most intricate of all—Bach. Only study the last-named thoroughly and the most complicated of my works will seem clear.' Half his admiration for Mendelssohn was devoted to 'the Master who was the first, by the strength of his own enthusiasm, to revive the memory of Bach in Germany'; almost the last work which occupied his failing powers was a set of pianoforte accompaniments to the violin and violoncello sonatas of the great Cantor. No doubt he gained something from Weber and Schubert, but his relation to them was far less intimate. From first to last his ideal in musical expression was 'the great and lofty art of the ancestor of harmony.'

Bach and Jean Paul—polyphony and romance—these are the two keys which unlock the mystery of Schumann's work as a composer. His own individuality remains unimpugned; all artists are in some degree indebted to the continuous growth and development of previous work; and Schumann's method is no more derivative than that of Beethoven or Handel. The formative conditions of genius are those by which it is trained, not those by which it is created, only in all cases the training must be efficient if creation is to lead to maturity. At the same time it is of considerable interest to notice three main points in which his education told upon his style. It may be impossible to explain the life; it is both possible and profitable to dissect the organism.

First, his career as a Composer is unique in the history of Music. There is no other instance of a musician who applies himself successively to each department of his Art, masters it, and passes on to the next. Almost all his great pianoforte works were written before 1840, then came a year of song writing, then a year of symphony, then a year of chamber music, then *Paradise and the Peri*. Schubert's songs cover the whole period of his productive life; Beethoven's first piece of concerted music is Op. 1, and his last Op. 135; Haydn's symphonies extend over nearly half a century. The other great Masters, in short, seem either to have had the forms always at hand, or, like Wagner and Berlioz, to have left some altogether untouched. Schumann employs every medium in turn; but he fetches it from outside, and puts it back when he has finished with it. No doubt he wrote songs after 1840, and orchestral compositions after 1841; but it is none the less noticeable that he devoted himself exclusively to the different forms when they first came under his hand, and that almost all his best work may be divided into a series of detached groups, each produced in one particular manner at one particular time. Surely we have here the indirect working of a logical, deliberative mind—a mind that has been trained into special habits of purpose and selection. In the very character of his method Schumann is actuated by psychological forces different from those of his predecessors in the Art.

The second distinctive point is his system of melody. All tune implies a certain fundamental unity—otherwise it would be chaotic, and a certain variation of detail—otherwise it would be monotonous. This identity in difference can be attained in two ways, which we may call respectively the Continuous and the Discrete. In the former a series of entirely different elements is fused into a single whole: no two of them are similar, yet all are so fitted together that each supplies what the others need. In the latter a set of parallel clauses are balanced antithetically: the same rhythmic figure is preserved in all, and the differences depend entirely upon qualities of tone and curve. The former is the typical method of Beethoven, the latter that of Schumann. Take, for instance, the opening subject of Beethoven's violoncello sonata in A. No two bars present the same figure, yet the whole is a unity. Take the longer melody which opens the slow movement of the *Sonata Pathétique*. It contains almost as many figures as there are bars, yet the effect is of a single and perfect sentence. Of course Beethoven employed both methods, as he employed every other mode of musical expression, but it is incontestable that in the power of varying and developing his figures is to be found one of his greatest claims to supremacy as an artist. This power Schumann · seldom or never brought into active operation. In the opening movement of his pianoforte quintett, to take an instance from the most familiar of all his works, the first four bars contain two clauses, upon which are built the whole of the first subject and the transition; while the first two bars of the second subject contain the clause upon which the whole of the succeeding melody is constructed. In the last movement of the D minor trio, in the cantabile tune of the first *Novellete*, in the well-known theme of the *Bilder aus Osten*, in a hundred other examples, we find a definite square-cut scheme, exactly analogous to the structure of a stanza of verse. There are very few of Beethoven's instrumental melodies to which it would be possible to adapt metrical words; there is scarcely one of Schumann's which could not be so treated. His relation to poetry extends even to the fact of versification.

Hence his melodies are much easier to analyse than those of Beethoven. Indeed it often happens that the melodic phrase is obvious—almost commonplace—and that the value of the tune depends upon the skill of its treatment, and especially the richness of its harmonisation. The charming little waltz in the Papillons is simply an ascending and descending diatonic scale; the very effective opening subject in the slow movement of the pianoforte quartett is a series of sevenths; and similar instances may be found in the scherzo of the pianoforte quintett and in many of the songs. Sometimes, too, he took his theme from the 'musical letters' in a word, witness the Abegg variations, the *Carnaval*, and the fugues on the name of Bach, and though this has been done by other Composers, yet none have treated the matter so seriously or with such earnestness of purpose. The *Carnaval*, in particular, is an astonishing instance of the effects that can be produced out of five notes. But it is only very rarely that Schumann's tunes approach the 'divine unconsciousness' of the *Appassionata* or the A major symphony. They have their own character, their own vitality, but the genius that gave them birth was to some degree affected by the preoccupations of an external interest.

The third point is Schumann's comparative indifference to what is technically known as musical form. When he writes about the constituent elements of Music he almost always specifies them as melody and harmony—the 'king and queen of the chess board'—without any mention of that relation of subjects and distribution of keys by which the laws of structure are constituted. This indifference is still more noticeable in his estimate of other men's work. Schubert's C major symphony, Schunke's pianoforte sonata, Böhme's string quartett are discussed with little or no reference to their construction; while, strangest of all, Berlioz's *Symphonie Fantastique* is treated as the legitimate outcome of the system established by Mozart and Beethoven. So it is with his own compositions. Except the symphony in B-flat all his orchestral works are in some degree experimental, and in one of them, the symphony in D minor, he practically abandons the old scheme altogether; his pianoforte sonatas are only sonatas in the sense in which Don Juan is an epic; his quartetts, although they keep the elementary laws, yet show that there is much difference between obeying rules and mastering them. His two finest examples of structure are the pianoforte quintett and the overture to *Manfred;* and even these exhibit a sense of effort which place them on a lower level than the concealed art of Beethoven or Brahms. No doubt it is perfectly admissible to seek after new forms. In this respect, as in every other, Music must be allowed free permission to advance. But, if we are to acquiesce in a substitute for the earlier methods, we must be assured that it is at least as capable as they of satisfying our requirements. And at present it is not too much to say that, except in the one detail of the 'transference of themes,' Classical structure has not seen any discovery of importance since the publication of the Rasoumoffsky quartetts. It must be remembered that in this respect there is a marked difference between Schumann and Berlioz. The latter simply shows a want of acquaintance with the laws of construction. The former knows the laws, but underrates their importance. Schumann is far the greater musician of the two, but though his error is less apparent it is not less existent.

There are three possible reasons why a Composer of such brilliant genius and such unwearied industry should have displayed this weakness. First, that Bach wrote before the great cyclical forms were established, and could therefore give his devoted student little or no assistance in dealing with them. Second, that of all modes of musical expression form is the most abstract—the most essentially musical. Melody and harmony may have some rough analogues outside the limits of the Art: the laws of structure have none. Hence they constitute an inner shrine to which only the most single-hearted musicians can penetrate; and he who visits the Temple with any other prepossession — even of poetry itself — must be content to worship among the people. Third, that the whole tone of Schumann's thought was lyric. A very large number of his works consist of short detached pieces, in which there is neither need nor scope for any elaborate system of construction. Hence he grew habituated to the methods of conciseness and concentration, and his sustained efforts were hardly more congenial than the tragedies of Heine or the historical dramas of Uhland.

In one further respect the character of his work was affected by his general habit of mind. No other Composer has ever submitted his music to so much alteration and recension. The later editions of the *Davidsbündlertänze*, the *Études Symphoniques*, the *Impromptus on a Theme of Clara Wieck*, and other of the piano compositions, are full of variant passages, which range in importance from the correction of a detail to the complete restatement of a whole number. No doubt this form of self-criticism has existed to some extent among artists of all ages: Handel rewrote part of the *Messiah*, Berlioz of the *Symphonie Fantastique*, and recently Brahms has given to the world a new version of his first pianoforte trio; but in no other case has the critical faculty manifested itself so persistently or attached itself so frequently to the printed page. Here again we have evidence of a mind trained in a different school from that of Haydn and Mozart. They made their point once for all with an unerring certainty of intuition: Schumann weighs, deliberates, and finally revises.

As a writer for the pianoforte he may be said to rank beside Schubert. He has less melodic gift, less sweetness, perhaps less originality, but he appreciates far more fully the capacities of the instrument, and possesses more power of rich and recondite harmonisation. His polyphony was a new departure in the history of pianoforte music, based upon that of Bach, but exhibiting a distinctive colour and character of its own. The beauty of his single phrases, the vigour and variety of his accompaniments, the audacity of his 'bitter-sweet discords,' are all so many claims on immortality : hardly in the whole range of the Art have we such intimate household words as *Warum*, and *Träumerei*, *Carnaval* and *Humoreske*, *Kreisleriana* and *Novelletten*. His spirit, too, is essentially human. No Composer is more companionable, more ready to respond to any word and sympathise with any emotion. There are times in which we feel that Bach is too remote, Beethoven too great, Chopin too pessimistic ; but we can always turn to Schumann with the certainty that somewhere in his work we shall find satisfaction.

Among minute points may be mentioned his frequent use of syncopation, sometimes picking out the melody for emphasis, sometimes retarding it to half-speed, oftener traversing the rhythm altogether ; his fondness for long sustained organ chords, as in the *Humoreske* and at the end of the *Papillons;* and his peculiar habit of placing his theme in the middle of the harmony and surrounding it on both sides with a 'transparent fabric' of arpeggios. Of more importance is his employment of new lyric and narrative forms for the pianoforte : the former of which may be illustrated by the detached yet interconnected numbers of the *Blumenstück*, a Leiderkreis without words ; the latter by the structure of the first *Novellette*, in which the distribution of keys is based upon the interval of a major third (F, D-flat, A) instead of the old stereotyped relations of tonic and dominant.

A special word should be said on Schumann's position as a writer of variations. There are two points of view from which this device can be regarded. The Composer may consider the melody as the essential feature of his theme, and occupy himself solely with embroideries and arabesques; or he may take his stand upon its harmonic structure, and reproduce the thought that it contains in different modes of expression and phraseology. The one is, roughly speaking, the method of Mozart and Haydn —it is simpler, more rudimentary, more easily exhausted; the other, which is practically inexhaustible, is the method of Brahms. Beethoven represents the turning point between the two. In the slow movement of his pianoforte trio in C minor (Op. 1, No. 3) he gives us a developed example of the earlier form; in the Diabelli variations we have the finest existing instance of the later. Schumann, of course, is an uncompromising exponent of the second system. Indeed he is sometimes over-zealous in his anxiety not to adhere too closely to the melody of his subject. The set of variations for two pianos, though it atones for its freedom by its extraordinary beauty and charm, yet contains two episodes in which the theme is practically abandoned. It is in the *Études Symphoniques* that his power of variation is shown at its best. They also push freedom to its utmost limit, but they never lose touch with their original text, and in richness, brilliance, and vitality they are almost worthy to rank beside the highest efforts of Schumann's great successor.

After the pianoforte works come the songs. Here again Schumann's position can be stated by a single contrast. As absolute Music his songs have less value than those of Schubert, he has never given us a tune like the 'Litanei' or 'Sei mir gegrüsst'; as illustrations of lyric poetry they are unsurpassed in the whole history of the art. With him the terms 'words' and 'setting,' 'melody' and 'accompaniment,' lose their distinctive meanings; all are fused into a single whole in which no part has the pre-eminence. He follows every shade of the poet's thought with perfect union of sympathy, he catches its tone, he echoes its phrase, he almost anticipates its issue. It is not too much to say that no man can understand Heine who does not know Schumann's treatment of the 'Buch der Lieder.'

His songs are interesting also in certain matters of form. He was the first Composer who ventured to end with an imperfect cadence, if the words were abrupt or inconclusive, as for instance, 'Im wunderschönen Monat Mai' and 'Anfangs wollt' ich fast verzagen.' Often, too, he ends his earlier verses with a half-close, and so makes the song continuous throughout, as in 'Mondnacht' and the 'Lied der Zuleika.' Another point is his curious use of declamatory passages, neither exact melody nor exact recitative, as in 'Ich grolle nicht.' But no analysis can do justice to the beauty, the variety, and the profusion of his lyrics. The Composer of 'Frühlingsnacht' and 'Widmung,' of 'Die Löwenbraut' and 'Die beiden Grenadiere,' of 'Schöne Wiege' and 'Er der herrlichste von allen,' has assuredly some claim to be considered the most poetical of musicians.

Robert Schumann

The qualities required for a successful treatment of the orchestra are precisely those in which, comparatively speaking, Schumann was most deficient, and it is not therefore surprising that his orchestral compositions should be of less value than his works for the voice or the pianoforte. The symphony stands to Music as the epic to Poetry: it is the broadest, most sustained, most heroic of all forms of expression. Hence it cannot easily be attained by a Composer whose gift is for short flights and rapid movements, whose manner of thought is concrete, whose best writings are those which give most scope for the display of brevity and concentration. No doubt Schubert has left us one brilliant instance of a lyric symphony, but, apart from the difficulty of judging a work by two movements, it remains an exception. Schumann, at any rate, seems to lose his bearings among the 'swelling and limitless billows.' In the opening allegro of his C major symphony, for instance, the exposition is vigorous and concise enough, but before the end of the movement his boat has refused to answer to the helm, and gone drifting off into strange and unknown regions. Again, in the finale of the same work, he finds that the materials presented at the outset are inadequate, discards them half-way through, and introduces an entirely fresh subject. It is hardly unfair to say that the only thing which holds the movement together is a single two-bar phrase containing a diatonic scale. The same vagueness of outline is to be found in his symphony in D minor, originally called by the more appropriate name of *Symphonische Fantasie*. And it may be submitted that these are not really new forms, since they lack the organic unity which form implies. If they are to be taken as experiments it must be in Bacon's sense of 'mera palpatio.'

On the other hand the lyric movements—the scherzos and adagios—are always beautiful. Here Schumann was in his element, he was dealing with forces which he knew how to control, and his success was complete and indisputable. It is only necessary to recall the larghetto of the first symphony, or the exquisite romance from the second, or the Volkslied from the third, to see that within the limits of a narrower form Schumann could well display his power of musical expression. Indeed his first symphony is almost a masterpiece throughout, and his others, even the most indeterminate, contain separate thoughts and phrases for which we may well be grateful. It is only when we compare him with the great symphonic writers, Brahms and Beethoven and Mozart, that we see evidence of weakness and imperfection.

It is usual to depreciate Schumann's power of orchestration, and indeed there can be little doubt that the general texture of his scoring is somewhat thick and heavy, and that he too frequently writes for the band passages that seem to owe their inspiration to the pianoforte. Still, he has supremely good moments—the bassoon in the adagio of the C major symphony, the trumpets in the *Manfred* overture, the violin solo of the symphony in D minor—and often what he loses in transparency he supplies in warmth and richness of colour. Among his mannerisms may be mentioned a persistent habit of breaking up his string phrases into rapid repeated notes, and an almost restless change of pitch in his use of the transposing instruments.

Three of his concerti are published, one for pianoforte, one for four horns (a curious revival of the old 'concerto grosso'), and one for violoncello. Of these the pianoforte concerto is the best known and the most valuable. It consists of a brilliant opening fantasia, a light, graceful intermezzo, in which the second subject is ingeniously developed out of a phrase in the first, and a stirring finale in Schumann's best style of composition. The concerto for four horns is seldom or never given, owing to the extreme difficulty and compass of its first solo part; but it may be noticed that the allegro is more regular in form than the general run of Schumann's orchestral works, and that the romance is scored with unusual care. The violoncello concerto has a fine manly first movement, a very beautiful though very short adagio, and a rather diffuse finale, in which, however, the capacities of the solo instrument are treated with considerable skill.

A Composer who writes pianoforte passages for the orchestra has but an ill augury in approaching the special technique of the string quartett. No form of composition demands more exact perfection of style, more intimate sympathy with the medium employed. Every phrase is salient; every note shows through; there is no possibility of covering weak places or condoning uncertainty of outline. Hence there is little wonder that Schumann's three essays in this field should rank among his comparative failures. The three opening allegros have great charm of melody, and in two of them the structure is firm and solid; the sectional movements exhibit

Schumann's usual power of dealing with lyric forms, but the rest show a continuous sense of effort which is inadequately repaid. Many passages, too, even in the more successful numbers, are alien to the style of the quartett, and recall methods of treatment which would be more appropriate to the orchestra. The case is very different in the concerted works for pianoforte and strings. Here the medium is pastel in place of water-colour; the new instrument brings with it an entirely new means of expression, and one, moreover, of which Schumann was a consummate master. At the keyboard he was once more at home, and his work in this department of the Art may rank among the most genial of his inspirations. Indeed, this particular form lays most emphasis on the qualities of romance and least on the technical gifts of absolute Music. Mozart's pianoforte trios are weaker than his string quartetts; Schumann, who is beaten by the strings alone, has only to add the pianoforte and his victory is assured.

As a dramatic writer he displays the same strength and weakness as Byron, with whom he has often been compared. Both possessed a considerable gift of description; both were steeped in Romanticism; both were too intensely subjective to succeed in that essential of the drama—characterisation. In *Genoveva*, for instance, the whole background of the opera is vividly depicted in the strong chivalrous overture, but the *dramatis personæ* are drawn with an uncertain hand, and even the situations are imperfectly presented. Golo's first song is far too beautiful to be wasted on a villain; the supernatural element is clumsily treated throughout; Siegfried, except for one moment, is a mere lay figure; and even the heroine fails to retain the interest which ought to centre about a title-rôle. No doubt in this, as in Weber's *Euryanthe*, much allowance must be made for a weak libretto, but it may be remembered that Schumann himself chose the subject and modelled the words. He treated it, in short, as a psychological study, than which the stage can follow no more fatal ideal.

Much the same may be said of *Manfred*. The incidental music is most successful where it deals with description, least so where it deals with action, and at best does not approach the superb force and splendour of the overture. In this Schumann's orchestral writing reaches its highest point. From the first note to the last it is as magnificent as an Alpine storm, sombre, wild, impetuous, echoing from peak to peak with the shock of thunder-clouds and the clamour of the driving wind.

In *Faust* we rise above the tempest. The overture and the earlier scenes need not here be considered, for they were written when Schumann's powers were beginning to fail under the stress of disease, and so cannot justly be estimated in relation to his normal work. But in the scene of Faust's salvation we have an incontestable masterpiece. It may be, as some critics have asserted, that the last half of the Chorus Mysticus is something of an anti-climax, that in neither of its two alternative versions does it 'breathe the pure serene' of the other numbers. In any case the whole work is noble music, vast in scale, lofty in spirit, a worthy interpretation of the great poem that summoned it into being. The only fit analogue with which it may be compared is the third act of *Parsifal*, opening with the solemn quietude of the Hermitage and closing with the Eucharistic strains that ascend to the gate of Heaven itself.

Among Schumann's cantatas *Paradise and the Peri* stands pre-eminent. It is easy to see how readily he would be attracted by the subject, and how fully he would avail himself of the opportunities afforded by its warm imagery and its suggestions of Oriental colour. The artificial glitter of Moore's verse is mercifully obscured in a translation: only the thought is left for the Composer to decorate as he will. Nowhere is Schumann's treatment of a libretto more thoroughly characteristic. All his favourite devices are here—long rhetorical passages, hovering between tune and recitative, single melodic phrases of great beauty, rich almost sensuous harmonisation, even the broad sustained chords which form such a distinctive feature in his pianoforte music. It is, in short, an abstract and epitome of the Romantic movement, a scene of fairyland admirably painted against a background of human interest and emotion. Of other choral works for the concert room two deserve special mention: the exquisite *Requiem for Mignon*, and the bright, tuneful *Pilgrimage of the Rose*. The rest belong to Schumann's period of exhaustion, and lie outside the limits of fair criticism.

At the same time no account of his compositions would be complete without some reference to the sacred music, which he declared to be the 'highest aim of every true artist.' Yet his own work in this field is singularly scanty. The two so-called motets are rather inconspicuous, the '*Altkatho-*

lisches Requiem' is but a beautiful song, not much larger in scale than Schubert's '*Ave Maria*,' and beside them we have only two works—the Mass and the Requiem—left for examination.

Of these the Requiem is undoubtedly the finer. In the Mass Schumann is approaching too closely the unfamiliar region of Absolute Music; its style demands an austerity, a self-repression to which he had never grown accustomed. Further, with all his experience as a song writer, he had not concerned himself with the peculiar capacities of the voice, and hence was unprepared for the special treatment of counterpoint which all tradition has connected with the Kyrie and the Credo. Hence, although his Mass contains some good episodes, notably the Offertorium, which he added to the orthodox text, it cannot be regarded as certainly successful. In the Requiem, on the other hand, we have two of the finest things that Schumann ever wrote: the opening number, and the portion which contains the 'Qui Mariam absolvisti,' the 'Confutatis,' and the 'Lacrymosa.' It is hard to believe that the mind which conceived that wonderful music was already tottering to its fall.

So much has been said about Schumann's work as a critic that it is hardly needful to recapitulate the story of the *Neue Zeitschrift* or to re-estimate its position in musical history. But there is one misconception which it is advisable to clear away. Many men have followed Dr Hueffer in supposing that Schumann restricted his judgment to examples of the style in which he was especially interested, and that even within these limits his method is purely subjective, dealing not with fundamental principles of the Art but with personal impressions derived from individual works. For such a theory there are two possible excuses: first, his comparative silence with regard to the great masterpieces of musical form; second, his fondness for discovering fantastic meanings and analogies—the 'jolly wedding' in the finale of Beethoven's seventh symphony, the 'ball big with fate' in Chopin's waltzes, the 'tournament' in one of Mendelssohn's songs without words. But this is only the surface of his criticism—a single aspect, and that the least important. To sum up his conclusions from so narrow a standpoint is at once unjust to him and misleading to his readers.

No artist in the whole history of Music has ever displayed a broader range of sympathy. The critic who could offer cordial admiration to Palestrina and Chopin, to Bach and Berlioz, to Sterndale Bennett and Brahms, scarcely deserves to be regarded as the advocate of a single school. He speaks of Haydn and Mozart as men speak of Chaucer and Shakespeare; of Beethoven's music he says, 'we almost forget thinking and hearing while subdued by it'; and yet with two at least of these Masters his own method had little or nothing in common. More remarkable still is his generous readiness to praise everything that came from Mendelssohn. In Leipsic and Berlin a foolish attempt was made to set the two Composers in opposition, as if loyalty must always imply partisanship. Schumann, however, remained outside and above the whole controversy, and filled article after article with the warmest eulogy of a musician whom he had every reason to regard as his rival. No doubt there have been unselfish artists in every age, men who are capable of welcoming good work from whatever source it proceeds, but we may look long and wide before we find a nobler instance of self-effacement and devotion.

Yet there was nothing undiscriminating in his enthusiasm. Addison complimented until his commendation lost its value. 'Everyone,' says Thackeray, 'had His Majesty's cheap portrait surrounded with diamonds worth twopence apiece.' Goethe distributed his favour so ill that 'to be praised by him was a brevet of mediocrity.' But Schumann knows how to chastise, though he does it with a reluctant hand. He finds fault with the harmony of the *Symphonie Fantastique* while he admires its boldness of conception; he detects the 'musical triviality' of *Tannhäuser* while he does full justice to its poetic value; he points out the mannerism of Spohr, the staginess of Rossini, the virtuosity of Liszt, without falling into the error of believing that a composer who is weak in one respect must be weak in all. Only in dealing with Meyerbeer does his tone rise into denunciation. 'In *Il Crociato* I still counted Meyerbeer among musicians,' says Florestan, 'in *Robert le Diable* I began to have my doubts, in *Les Huguenots* I place him at once among Franconi's circus people.' And in the operatic note book the performance of *Le Prophète* is marked with a simple cross, a 'Hic Jacet' under which the remains of a dead reputation are left to moulder. Yet, in spite of all, he acknowledges Meyerbeer's ability; it is the deliberate degradation of high gifts to ignoble uses that he attacks. Of

Les Huguenots in particular he says, 'The work does not contain one pure idea, one spark of Christian feeling. All is made up, all appearance and hypocrisy. Talent there is, polish, instrumental cleverness, considerable variety in forms; but what is all this compared with the coarseness, immorality, and unmusical character of the whole? Thank Heaven there can be nothing worse, unless we transform the stage into a scaffold.' It must be remembered that this was written at a time when Meyerbeer's operas were regarded as the legitimate offspring of *Fidelio*. Assuredly one of Schumann's many claims upon our regard is that he was the first musical critic to expose and castigate that brilliant impostor.

That his criticism had a method must be plain to everyone who takes the trouble to study his writings. On the one hand a rooted disbelief in the permanence of traditional laws, on the other a sturdy opposition to all cheap effect and all facile prettiness—between the two a cordial recognition of all earnest workmanship, whatever its nature or style—these were the main principles in accordance with which he delivered judgment. More than any other artist he realised the great truth that every era in Art is a period of transition; that it not only sums up the results of past thought but prepares the way for new forces and future types of development. 'Onward to the light' was his watchword, and the history of human progress contains no higher command.

It may be that much of his work will not survive the attack of Time. There are few men who do not find that the greater part of their life's record is written in water. But something at least will remain. He is not only the best representative but the virtual founder of a distinct style in Music; his sense of beauty is often exquisite; his feeling pure, manly, and chivalrous. So long as melody possesses the power to soothe, to comfort, to sympathise, so long shall we turn in gratitude to one who could transmute the sorrows of his own heart into an elixir for the cure of others. After all we have no right to require that an artist's whole gift should consist of masterpieces. We do not judge Wordsworth by his stories of the nursery, or Shelley by his two attempts at burlesque, we take the Ode and the Sonnets, Prometheus and Adonais, and let the failures go. In like manner we can discard some of Schumann's compositions as uninspired, but when we have done so there will still be left a legacy that may enrich Music to the end of the world. It matters little whether his monument be large or small, in either case it is imperishable.

RICHARD WAGNER AND THE REFORM OF THE OPERA

A musical thought is one spoken by a mind that has penetrated into the inmost heart of the thing, detected the inmost mystery of it, namely, the *melody* that lies hidden in it: the inward harmony of coherence which is its soul, whereby it exists and has a right to be in this world. All inmost things, we may say, are melodious: naturally utter themselves in Song. The meaning of Song goes deep. Who is there that in logical words can express the effect Music has on us? A kind of inarticulate, unfathomable speech which leads us to the edge of the Infinite, and lets us for moments gaze into that.
       CARLYLE: *The Hero as Poet.*

Richard Wagner
AND THE REFORM OF THE OPERA

I

A STRUGGLE FOR EXISTENCE

In the closing years of the 16th century a few Florentine gentlemen used to meet together at the Palazzo Vernio to discuss æsthetics in general and Music in particular. They were mainly men of some note: Vincenzio Galilei, the famous father of a more famous son; Rinuccini the poet; Giulio Caccini, whose voice and lute were in evidence at every serenade in the city; and, above all, the ducal Maestro di Cappella, Messer Jacopo Peri. Their most intimate subject of discussion was the revival of Greek tragedy, partly as a contribution to the New Learning, partly as a protest against the Contrapuntal School, which had just suffered a serious blow in the death of Palestrina. Like Wagner they were 'not musicians.' They had little or no sympathy with the academic methods on which was founded the musical education of their time; they were indifferent to rules, impatient of restraints, and especially anxious to uphold the dramatic ideal in the face of all competitors. No doubt their choruses had to be modelled, more or less, on the lines of the madrigal, but the main part of their drama was centred in the actors and in the free declamatory recitative through which the monologues were to be presented. There was, of course, no question of aria, no interruption of the plot to glorify the hero with roulades and cadenzas, only that intensification of the tones of ordinary speech in which, as tradition held, the iambics of Æschylus and Sophocles had been delivered. After some preliminary essays Rinuccini and Peri combined their forces and effected one of the greatest of musical revolutions in the production of the first opera.

For some time the new form maintained its original purpose, entirely subordinating the musical to the dramatic aspect, and aiming at nothing more than the impressive and dignified utterance of the poet's words. Then, as was natural in Italy, the melodic side began to claim equality of importance, until at last in Alessandro Scarlatti it found a champion, through whom it gained preeminence over the libretto. From his day the composer of Italian opera grew more prominent, the poet retired further and further into the background, the value of the verse declined as its honour diminished; finally, the descendant of Œdipus and Agamemnon came to consist of a series of pleasing melodies strung together on the slenderest thread of story, and as independent as possible of the uninspiring lyrics with which they were connected. It is not necessary to consider here whether Scarlatti's ideal was higher or lower than that of Peri; the point is that it was different, that it represented a new departure in the development of the Art. The two collaborators who produced *Dafne* and *Euridice* have handed down their names to posterity side by side. Nowadays everybody knows who composed the music to *Norma* or *Semiramide* — no one either knows or cares who compiled the book.

Meanwhile, at the court of Louis XIV., Lulli was establishing the traditions of his native Florence. In many respects he carried on his work under altered circumstances. He had a comparatively large and efficient orchestra; he had an audience with a special taste for spectacular display; he had the heritage of half a century's progress in instrumental music. But while in ballet and overture he far extended the limits by which his predecessors had been confined, he endeavoured at the same time to maintain the dramatic force and unity of his plot, and to illustrate characters and situations by appropriate musical expression. In one word, he represented the music and the poetry as comrades, not as rivals.

After Lulli came a reaction, and with Graun and Hasse, with Pergolesi and Paisiello, the methods of the concert room once more prevailed over those of the stage. Opera began to form certain purely musical conventions, which, however valuable in themselves, were inconsistent with the motion and continuity of a dramatic story. Addison's 'Rosamund' is a striking instance of a true poet's failure to satisfy the new requirements, and its unfortunate author may be forgiven if for once he forgot his usual amiability and protested that 'Music renders us incapable of hearing sense.' In Italy Metastasio made a gallant effort to compromise between the two ideals, but Goldoni, a far greater dramatist, threw up libretto writing in disgust, and turned with a breath of relief to the freer atmosphere of comedy. Then for the second time arose an operatic Composer who endeavoured to recall the Art to its original purpose. Gluck may be called the Wagner of the 18th century. Starting as a half-hearted member of the accepted school, he soon broke away, declared war against convention and restraint, used his music solely as a means of furthering the dramatic action of the play, disregarded the scowls of contrapuntists and the tearful pleas of prima donnas, and set again upon the stage a form of opera which the influence of Cuzzoni and Senesino had seemed likely to banish altogether. When aria was appropriate he could write 'Che farò' or 'Au faîte des grandeurs;' where the situation demanded rapid movement not all the Conservatism in the world could induce him to delay it. He developed his characters down to the minutest detail, followed the course of the story with the most scrupulous fidelity, and took every opportunity of enhancing the emotional force of the scene by some telling effect of figure or orchestration. A single instance will suffice. A certain critic found fault with Orestes' exclamation, 'Le calme rentre dans mon cœur,' on the ground that the agitated accompaniment belied the quietude of the words. 'No,' said Gluck, 'he mistakes physical exhaustion for calmness of mind. He has just killed his mother.'

But Gluck's reforms were soon swept away in the magnificent outburst of Absolute Music which spread over the world from Vienna. Nothing could be less dramatic than Mozart's scheme of opera. Indeed, in after days Zuccalmaglio proposed to fit him with new libretti, on the ground that the words of *Don Giovanni* were dull and those of *Zauberflöte* unintelligible. The project was never carried out, but its very conception is significant. We can hardly imagine anyone suggesting a new text to *Orfeo*, much less to *Tristan* or *Meistersinger*. Then came *Fidelio*, reconciling the two ideals in the noblest dramatic music of the age; but there was only one Beethoven, and he wrote only one opera. And meanwhile Italy was following its accustomed method, and turning out score after score of smooth, melodious, conventional arias, which sounded, as Coleridge said, 'like nonsense verses.'

Up to Beethoven the history of opera presents rather a crude series of alternate reactions. After Beethoven the movement becomes more gradual, and Wagner may be regarded as the climax of a long crescendo that begins with Weber and Marschner and the other Composers of the Romantic school. Assuredly his theory of the stage was not an innovation. The subservience of dramatic music to the scenes that it is intended to illustrate is an ideal as old as opera itself; Wagner's work has simply been to sum up, at any rate for the present generation, the same tendencies which can be observed in the compositions of Gluck, of Lulli, and of Peri. 'He calls our attention,' says M. Rockstro, 'not to a new creation, but to a necessary reform.' Like all artistic revolutionaries he destroys only to rebuild; and to rebuild, moreover, on the old site, in accordance with the plans of the original architect.

Among the influences which assisted to form his character must be counted not only the forces of historical tradition but the more intimate action of heredity and early training. His father, who was clerk to the city police courts at Leipsic, is described as a cultivated linguist, with a taste for poetry and the drama, ready even to unbend from his official dignity and bear his part as an actor among the Leipsic *dilettanti*. His mother was a refined, intelligent woman, 'whose sweet ways and lively disposition had a special charm for artists.' Of the elder children three became famous in the theatre or the concert room; and thus from his earliest years the Poet-Composer grew up in a more congenial atmosphere than has surrounded the childhood of most musicians.

He was born on May 22, 1813. Before he was six months old his father died, leaving a widow and eight children, the eldest only fourteen years of age, to subsist as best they could on the meagre pension afforded by the Saxon Government. For a time the shadow of poverty lay heavy on the little house in the Brühl, but in 1815 Frau Wagner married a certain Ludwig Geyer, actor, playwright, portrait-painter, and general Bohemian of genius, and carried the family to Dresden, where her husband had a permanent post in the Hoftheater.

Geyer seems to have noticed early that there were signs of exceptional ability in his youngest step-son. With the usual wrong-headedness of enthusiasm he proposed to make him a painter, but the boy had no capacity for drawing, and preferred to spend his time, like Schumann, in picking out tunes on the piano. It is curious, by the

way, that genius should so often have received its first education in a wrong artistic school. Botticelli was brought up to be a goldsmith, Benvenuto Cellini to be a musician, Molière learned his first lessons of design at the tapestry loom, and amid this company is the sad little figure of Richard Wagner, urging a reluctant pencil in lesson hours, and flying off to the keyboard as soon as the clock set him free.

In 1822 his education began in earnest. He was entered under the name of Richard Geyer at the Dresden Kreuzschule, and began at once to show a hereditary aptitude for languages and a hereditary fondness for the drama. He did not make much of Latin, which he found uninteresting, but by the time he was thirteen he could translate the first half of the Odyssey out of school hours, and had made much progress with English, to which he was attracted by the delights of reading Shakespeare. He soon began to write imitation Greek plays, and at the age of fourteen produced a grand Shakespearian tragedy, in which he killed forty-two characters during the first four acts, and had to recall some of them as ghosts in order to provide any *dramatis personæ* for the fifth. Meanwhile he was taking pianoforte lessons with much less success. His teacher, a good, conscientious man, soon gave him up in despair, and declared that he would never become a pianist, a prophecy which, as Wagner adds, was abundantly justified by the event. It must have been disheartening to an honest professor that he should leave his pupil to practise scales and come back to find the young rebel with all his fingers on the wrong notes, hammering out as much as he could remember of the overture to *Freischütz*.

For a few years Weber shared with Homer and Shakespeare the whole flood of Wagner's adoration. The boy was intensely patriotic; he even refused to accept *Don Giovanni* because of its Italian words; and all his musical enthusiasm centred round the composer of *Freischütz* and *Euryanthe*. But in the spring of 1827 he learned through the newspapers that a musician called Beethoven had just died at Vienna, and, struck by the obituary notices, began to study some of the Master's compositions. In the same year Frau Geyer, now advanced in her second widowhood, returned to Leipsic, where her eldest daughter Rosalie had an engagement at the town theatre, and so gave Wagner an opportunity of maturing the fresh acquaintance by hearing *Egmont* and the *Choral Symphony* in the Gewandhaus. Thenceforward his fate was settled. Through Beethoven's music he found a new world open before him, and after a few days of almost ecstatic wonder and delight determined that he would devote his whole life and work to its exploration.

Then, of course, came difficulties. Frau Geyer recollected the pianoforte lessons at Dresden and shook her head, intimating pretty plainly that it would be more profitable to cultivate the Classics in the Nicolaischule than to meditate a Muse who promised to be unusually thankless. As a concession she allowed him to study harmony with a certain Herr Gottlieb Müller, and the result seemed entirely to fulfil her expectations. After a few lessons Herr Müller declared that his pupil was idle and refractory;

that he would do nothing but talk nonsense about the personality of the notes, and other fantastic absurdities; that, in short, it was useless to imagine that he had any gift or aptitude for serious music. As a matter of fact Wagner had fallen under the spell of Hoffmann, and insisted on treating composition from the standpoint of the *Fantasiestücke*. At school he fared little better. The authorities placed him in the third class, whereas at Dresden he had sat in the second, and after such an insult no boy of spirit could think of doing any work. Besides, he was spending all his time in making surreptitious copies of Beethoven, and had no leisure to bestow on irregular verbs. So that, when he finally shook off the dust of his school days and entered at the University of Leipsic, he was no further advanced, in the eyes of his family, than he had been three years before.

In reality his character was forming under potent influences. 'I doubt,' said Dorn, 'whether there ever was a young musician who knew Beethoven's works more thoroughly than Wagner in his eighteenth year. The Master's overtures and larger instrumental compositions he had copied for himself in score. He went to sleep with the quartetts, he sang the songs, he whistled the concertos (for his pianoforte playing was never of the best); in short, he was possessed with a *furor Teutonicus* which, added to a good education and a rare mental activity, promised to bring forth rich fruit.'[1] About the same time he made the acquaintance of a Revolutionary poet called Heinrich Laube, a curious German combination of Blanqui and Théophile Gautier, who appears to have

[1] *Neue Zeitschrift*, 1838, No. 7. *Grove Dictionary*, Vol. IV. p. 348a.

spent half his time in 'shocking the bourgeois,' and the other half in undergoing terms of imprisonment for political offences. Laube was the editor of a 'society' paper, *Die Zeitschrift für die Elegante Welt*, and the author of several romances, one of which, *Das junge Europa*, took a firm hold of Wagner's boyish imagination. Soon the two were sowing their intellectual wild oats together in lavish handfuls. There was no cause so desperate that they did not champion it; no law so needful that they did not clamour for its abolition. The object of their most persistent attack was the institution of marriage, which Laube denounced as immoral and Wagner as unjust, nor could the most vociferous of our own reformers exceed the fervour with which these two unfledged enthusiasts called upon all respectable German households to throw off the galling chains of domestic life and establish a universal Agapemone.

In 1830, the year of his matriculation, Wagner succeeded in finding a composition master to suit his somewhat imperious requirements. It was growing necessary, for he had hitherto studied or refrained from study, more according to his own fancy than on any intelligible system, and 'a self-instructed man,' as Dr Johnson said, 'has a very ignorant fellow for his teacher.' Weinlig possessed not only the knowledge which one might expect in a Cantor of the Thomasschule, but in addition a gift of tact and sympathy unusual among the occupants of an academic chair. He was to Wagner what Dorn was to Schumann, or Lesueur to Berlioz, the one guide who could inspire some confidence and command some attention. Instead of beginning with dreary rules and uninteresting technicalities, he taught his anatomy from the living subject, gave his pupils a sonata of Mozart or Beethoven to dissect, pointed out the beauties, displayed the laws of structure in their most perfect embodiment, and thus started, as all teachers ought to start, with the method of encouragement rather than the method of prohibition. It is a thousand times more stimulating to say 'this is right' than to say 'the other is wrong.' Further, he entirely won Wagner's heart by apologising for setting him fugues. 'You will probably never want to write one,' he admitted, 'but the practice will give you facility,' an admirable sentence which almost sums up the value of strict counterpoint to a modern composer. As a natural result the lessons were keenly appreciated, there was no more talk of idleness or insubordination, and at the end of six months Weinlig could dismiss his new scholar with the kindly words, 'You may go now, for you have learned to stand on your own legs.'

Of the compositions of this year two are published —a sonata in B-flat and a polonaise for four hands in D. The former, which is the more important work of the two, is closely modelled after Beethoven's early manner, and thus shows clear though indirect signs of the style and influence of Mozart. The adagio is specially Beethovenish, and the whole, as Mr Dannreuther says, 'a piece of solid schoolwork without a trace of Wagner.' Much the same is true of the symphony in C major which followed in 1832, the famous symphony which Wagner afterwards offered to Mendelssohn for performance at the Gewandhaus, and which mysteriously vanished out of the sum of things until it was discovered in an old trunk nearly forty years later. What Mendelssohn did with it has never been satisfactorily determined ; at any rate he spared Wagner the pain of a refusal by leaving his application unanswered.

In the summer of 1832 Wagner paid a visit to Vienna, hoping that his new symphony might gain a hearing in the city from which it had drawn its inspiration. Unfortunately *Zampa* already occupied the field, with the whole Viennese public at its back, and the invader was compelled to retreat in some confusion. On his way home he stopped at Prague, and there wrote his first libretto, *Die Hochzeit*, a rather brutal tragedy which he afterwards had the good sense to destroy. But meanwhile the more material problems of life began to press for a solution. He was now nineteen ; money, which had never been very plentiful, was growing scarcer ; the attractions of the philology class at Leipsic were neither very inviting in themselves nor very promising for the future ; on all grounds he felt the need of a settled career, in which he could carry on the work that he found most congenial, and at the same time earn enough to satisfy his necessities.

At the appropriate moment his brother Albert, who was then acting as stage manager at Würzburg, offered him the post of chorus master, with a salary of ten thalers a month. The sum was not large, but the position had two advantages — it gave leisure for composition and a possible opportunity for performance. Wagner entered upon his new office in the middle of 1833, and at once set to work on an opera in three acts—his first essay in the field of dramatic music. Nothing could have been more incongruous than his choice of subject. We can hardly imagine Victor Hugo constructing a play out of a fable of La Fontaine, yet it is not more unlikely than that the future composer of *Siegfried* should turn for inspiration to the author who wrote the ' Loves of the Three Oranges.' This, however, is precisely what happened. The plot of *Die Feen* is borrowed, with very slight alteration, from one of the fairy extravaganzas with which Carlo Gozzi drove Goldoni off the Venetian stage. It is a dainty, delicate little nursery tale, full of grace and charm, but in no way exemplifying the *furor Teutonicus* upon which it broke as an episode. Indeed, Wagner must have forgotten his antipathy to Italian Art when he set himself to exorcise by the power of Music the enchanted form of his Donna Serpente.

Stranger still, his completion of *Die Feen* was followed by a period of enthusiastic admiration for Auber and Bellini. Of the former's *Masaniello* he said, 'It is one of the finest music dramas in existence'; on the latter's *Capuletti e Montecchi*—the very opera which three years before had embittered Berlioz's stay at Florence—he wrote an article in Laube's paper, some of which deserve epitomising. 'We have no German opera,' he declared. 'We are too critical, too well educated to be satisfied with simple, living humanity. . . . I shall never forget the effect which was produced upon me by Bellini's work. I was weary of instrumental complications, of musical symbolism. Here at last I discovered a fountain of pure and noble melody. . . . I do not mean that we are to be ousted from our places by French and Italian Composers, but I do mean that if we are to win the field we must stand to our guns. Let us throw off this counterpoint which shackles us, let us be men, let us dare to adopt new methods and employ new weapons. The Master who gains the day may not follow the style of Italy or France, but he will assuredly avoid that of our present Germany.' No doubt much of this ebullition is due to Madame Schröder-Devrient, whom Wagner first heard in the part of Romeo; but, with all allowance, it is a sufficiently remarkable preparation for *Oper und Drama*.

Unfortunately the theatre at Würzburg proved incapable of presenting *Die Feen* to the public, though a few numbers were rehearsed with some success, and the Composer therefore set off to Leipsic with his MS. to try his chances in his own native town. By that time Dorn had gone to Riga, but Ringelhardt, the director of the Municipal Theatre, accepted the work very graciously, and put it in a drawer, where it remained. The first performance was given at Munich on June 29, 1888. That is the way in which impresarii encourage rising genius.

Meanwhile the influence of Bellini and the melodists was converging with that of Laube and the Revolutionaries, and the resultant of the two forces took shape in Wagner's second opera, *Das Liebesverbot*. It is usual to speak of this work as 'based upon *Measure for Measure*.' In reality it is an audacious apology for Free-Love, which owes to Shakespeare nothing more than the bare outline of its plot. Angelo is replaced by a German precisian, who is drawn as Puritans were drawn by our Restoration dramatists; his edicts are ridiculed, his prohibitions transcended, and at last the climax is attained in his own unwilling conversion to the new social doctrine preached by Claudio and Isabella. The scene is Palermo, the time is Carnival, the whole story as joyously unashamed as a plot of Aristophanes. It is, in short, an outburst of adolescent passion, for which its Composer soon made atonement in the nobler figures of Senta and Elisabeth.'[1]

The libretto was written during the summer of 1834. In the autumn Wagner obtained the conductorship of the little town theatre at Magdeburg, and set to work in earnest at the music of his opera, that he might have the pride of producing it upon his own stage and with his own cast. Unluckily the finances of the theatre were in a very unsatisfactory state, and the new director had to devote himself to the ordinary routine of his office in order to please his public and maintain his position. But at the end of the season of 1836 he ventured to advertise two performances of *Das Liebesverbot*—the first for the benefit of the manager, the second for that of the composer and conductor. It was a desperate neck-and-neck race with Fortune. On the first night the house was crowded, but the singers, already mutinous for arrears of salary, proved utterly incapable of performing their parts, and the result was chaos. On the second night the audience, according to Wagner's own account, 'consisted of his landlady, her hus-

[1] See Wagner's pamphlet, *Das Liebesverbot, Gesammelte Schriften*, Vol. I.

band, and a Polish Jew.' Worse still, Claudio took to rehearsing his lines with too much vehemence, a jealous husband interposed, there was a free fight in the green room, and at last an agitated and dishevelled conductor had to appear before the curtain and announce that the performance could not take place. Next day the Magdeburg theatre closed its doors and retired into bankruptcy.

This was not an encouraging *début*, but there was still a gleam of hope remaining. Schumann's paper had printed a few kindly words about the new opera, and, after all, Leipsic was a much better field of action than these small provincial towns. Once established there it would be easy to forget past disappointments and to use adversity itself as a stepping-stone to success. Besides, Ringelhardt would surely have too much conscience to treat the second work as he had treated the first. He must accept it if only to atone for his neglect of *Die Feen*. Perhaps Schumann himself would come to the first night, then there would be a leader in the *Neue Zeitschrift*, and then fame and affluence. The Fates, however, determined otherwise. Ringelhardt's only comment on the opera was an expression of wonder that it had passed the censors; his only conclusion about it, that under no circumstances should it be produced at his theatre. An application to Berlin was equally unsuccessful, and at last Wagner, almost penniless, was compelled to cut down his ambitions and try his fortune again in a smaller sphere.

This time he selected Königsberg, partly because it was an untrodden field, mainly because a certain Wilhelmina Planer was acting there as 'Erste Liebhaberin.' She had been a member of the Magdeburg company, and under her influence Wagner was beginning to doubt whether his tirades against marriage were altogether scientific, and whether, at any rate, it was not the part of a philosopher to recognise that all rules admitted of exceptions. Before the end of 1836 he had completely satisfied himself on this point, and his wedding took place in the latter part of November, about the same time as Laube's. There is much food for thought in the simultaneous conversion of these two abolitionists.

Shortly after his marriage Wagner was made director of the Königsberg Opera, to which he had already submitted his credentials in the shape of a concert overture entitled *Columbus*. But the salary was poor and the work heavy; there was little time for composition; even the daily routine was harassed by a host of petty cares and trivial anxieties. He did, indeed, ask Scribe to fill in the outline of a libretto on a novel of Henrich König's, of course without eliciting any answer; but beside this his only production during the year was an overture to 'Rule Britannia,' described by Dorn as a mixture of Bach, Beethoven, and Bellini. Even this triple alliance was not strong enough to win the day. The season of 1837 was an unbroken series of defeats, at the close of which the theatre followed the example of Madgeburg and capitulated into the hands of its creditors. The overture was sent to try its chances in England, but it was insufficiently prepaid, Sir George Smart refused to take it in, and the score is now supposed to be lying in some forgotten corner of St Martin's-le-Grand.[1]

Thrown once more upon the world, Wagner took refuge at Riga, where Dorn's influence procured him another directorship. The new appointment was a considerable advance on its two predecessors, the company was excellent, the public appreciative, and the manager a perfect model of energy and resource. Then, as often happens, prosperity itself began to engender a feeling of restlessness. The provincial stage grew too small for Wagner's ambition; there floated before his eyes dazzling visions of the Grand Opera at Paris, where he might have Rubini to sing for him and all the court of Louis Philippe to applaud. While his discontent was taking shape he fell in with Bulwer Lytton's *Rienzi*, and at once began to turn it into a libretto of larger dimensions than anything which he had yet attempted. All through the work he kept the Académie de Musique in view: its splendid chorus, its magnificent opportunities for spectacular effect, the first tenor in Europe at the footlights, and beyond them an audience which had made the fortune of Auber and Meyerbeer. By the spring of 1839 the first two acts were finished, and in the summer of the same year Wagner set sail, with his wife and a large Newfoundland dog, bound, like his own Columbus, for the discovery of a new continent.

Columbus, however, was not a good sailor, and the voyage, which lasted three weeks and a half,

---

[1] The same story is told of the *Columbus* overture, which was apparently sent to Jullien from Paris. It is a little unlikely that the misfortune should have occurred twice over.

was miserable enough to have propitiated the most
adverse destiny. The only incident was a narrow
escape from shipwreck off the coast of Norway,
where the sailors, by way of precedent, told the
passengers the story of Vanderdecken and the
Phantom Ship. After a few days stay in London
Wagner crossed over to Boulogne, making the acquaintance of some friends of Meyerbeer on the
boat, and at once proceeded, with a new letter of
introduction, to the great man's presence. Meyerbeer
was profusely affable, praised the book of *Rienzi*
until his visitor suspected him of wishing to buy it,
complimented *Das Liebesverbot*, discussed the possibilities of success in Paris, and finally closed the
interview with an abundance of good wishes and a
sheaf of commendatory letters. It is a difficult
matter to decide at this distance of time the
precise extent of the obligation owed by Wagner
to the Composer whom he afterwards so fiercely
attacked. On the one hand it is urged that
Meyerbeer befriended him when he was in sore need
of assistance and found himself repaid with the
black ingratitude of *Oper und Drama* and *Das
Judenthum in der Musik*. On the other hand it
is asserted that Meyerbeer had a keen eye to the
main chance, that he recognised in the newcomer
a possible lieutenant of some value, that letters of
commendation, especially to bankrupt theatres, are
easily written, and that, after all, musical criticism
ought not to be affected by any bias of personal
relation. Wagner's own view of the case may be
summed up in the following extract from a private
letter written in 1847.[1] 'I am on a pleasant footing

[1] Quoted in *Grove*, Vol. IV. p. 358*a*.

with him, and have every reason to value him as a kind and amiable man. But if I try to express all that is repellent in the incoherence and tawdriness of our present operatic music I arrive at the conception Meyerbeer.' Indeed there can be no doubt that the Composer of *Robert le Diable* deserves as a musician all the ill that can be said of him; the only question is whether his *protégé* was the man to say it, and whether it should have been expressed in so strident a tone. At all events Wagner accepted the recommendations, swallowed the compliments, and took his departure in the full confidence that he carried in his trunk the bâton of the Grand Opera.

Paris in 1839 was at the zenith of its brilliance. Hardly in the golden age of Florence or Athens could so much genius have been collected within the limits of one single city. Pass along the Boulevard des Italiens and you would see Rossini 'looking,' as Berlioz said, 'like a retired satyr,' or Prosper Merimée turning over the leaves at a bookstall, or Roger on his way to a rehearsal at the opera house. Cross over to the Rue Bergère and you would meet Auber and Halévy discussing a point of orchestration, or Cherubini explaining to Habeneck why *Romeo* had deserved to fail at the Conservatoire concert. Among the audience at the Français would be Victor Hugo, cold, correct, and stately; Dumas, with his shock of hair and his broad genial face; Musset, as pale and silent as a ghost; Barbier, meditating a new satire; and Béranger, humming the refrain of his last ballad. At Hiller's, in the Rue St Florentin, Baillot and Thalberg would be playing violin sonatas which could make Nourrit forget his triumphs and Fétis his failures. At Corot's, in the Faubourg Poissonière, would gather Vernet and Décamps and Delaroche, to learn the latest news of Ingres, or debate the methods of the Barbizon school. But the climax of all was the famous *salon* in the Cour d'Orléans: Chopin at the piano, Heine curled up in a corner of the sofa, Mickiewicz listening, in the very abstraction of happiness, to the melodies of his native Poland, Gautier and Delacroix, Liszt and Daniel Stern, Lamennais the bishop, and Boscage the actor, and, in the centre of the group, 'the large-souled woman with the manly brain,' whose name was a household word wherever the French language was spoken. Amid such a gathering there was very little chance for an obscure German Composer, without money, without friends, without reputation, and with nothing but a couple of scores—one of them unfinished—to represent his whole available capital.

He arrived in the latter part of September 1839, and established himself in a dingy little house near the markets. At first Fortune seemed inclined to be favourable. Joli, the director of the Théâtre de la Renaissance, accepted *Das Liebesverbot*, Dumersan translated the text, Pillet and Habeneck greeted the new composer with their most amiable smiles and their most graceful compliments. True, Heine did not display any great cordiality, but Heine, as everyone knew, was a determined opponent of Meyerbeer and all his works; and if Rossini treated the Music of the Future as a joke, he was equally impartial in his attitude towards the Music of the Present. For a time Wagner believed that his victory was assured, and with all the confidence of six-and-twenty set about removing his lodging to a more fashionable quarter, and ruining himself by extravagant orders and expensive purchases. Then came the crash. On the very day on which he changed houses he learned that the Théâtre de la Renaissance had failed, and that the prospects of *Das Liebesverbot* were closed indefinitely. There was no chance at the Grand Opera, an attempt to get a *vaudeville* performed at one of the Boulevard theatres was equally unsuccessful, and at last Wagner returned to his garret, with all his hopes destroyed and all his ambitions overthrown.

Then followed a hard struggle to escape actual starvation. He applied for a place as chorus singer: it was refused. He tried his hand at writing songs: they were pronounced too serious for the popular taste. In despair he accepted a commission from Schlesinger to make a pianoforte arrangement of Donizetti's *Favorita* and to do odd jobs of scoring dance music for quadrille bands. Even this did not bring in enough to supply him with the bare necessaries of life, and if it had not been for the assistance of his friends he would have literally died of hunger. In his account of the first performance of Halévy's *Reine de Chypre* he sketches a figure of which it is only too easy to recognise the original. The theatre is crowded from floor to roof; all the wealth and brilliance of Paris are in the boxes; along the stalls sit the German impresarios who have come to carry off the last operatic triumph to Dresden and Weimar; and in a far corner stands a young musician, with pinched face and haggard eyes, praying for the success of the piece that he may earn a few francs by a *pot-pourri* of its melodies.

Through all these evil days he was supported

by the courage and devotion of his wife. She administered his scanty resources, she did all his household work single-handed, she soothed him in anxiety, comforted him in disappointment, and met reverse after reverse with the same unselfish affection and sympathy. We are told that Minna Wagner never appreciated her husband, that she never understood his ambitions or believed in his genius. In that case her conduct was little short of heroic. With all the faith in the world her privations would have been hard to endure; they were a thousand times harder if she had no hope of a larger issue in which the straitened life should expand. With the full certainty of an ultimate success she might have been forgiven if the present misery had sometimes wrung from her a word of complaint; as it was she bore his burden in addition to her own, and bore it with unremitting cheerfulness and untiring patience.

At the beginning of 1840 Wagner was prostrated by an attack of erysipelas, brought on partly by exposure and partly by want of food. The fancies of his sickbed formed themselves into sound, and the earliest result of his recovery was the magnificent orchestral piece published afterwards as '*A Faust Overture*.' Apart from the 'autobiography' which most of Wagner's critics have found in its themes, the work is noticeable as the first real expression of its Composer's personality. There are still traces of Beethoven and Weber—there are even some of Berlioz —but the true parentage of the ideas is as unmistakable as their treatment. No other musician could have written the marvellous passages for strings in the introduction, or the melody, with its curious anticipation of *Lohengrin*, which opens the second subject. It is worth adding that the overture was originally intended as the first movement of a Faust symphony, and that Wagner in after days was very angry with admirers who professed to find in it a complete exposition of Goethe's poem. 'There is no Gretchen,' he wrote to Liszt, 'only Faust in the solitude of his study.' Even that is probably an afterthought, and the music may well be left to tell its own tragic story without the intervention of a programme.

Towards the middle of the summer Meyerbeer appeared in Paris, and at his recommendation Wagner submitted to M. Pillet a sketch for a new opera on the subject of the Flying Dutchman. The director read, approved, and offered to buy the sketch for £20, in order to have it set by his chorus master Dietsch, 'to whom he had promised a libretto.' Under the circumstances such a proposition was nothing less than an insult. Wagner indignantly refused, and demanded back his MS. M. Pillet temporised until Meyerbeer was out of the way, and then confiscated the sketch and sent the money. He knew well that he had nothing to fear from the protests of a penniless musician, and even had the brutality to close the last interview by saying, 'In any case there is no possibility of producing a work of yours during the next four years, and by that time you will have thought of a new plot.' This gave the *coup de grâce* to all Wagner's chances of a hearing in Paris. There was no one to help him. Meyerbeer had gone, Berlioz was just starting on his first visit to Germany, Liszt was antipathetic, and the other musicians 'too busy to show any kindness.' At last, with the inspiration of despair, he completed *Rienzi*, which had lain untouched ever since his arrival, and sent it off to Herr von Lüttichau, the Intendant at Dresden. It was his first confession of defeat.

Another winter passed, with the same dreary round of drudgery and privation. In the spring the *Columbus* overture was performed at a private concert of Schlesinger's, but it produced no effect, and shortly afterwards the score disappeared. As a small compensation from the Fates, Wagner succeeded in subletting his rooms in Paris and retired to Meudon, where he set his own version of the Flying Dutchman. It was Walther's *Preislied* against Beckmesser's. Dietsch took eighteen months over *Le Vaisseau Fantôme*, which had a run of one night and was then withdrawn from the stage. Wagner finished *Der Fliegende Holländer* in seven weeks, and the music is as fresh to-day as when it was written. During the same year he began to vary the monotony of hack work by sending *feuilletons* and articles to the *Gazette Musicale*, the *Neue Zeitschrift*, and the *Dresdener Abendzeitung*.[1] Many of them, as one might expect, are rather bitter in tone, but they are all forcibly conceived and clearly expressed. Compared with his later treatises and pamphlets they are like Carlyle's early writings beside Sartor Resartus: there is the same strength of purpose, the same uncompromising sincerity, but the style is simpler and more lucid. Two of the *feuilletons*, 'A Death in Paris' and 'A Visit to Beethoven,' attracted the notice of Berlioz, who wrote a favourable critique of the latter in the *Journal des Débats*. It is not known what opinions Berlioz expressed of the two articles on '*Der*

[1] They are all to be found in the first volume of the collected works.

Freischütz, in Paris' which followed about the end of the year.[1] Perhaps, as they were sent to the Dresden paper, he was spared the annoyance of reading them.

Having finished *The Flying Dutchman*, Wagner began to look about him for a new subject. At first he was attracted by the history of Manfred von Hohenstaufen, but before he had done more than sketch a libretto he met with a popular version of the Tannhäuser legend, and at once saw the immense opportunities which it offered to the dramatist. His early reading of Hoffmann had already made him familiar with the contest of the Minnesingers at the Wartburg, the ballad before him gave a precedent for combining the two romances: further research led him to Wolfram von Eschenbach and the stories of Lohengrin, Parsifal, and Titurel. This was exactly what he wanted. He had already begun to formulate his favourite doctrine that the true basis of opera is popular and democratic; that it is the development of national legend and the outcome of national feeling. Here was a pure mass of virgin treasure, a Rheingold which, if he had the skill to forge it, would give him the mastery of the world. In the midst of all these preparations news came that his *Rienzi* had been accepted at Dresden, and that his presence was required to direct the rehearsals. The revulsion was almost too great. For three years he had suffered every torment which adversity could inflict: now at a single stroke he was liberated from his fetters. It was no ordinary theatre that had offered him welcome, no *baraque* of the boulevards, with a dishonest manager and an

[1] See p. 109.

empty cash-box: it was to Dresden that he was going, to an opera house as great as the Académie de Musique itself. Tichatschek, the first tenor in Germany would sing Rienzi, Madame Schröder-Devrient would sing Adriano, the King of Saxony would be present—there was no end to the vista which began to open. Half wild with joy he flew round Paris to say farewell to his few intimates, gathered up his remaining manuscripts into a bundle, and set off with his wife as fast as the loitering *diligence* could carry them. All through the journey he poured out his projects for the future. *Rienzi* was bound to succeed, then would come *Tannhäuser*, then *Lohengrin: The Flying Dutchman* would probably be given at Berlin, where Meyerbeer was in command: once established at the centres there would be no difficulty about getting a foothold in the provincial towns: before long there would be a Wagner opera on the stage of every theatre in Germany. France had rejected him : he would leave her to her *vaudevilles*. For the future he would preach his message in his own tongue and to his own countrymen. To all this Minna Wagner listened with her usual placid acquiescence. At the bottom of her heart she had very little faith in these golden dreams ; but she was not the woman to chill her husband's enthusiasm by unseasonable memories. At any rate Dresden would be better than Paris. No doubt Richard was over-sanguine. Still, his opera had been accepted, and whether it succeeded or not there would be some money to come in. For a time, at least, they would have respite from all the scheming and pinching of the past three years, and after that there might be a chorus mastership vacant, or perhaps another conductorship in some provincial theatre. So the two travelled homeward, strangely different in their anticipations of the new life, yet united through all differences in the bond that they had welded by community of suffering.

II

ART AND REVOLUTION

WHILE the preliminary arrangements for *Rienzi* were getting under way Wagner took a holiday at Teplitz, and occupied it with his usual energy in completing his sketch for the libretto of *Tannhäuser*. On his return he found everything in train. Reissiger the conductor was well disposed towards the new work; Fischer the chorus master was enthusiastic; Tichatschek, Wächter, and Schröder-Devrient exerted themselves to the utmost, and studied their *rôles* with a respect which artists of established reputation have not always shown to the writings of an unknown composer. The first performance took place on October 20th to a crowded and appreciative audience. It lasted from six o'clock till midnight, and not only was the interest maintained throughout, but when Wagner came down the next morning to make some excisions the whole cast protested against the curtailment of a single scene. 'I won't have it cut,' said Tichatschek, 'it is too heavenly.' Within the next ten days two more performances were given at increased prices. Before the end of November some of the numbers were presented at a Gewandhaus concert in Leipsic, and by Christmas the musician who a year before had been starving in the streets of Paris found himself an acknowledged hero, *fêted* by his fellow-artists, and received with acclamation by the public.

Success followed success with an almost bewildering rapidity. On January 2nd *The Flying Dutchman* made its *début*, and a month later Wagner was appointed Hofkapellmeister in succession to Morlacchi. The duties were sufficiently onerous — a performance at the theatre every night, the principal direction of the church music at the Hofkirche, and numberless other services and responsibilities which an official position almost invariably entails. There was a special danger, too, in the occupation of a quasi-academic chair. Wagner was a born revolutionary, a man of the people, who had little regard for prescriptive right, and still less power of adapting himself to methods or objects with which he was out of sympathy. It is therefore to his credit that he hesitated a short time before accepting the Royal bâton, though, once accepted, he made up his mind to use it in his own way.

Naturally he provoked some opposition. His vigorous, impetuous readings of the great operas produced an outcry from critics who were accustomed to the old jog-trot habits of Morlacchi and Reissiger. His uncompromising directness of speech gave offence in many quarters where he would have found it more politic to conciliate. Even his orchestra divided into parties. The more intelligent members recognised the genius of their new director, and worked enthusiastically to satisfy his exacting demands. The more careless and slovenly grumbled at the long rehearsals, the strict discipline, and the imperious insistence on every *nuance* of

expression. At the same time, too, Wagner's own
manner of composition was developing, and so passing beyond the intelligence of his auditors. *Rienzi*
had been near enough to the methods of Meyerbeer
and Spontini for the average man to recognise it as
a familiar voice. *The Flying Dutchman*, which is
much more distinctive in style, began to rouse some
hostility, which gathered over *Das Liebesmahl der
Apostel*, and finally broke in a storm upon the
appearance of *Tannhäuser*. Nevertheless the conductor went his own way. He had his position
assured, he was perfectly confident in the truth of
his own ideal; adverse criticism might annoy him,
but it could not affect his judgment. As for the
band, it was there to work and not to complain.
His business was to make it efficient, and whatever
the cost, he proposed to carry out his intentions to
the letter. Indeed, martinet as he was, his earnestness and decision soon made him respected, and
his ready humour helped to convert respect into
popularity. It is said that he once quelled his
trombones at a rehearsal with the courteous rebuke,
'Gentlemen, gentlemen, we are not marching round
the walls of Jericho.'

Meanwhile his reputation was extending to other
parts of Germany. Spohr gave *The Flying Dutchman*
at Cassel in the summer of 1843, *Rienzi* appeared at
Hamburg the next year; the *Neue Zeitschrift* published a cordial eulogium of Madame Schröder-Devrient as Senta, Laube's paper gave a long
biography of the new Composer, and circulated his
portrait among the *dilletanti* of Leipsic. Soon, however, Wagner received an even more tremendous
compliment. Spontini came to Dresden to conduct

a performance of *La Vestale*, and condescended to say that he had heard *Rienzi*, and that he considered it a work of genius. He even invited the Composer to the honours of collaboration. 'I see in your score,' he said, 'an instrument called a bass-tuba. I do not wish to banish that instrument from the orchestra. Please write me a part for it in *La Vestale*.' All through the interview Spontini was at his best. 'Opera has reached its climax,' he declared. 'I find it impossible to surpass my preceding works, and you will hardly venture to suggest that anyone else will succeed where I have failed.' Wagner timidly hinted that there were perhaps new subjects, such, for instance, as Mediæval German legends, which might offer an opportunity for the future. Spontini looked at him with surprise and compassion. 'In *La Vestale*,' he said, 'I set a Roman subject, in *Fernando Cortez* a Spanish one; in *Olympie* I took my story from Macedonia, and in *Agnes von Hohenstaufen* from Germany. There are no others worth mentioning.'

In spite of this discouraging assertion Wagner continued to work at *Tannhäuser*, of which he completed the revision shortly before the end of the year. It was a little delayed by the great public funeral of Weber, on December 14th, but by the beginning of 1845 the opera was ready for rehearsal, and in the following October it was produced. The result was by no means an unqualified success. Tichatschek was magnificent in the *title rôle*; Joanna Wagner gave an admirable reading of Elisabeth; but Madame Schröder-Devrient could make nothing of the Venus music, and the whole first scene, with its introductory ballet, puzzled rather than pleased the audience. Indeed the reception throughout was exactly what might have been expected. The march in the second act was applauded to the echo, the 'Hymn to the Evening Star' politely tolerated, and the scene of 'Tannhäuser's pilgrimage' endured with undisguised weariness. After the performance Wagner was overwhelmed with suggestions and criticisms. 'You ought not to write things which people can't sing,' said his prima donna. 'You ought never to have let Tannhäuser die at the end,' protested Herr von Lüttichau; 'Weber would have made him marry Elisabeth.' Even Schumann, who had recently settled in Dresden, professed himself unconvinced, though with his usual generosity he preferred to reserve judgment for another hearing. No doubt there are many imperfections in *Tannhäuser;* some of it is conventional, some is even trivial and commonplace. But there are two points which deserve to be emphasised: first, that the opera as a whole is a very important step in the direction of the true music-drama; and second, that, with very few exceptions, the critics doled out their scanty praise to the worst musical numbers and poured the full measure of their denunciation upon the best. We at the present day, rich with all the legacy of *Siegfried* and *Parsifal*, could readily dispense with the theatrical glitter of the Wartburg scene; but we would not lose the splendour of the overture or the sombre tragedy of Tannhäuser's expiation. In the former case Wagner is still struggling to free himself from an alien phraseology; in the latter he speaks with all the fervour and eloquence of a poet who has mastered his own means of expression.

The summer holiday was spent as usual in libretto sketching among the Bohemian mountains, and at its close Wagner returned to Dresden with the materials for two new opera books—*Lohengrin* and *Meistersinger*. The former began to occupy him at once: for the latter he wrote one or two numbers, notably the quintett at the end of the second act, and then laid it aside until a more fitting opportunity. Indeed, during the years 1846-1848 there were many difficulties in the way of composition. There was a long and anxious correspondence with the publishers who had brought out his last three operas. The edition was not selling well, and the Composer found himself liable for a large sum towards the expenses of printing. Then there were special performances of Gluck's *Iphigenia in Aulis* and Beethoven's *Choral Symphony*, both of which involved considerable labour and much controversy with the critics. Then followed an unsuccessful visit to Berlin, where, after long hesitation, the management had decided to give *Rienzi*. Meyerbeer absented himself from the performance, and his partisans on the press took advantage of a maladroit apology which Wagner had offered at one of the rehearsals and fell foul of the work from beginning to end. In tones of dignified protest they declared it to be an insult that any musician should present to the Prussian capital an opera for which he was himself compelled to crave indulgence. Such things might satisfy Dresden, but a city which could boast the presence of such masters as Meyerbeer and Mendelssohn could not be expected to waste its time over a local Kapellmeister and his 'aberrations of youth.' Besides, the work was dangerous. It was full of allusions to liberty, and other such unmentionable topics. The censors had wisely refused to licence Beethoven's Ninth symphony unless the word 'Freiheit' was removed from the ode and the word 'Freude' substituted; they would surely not permit themselves to be outraged by an ignorant *sansculotte* who had come to demoralise Germany with the methods of his favourite Paris.

It is certainly true that about this time Wagner was beginning to engage in politics on the revolutionary side. As early as 1845 there had been an outbreak in the streets of Dresden, the soldiers had lost their heads and fired upon the mob, and the Hofkapellmeister had denounced the 'butchery' with such indiscreet zeal that he was compelled to make a public apology to the Government. During the next two years he was gradually forced into the cause which his ardent temperament and democratic sympathies rendered especially congenial. His greatest friend was August Roeckel the 'patriot.' His partisans were all men of the people, his chief opponents held official positions in and about the court. His new opera was 'indefinitely postponed' by Herr von Lüttichau and a course of Donizetti put on in its place. Once more he felt the pressure of money difficulties and the annoyance of empty pockets and exacting creditors. His careful and elaborate scheme for the reform of the Dresden theatre was treated with derision by the Minister to whom it was submitted. There is no need for wonder that he grew daily more discontented with his position and more embittered against the antagonism that surrounded him on every side. Not that he neglected his work. Beside the routine duties, which were all punctually fulfilled, he completed *Lohengrin* by the beginning of 1848, and in the course of the same year wrote a set of historical essays, an introduction to the *Nibelungenlied*, and a great part of the text of *Götterdämmerung*. But not even the labour that he delighted in could physic the pain of neglect and isolation. The more he brooded over his projects of reform the more did his republicanism assume shape and consistency. The more he reflected upon his own troubles and disappointments the more willing did he become to welcome any change in the conditions of his life. Like most revolutionaries he found impulse in his convictions and opportunity in his circumstances. The train was laid, the spark was ready to fall, the inevitable explosion was only a matter of time.

He began with a paper on the reform of the Monarchy, read before a Radical Association of which he and Roeckel were both members. The greater part of it is taken up in a Utopian attempt to reconcile Personal with Republican government, by 'declaring Saxony a free state,' and establishing the Royal House in a sort of hereditary archonship. It even proposes that the king shall be requested to sign the petition by which this change is to be brought about, and significantly hints that to doubt his willingness to comply is 'to pronounce the monarchical death warrant.' On other matters it speaks with more distinctness. The abolition of the first chamber, the suppression of all ornamental offices and dignities, manhood suffrage, universal conscription in place of a standing army, and the substitution of exchange for currency are the five points of this remarkable charter, to all of which His Majesty Friedrich August II. was expected to subscribe. Apparently the expressions of loyalty which are scattered over the essay saved its author from prosecution, but it is noticeable that at the Festival of the Hofkapelle in September Wagner was the only official who did not receive any mark of royal favour. At the same time, too, his friend Roeckel was dismissed from the post of assistant conductor in consequence of a more daring publication on the reform of the Saxon military system. During the winter there was an election to the second chamber, at which the Republican party carried ninety per cent. of the seats. As soon as the House met it insisted on the acceptance of the recent 'Frankfort Convention,' which had proposed to unite all Germany into a single democratic federation under the Archduke John of Austria. Of course the measure was vetoed by the Upper House, and then followed stormy debates, fierce leaders in Roeckel's paper *Die Volksblatte*, and continuous popular agitation in which Wagner took part. On the 3d of May the chamber was dissolved, and two days afterwards men were fighting at the barricades.

In later times Wagner grew somewhat ashamed of his connection with the outbreak, and some of his biographers have endeavoured to minimise it into a philosophic sympathy with the general objects of the Revolution. But the facts are too strong to be disputed. It may be true that the account of his active participation in the riot is 'not corroborated' by the official indictment of the Saxon police. There is more significance in the fact that it is corroborated not only by his own letters at the time but by the certain testimony of eye-witnesses. 'I was everywhere,' he said to Edward Roeckel, 'and it was a mere accident that I was not arrested like the others.' It was he who rang the tocsin to call the mob into the streets; it was he who tore down lead from the roofs when the supply of ammunition ran short; it was he who superintended the convoys and distributed the rations.¹ One story is too characteristic to be omitted. August Roeckel was hurrying down to the scene of action, and dodging the Prussian bullets as they whistled along the roadway, when he met with a fellow-conspirator called Hainberger, also a musician and a devoted adherent of the Hofkapellmeister.

'Hullo,' said Roeckel, 'why are you not at the barricades?'

'Just left them,' said Hainberger. 'Wagner's there. He says that he's thirsty, and has sent me for an ice.'

After a few days' fighting the superior order and discipline of the soldiery began to make itself apparent. Gradually the populace gave way, the principal rioters were captured, and Wagner found that his only chance of escape was to leave Dresden as soon as possible. The Government had enough documentary evidence to condemn him, and a warrant was actually issued for his arrest. Without further delay he fled to Weimar, where Liszt was producing *Tannhäuser* as serenely as though there were no such things as revolutions in the

¹ The reader may compare the account of the Dresden revolution in Dr Praeger's 'Wagner as I knew Him,' with that in Mr Ashton Ellis' '1849, a Vindication.'

world. But in the midst of a rehearsal there came an excited messenger to say that the Composer was 'wanted;' Liszt flew off to the police office and secured an hour's delay; a post chaise was hastily provided; and when the warrant came to be served there was nothing but a faint cloud of dust on the horizon to indicate the whereabouts of the prisoner.

By some strange fascination he made his way to Paris, hoping that the city which had driven out Louis Philippe would show some sympathy with a republican exile. On his arrival he attempted to arrange with the editor of the *Journal des Débats* for the production of a series of articles on 'Art and Revolution.' But whether as composer or pamphleteer Paris would have none of him, and after a few weeks of fruitless negotiation he retired to Zurich, which was then, as now, the most hospitable refuge in Europe for political malcontents. There he set to work at once upon the exposition of his sociological and artistic theories. His imagination was still warm with memories of Dresden and the Fatherland Union, he was free to write without fear of prohibition or censorship, and during the next few years he poured out book after book and essay after essay with unceasing energy and enthusiasm. As a matter of fact he was not well suited to be the literary guide of a great movement. His writings are often suggestive, they are seldom convincing, more rarely still do they show any power of grasping both sides of a question or of treating opponents with moderation or tolerance. On the other hand, they contain many passages of real eloquence, and their earnestness of purpose is sufficient to atone for their occasional excess of zeal.

S

As pendants to his operatic work they possess great psychological value and interest, but it must always be remembered that their function is secondary. The arguments which have established the Wagnerian theory of opera are to be found not in *Oper und Drama* but in the pages of *Tristan* and *Parsifal.*

All this time *Lohengrin* was lying idly in the desk, buried under analyses of Æschylus and denunciations of Meyerbeer. Suddenly the Composer felt a touch of paternal compassion for his neglected score, and wrote off to ask Liszt whether there was any chance for it at Weimar. The answer was most reassuring. On August 28th there was to be a great festival in honour of Goethe's birthday— poets and musicians were coming from all parts of Europe—if Wagner would send his opera it should be performed with the best resources of the Weimar theatre, before an audience distinguished enough to do it justice. Preparations were made on an unusually large scale, Liszt himself conducted, and the result was a more unqualified triumph than had attended any work of Wagner's since the first production of *Rienzi.* 'From that memorable evening,' says Mr Dannreuther, 'dates the success of the Wagner movement in Germany.'

It may be said that Wagner's friendship with Liszt attained its majority on the same occasion. During the earlier days at Paris the two had been on terms of acquaintanceship but not of intimacy: Liszt took but little notice of the unknown stranger whose musical gifts certainly did not exhibit themselves at the keyboard; Wagner felt an unreasoning antipathy towards the brilliant, popular virtuoso, whose sincerity he suspected, and whose powers he was inclined to underrate. The appearance of *Rienzi* brought them into closer connection. In 1848 Liszt gave the overture to *Tannhäuser* at Weimar, and followed it by the performance of the entire opera early in 1849; then came the *émeute* and its consequences; and at last the production of *Lohengrin* cemented a union which lasted without intermission until Wagner's death. Too much has been made of the money relations which existed between the two artists. No doubt the poorer man was sometimes helped with loans, and even gifts, by the richer; but the fact is only a stumbling-block to those who believe that friendship is degraded by the weight of any material obligation. Rather it is honourable to both that the most fruitful source of discord in this quarrelsome world should have been powerless to impair in any degree the cordiality of their feelings. Look at the way in which money alienated Rousseau from one generation of Englishmen and Comte from another. Think how often artistic friendships have been transitory or one-sided, how often they have been poisoned by jealousy or severed by antagonism, and then turn for contrast to the thirty years' correspondence of these two men. To the last they remained comrades, animated by the same ideals, pursuing the same objects, working in the same cause with perfect sympathy and affection.

1851 passed quietly in the completion of *Oper und Drama*, but in the next year Wagner launched a thunderbolt which set the whole musical world of Germany in conflagration. This was the famous tract on *Das Judenthum in der Musik*, issued as a series of papers in the *Neue Zeitschrift* under the pseudonym of K. Freigedank. Its main contention may be stated in a few words. Starting with his favourite aphorism that true Music is essentially national in origin, Wagner goes on to maintain that the Jews are not, in any real sense of the term, a nation; that they have no organic unity, no common tongue, no settled dwelling-place; that, in short, they are aliens, adapting themselves to an external conformity with the countries that they have helped to colonise. Thence follows the inference that the music of Jewish Composers is a sham, a cleverly constructed automaton, painted and dressed into a semblance of humanity, but entirely devoid of any genuine life or any spontaneous movement. The conclusion is supported by examples drawn mainly from Mendelssohn, whose abilities are treated with considerable respect, and Meyerbeer, who is fiercely denounced as a mountebank and an impostor. Of course the whole position as stated is altogether untenable. The premises are far too crude to be accurate, and their uncertainty invalidates the whole deduction. There are many important facts of which the reasoning takes no account, such, for instance, as the intermingling of national streams and the increasing complexity of national development. Rossini had Jewish blood in his veins, but *Il Barbiere* is none the less Italian; Halévy was a Jew by birth and religion, yet Wagner himself praises *La Reine de Chypre* as a complete embodiment of the French spirit. In short, it may be true that the music which is most conspicuous for glitter and display is to be found among the writings of certain Jewish Composers; it is not true that the artistic work of a great people can be summed up as mechanical and factitious.

On the other hand, it is manifestly unjust to attribute the pamphlet to any motive of personal enmity. No doubt Wagner felt a repugnance to the Semitic race as a whole ; no doubt he regarded its members as hard, irreconcilable units, whom it would be difficult to fuse into his general scheme of German nationalism. But it is equally certain that he spoke from a conviction which, however wrong-headed, was absolutely sincere. He did believe that Judaism represented a false ideal in Art, and when he had once formed a belief, nothing could prevent him from proclaiming it at the top of his voice. The attack may have been intemperate in tone ; it was, at least, single-hearted in intention.

The pseudonym was, of course, transparent from the outset. Dr Brendel, the editor of the *Neue Zeitschrift*, formally refused to divulge the name of his correspondent, but no one had any doubt in the matter, and it is not surprising that Wagner's challenge was accepted with eager hostility. Even when he republished the work, seventeen years later, it was answered by a storm of tracts and articles, most of which evaded the point at issue, and insisted on treating the question as a personal encounter. Wagner was jealous of Meyerbeer, that was the long and short of it. He might conceal his meaning under fine phrases about patriotism and national unity, but he could not deceive the experienced eyes of his opponents. They knew to what excess of vituperation men could be moved by pique or envy, and they were determined that the true incentives of the controversy should be exposed to the whole German public. Jealous of

Meyerbeer! Jealous of a man who used to conciliate the mistresses of his critics in order to obtain favourable notices in the newspaper! It is not an accusation which there needs much eloquence to repel.

Meanwhile the author of all this disturbance was living on quietly at Zurich, conducting *La Juive* at the opera house, training up his pupil Von Bülow, and, above all, finishing the libretto of the *Ring*. Before leaving Dresden he had written a text on the subject of Siegfried's death, borrowed, with some alterations, from the *Nibelungenlied*. On reconsideration he felt that his poem did not tell its own story; that it did not sufficiently emphasise Brünnhilde's wrongs or justify her revenge, and he accordingly turned to the Eddas in which the earlier portions of the myth are related. Then came the question how to present his new material to the audience. It seemed impossible to incorporate it as narrative without clogging and impeding the action of the drama: the only feasible method was to construct a separate opera, which, in performance, should precede *Götterdämmerung* and explain it. For this there was already some precedent. *Rienzi* had occasionally been given in two parts: the first two acts on one evening, and the last three on the next; and further, the plan of two interdependent operas would be a step in the direction of Wagner's dramatic ideal—the system of Greek tragedy. He therefore set to work upon a poem which should describe the life of his hero: the forging of the magic sword, the combat with the dragon, the betrothal to Brünnhilde. Even so, the story was incomplete. The new libretto contained the furthest possible extreme of narration, more probably than any other opera book in existence, yet it did not give full account of Siegfried's parentage, or Brünnhilde's captivity, or the curse with which Walhalla itself was threatened. There was nothing for it but to trace back the story from Siegfried to Walküre, and from Walküre to Rheingold. Only by that means could the whole myth be adequately adapted to the requirements of the theatre. Thus the great Tetralogy was not a deliberate and systematic 'new departure': it was developed by gradual stages from the exigencies of its plot. The motive of the Eumenides would not be very clear to an audience unacquainted with the Choephoræ and the Agamemnon, nor should we gain much profit from the story of Faust's salvation unless we had been already told of his ambition and his fall.[1]

The four poems were finished early in 1853. In May there was a Wagner Festival at Zurich, to celebrate the Composer's fortieth birthday; and we are told that he broke down in attempting to return thanks for the ovation which he received. Indeed, his exile was beginning to weigh heavily upon his mind. With all his intemperate vehemence of manner, he was intensely, ardently patriotic: he had struck no blow that was not designed for the service of his cause, and it accentuated the bitterness of his position that his honour should come from his own country, which he could not enter. Germany was beginning to acknowledge his mission, to accept his leadership, and he must lie caged in his Swiss

[1] See Wagner's own account of the matter in 'Eine Mittheilung an meine Freunde' (*Collected Works*, Vol. IV.). See also the introduction to the four poems in Vol. VI.

canton, far away from the scene of conflict and the hope of victory. It is characteristic of the man that at no moment does he appear to have questioned the injustice of his punishment. For whole days he wandered among the hills above Zurich, denouncing the tyranny of his oppressors, and vainly challenging an enemy that he was powerless to meet.

At such a crisis his wife's homely consolations were of little avail. He soon fretted himself into illness, and was sent off to Italy, where the fit wore itself out in the soothing companionship of the olives and the sea. On his way home the passion for work returned; sketches and suggestions of the *Rheingold* music began to present themselves during a sleepless night at Spezia; once back at Zurich, he set himself in a fury of inspiration to pour out the flood of song that his sorrows had stricken from the rock. In May 1854 he completed the score of *Rheingold;* in June he began *Walküric;* by Christmas he had not only finished it, all except the instrumentation, but had in addition begun the first sketches of *Siegfried.* Then came a sudden and unexpected episode which for a short time retarded his progress.

At the beginning of 1855 the Directors of the Old Philharmonic Society in London were on the lookout for a conductor. Costa had resigned, Sterndale Bennett was not available, Spohr could not leave Cassel, Berlioz was engaged by the New Philharmonic. At the suggestion of Dr Praeger, M. Sainton brought forward Wagner's name at a committee meeting; it was accepted, and before the end of January an ambassador was sent out to Zurich to make a formal offer of the post and to settle arrangements for the coming season. On March 5th the new conductor arrived, and on March 12th he scored an undoubted triumph at his first concert. The audience was astonished beyond measure. It had come to see a blustering demagogue, a 'Marat of music,' whose one ambition was to guillotine the Classical Composers and establish a Republic of noise: it found a poet who could understand Haydn and Mendelssohn better than Costa himself, and who could give a reading of the *Eroica* that for the first time revealed its greatness. In spite of all assertions to the contrary there can be no doubt that Wagner was a great conductor. He had certain disquieting mannerisms; he used, for instance, to leave off beating when the orchestra was in smooth water, and resume at a difficulty or a climax; but he possessed extraordinary insight into the meaning of the works which he directed, and he was martinet enough to insist on an adequate fulfilment of his wishes. The Philharmonic band was soon delighted with him, and the public began to turn anxious eyes towards the newspapers to learn whether it might not applaud after all.

It was very careless of Wagner to neglect the old established custom of calling upon the musical critics and soliciting their good opinion. He would not have made much way with Mr Davidson of the *Times*, who had chivalrously announced the intention of 'not giving him a chance,'[1] or with Mr Chorley of the *Athenæum*, who had taken *Tannhäuser* as a personal insult, but he might have conciliated other leaders of the popular taste and induced them

[1] See Dr Praeger's *Wagner as I knew Him*, p. 227.

to treat his work with some show of impartiality. As it was he got all the worst of the controversy. The whole critical Press turned upon him with a unanimity which it very seldom displays, and excited itself almost to hysteria over the 'mass of incoherent rubbish' which he had the temerity to offer as a contribution to Art. The *Musical World*, for instance, regarded his compositions in the light of a 'reckless, wild, extravagant, and demagogic cacophony, the symbol of profligate libertinage.' It warned its readers that 'Wagner's theories were impious,' and that if they listened to the 'wily eloquence' of his followers they would 'find themselves in the coils of rattlesnakes.' The *Sunday Times*, a newspaper of some position, declared that Richard Wagner was a 'desperate charlatan, endowed with worldly skill and vigorous purpose enough to persuade a gaping crowd that the nauseous compound he manufactures has some precious inner virtue which they must live and ponder yet ere they perceive.' 'Scarcely the most ordinary ballad writer,' it continues, 'but would shame him in the creation of melody, and no English harmonist of more than one year's growth could be found sufficiently without ears and understanding to pen such vile things.' There seems to have been a singular want of urbanity about musical journalism in the year 1855.

Yet the concerts were uniformly successful in spite of the extraordinary length of their programme. The average was eight numbers: two overtures, two symphonies, a concerto, and three vocal pieces—a banquet for Gargantua rather than for the limited digestions of ordinary humanity. Wagner protested vigorously against this 'overfeeding,' but the conventions were too strong for him and the original scheme remained unaltered. His own works were very sparsely represented. At the second concert he introduced himself with the prelude to *Lohengrin*, at the fifth he gave the *Tannhäuser* overture, which was repeated by Royal command at the seventh; but except on these three occasions he kept himself entirely in the background. The Royal command was especially pleasing to him, as the *Times* had been making capital out of his political adventures, and declaring that it was outrageous for a loyal English society to place itself in the hands of an exiled revolutionary. The Queen was present at the performance, and received the Composer with that winning graciousness which Her Majesty has always shown to the great artists of every school and nation.

In the intervals of his official work Wagner was busily engaged in scoring *Walküre*, of which the first two acts were practically finished by the end of his visit. Shortly before his departure Berlioz arrived in London, and the two rival conductors had many opportunities of meeting, sometimes at Wagner's lodgings in Portland Terrace, sometimes at the house of M. Sainton or Dr Praeger. They were never really intimate. Although not dissimilar in aim, they were widely different in manner: the one vivid, eager, impetuous, treating life as a cavalry charge, and riding down opposition at full gallop; the other polished and self-contained, standing with his hand on the trigger, and a cartridge box full of epigrams at his belt. It should be added that the sense of constraint which usually manifested itself between them was in no way the fault of the

younger man. At Paris he had spoken warmly of
Berlioz as 'a musician who, at least, does not
write for money'; at Dresden he had taken great
trouble to secure his visitor an adequate reception,
many of his early letters to Liszt are full of allusions
to the French Composer and friendly complaints
against his 'unapproachableness.' Hearing that
Berlioz was in want of a libretto he had proposed
to offer him a dramatic sketch called 'Wieland der
Schmied,' and now, with his usual impulsive good
nature, he was endeavouring to better the material
fortunes of his rival by launching an audacious
petition to Napoleon himself. Probably Berlioz
never heard of the latter service, otherwise he would
have mitigated some of his indignation when, six
years later, the Emperor stopped the rehearsals of
Les Troyens and forced *Tannhäuser* upon his unwilling subjects. It was most unfortunate that an
accident should have thrown into antagonism two
musicians, of whom one at least was anxious to
maintain a relation of kindliness.

On his return to Zurich Wagner occupied himself
at first with the music of his Tetralogy. *Walkürie*
was finished in 1856, the first two acts of *Siegfried*
followed in 1857, and then, by a caprice of genius,
the Composer grew tired of his subject and turned
to the story of Tristan, which had already excited
his attention some years before. It was becoming
necessary that he should write a work which stood
some chance of performance, and while he was
hesitating the opportunity suddenly appeared from
the most unexpected quarter. One morning a
stranger knocked at the door of 'The Retreat,'
announced himself as an official emissary from the

Emperor of Brazil, and offered Wagner his own terms if he would compose a three act opera for the theatre at Rio. Never was there a stranger commission since Mozart received his mysterious order for the Requiem. In great surprise Wagner hesitated to give any final answer, but the suggestion crystallised his resolve, and he forthwith began the poem of *Tristan*. By the middle of 1859 the whole opera was completed—and the Emperor of Brazil had made other arrangements.

In any case it seemed absurd that a reputation which had crossed the Atlantic should find an insuperable barrier in the Rhine. Once more Wagner determined to organise a campaign against Paris which should induce that stubborn city to a capitulation. The conditions had altered for the better since 1840. M. Carvalho had superseded M. Pillet,[1] the perfidious manager of the Théâtre de la Renaissance had retired into his last bankruptcy, and though Dietsch was still at his post—Dietsch the Composer of *Le Vaisseau Fantôme*—yet he had never been sufficiently in the wrong to bear malice. The public, too, was wiser by twenty years of experience, and Wagner's own work had greatly advanced in power and maturity since the old days of *Das Liebesverbot*. Accordingly, in the spring of 1859, he started from Lucerne, stopped to finish *Tristan* at Lyons, and before the end of the year had established himself in a house near the Champs Elysées, confident in the justice of his cause and the strength of his artillery.

He began with three operatic concerts, which, in consequence of the enormous expenses of produc-

---

[1] See *Berlioz*, p. 120.

tion, resulted in a deficit of about £400. However, they succeeded in attracting popular attention, and during the spring and summer of 1860 there was hardly a journal in the boulevards which had not something to say about the Music of the Future. Cham fired off volley after volley of caricatures, alternately condemning *Tannhäuser* as a din and recommending it as a soporific. Perhaps the best of them is that in which an economical auditor, in place of the money for his seat, offers the ingenious plea, 'Monsieur, je suis le payeur de l'avenir,' but for the most part they are poor productions, ludicrously inexact in portraiture, and too uncertain of aim to rank very high as satire. There is nothing in them half so good as *Punch's* 'Promissory Notes,' or the delicious picture of Wagner's orchestra rescued from oblivion by M. Grand-Carteret.[1] Apart from these skirmishes, which by themselves would have done Wagner more good than harm, there was arising also a steady force of hostility. Berlioz declared against the invader, the critics for once ranged themselves under his command, all hands were summoned to the defence, and German Music was retreating in disorder, when Napoleon, at the instance of Princess Metternich, suddenly resolved to exhibit himself in the unfamiliar part of a *Deus ex Machinâ*. It was like a scene from the Iliad— Hector marshalling his ranks before the beleaguered city, Agamemnon baffled and irresolute in face of the serried spears, and the wise Pallas Athene bidding the Cloud-compeller show forth his power and interpose in the battle.

But against stupidity even the gods contend in

[1] *Wagner en Caricatures*, p. 107.

vain. The imperial fiat could compel the obedience of M. Carvalho, it was powerless against the disapprobation of the Jockey Club. The members of that notable body had two quarrels with *Tannhäuser:* first, that its author was a German, whereas they were French; second, that their only attraction, the ballet, occurred at the beginning of the opera, and so would be over before they had finished dinner. They therefore determined that they too would do something to vindicate National Art, and organised a claque of their own, with instructions to begin whistling before the curtain rose and to continue until they arrived. Never, not even at our O. P. riots, was there such a scene in a theatre. The two claques strove manfully against each other, the audience joined in the fray, the front row of the pit played on flageolets, while the gallery howled; finally, an opera which had been produced at a cost of £8000, with over 150 rehearsals, had to own itself defeated. A second performance was given on March 18th, five days after the first, and a third on March 24th, but it was all unavailing. At the former some qualified attention was given to the Venusberg music, but to nothing after it; at the latter the members of the Jockey Club appeared in force and saved the Capitol by their hisses.

The disaster was compensated, as disasters usually are, by an unexpected stroke of good fortune. Thanks to the entreaties of Princess Metternich, Wagner obtained leave 'to enter all German states other than Saxony,' an exception which was itself removed a year later. He at once availed himself of this remission of his exile, and after a few months of travel settled down on the Rhine near

Maintz, and began in earnest on the composition of a new opera — *Die Meistersinger*. He had written the first sketches at Teplitz in 1845, now he took the work in hand, and, with many interruptions, occupied himself during the next five years in its completion. Bright as it is the opera was written in the midst of troubles—fruitless endeavours to get *Tristan* accepted, gathering difficulties and disappointments in his home, and a steadily increasing pressure of poverty. At the beginning of 1864 he published the text of the *Ring* 'as a literary product.' 'I can hardly expect that I shall find leisure to complete the music,' he wrote, 'and I have no hope of living to hear it performed.'

Hope was nearer than he thought. On March 10, 1864, there ascended the Bavarian throne a boy of eighteen, whose reign was to revolutionise the Music of Europe. The new king inherited the artistic tastes of his grandfather, he had heard *Lohengrin* a short time before his accession, and one of his first acts was to despatch an equerry to Wagner with the laconic message, 'Come here and finish your work.' The offer was accepted with enthusiastic gratitude, preliminaries were speedily arranged, and by the beginning of the summer Wagner was settled at Munich, with a pension from the Privy Purse, and unlimited means of production at his disposal. But he went alone. The reverse at Paris had restored him to his country, the triumph at Munich found him separated from his wife. She had borne with him the troubles and privations of thirty years' adversity: she left him at the very threshold of his success. It is certain that he never consciously gave her pain; but the gentle nature, which had so well fulfilled its mission of comfort, found itself broken and bewildered by the stress of battle and the shock of victory. Gradually the old sympathy began to wane; Wagner found her cold and irresponsive; she in her turn began to feel bitterly the preoccupations of his public life. Then as a climax appeared Cosima von Bülow, the wife of his pupil and the daughter of his greatest friend. It became impossible for Minna to sit in silence and hear her husband discussing with another woman projects and ambitions on which she had no word to say. There is no reason here for a charge of infidelity, no stain of reproach or dishonour, only the 'little rift' which began unnoticed and widened until the whole music of her life was mute.

Wagner felt her loss with the most poignant regret. 'I am in the midst of profusion,' he writes to his friend Praeger, 'but my sense of isolation is torturing. With no one to realise and enjoy with me this limitless comfort a feeling of weariness and desolation is induced which keeps me in a constant state of dejection terrible to bear. . . . I who have praised women more than Frauenlob have not one for my companion.' These are not the words of a hard-hearted or unfaithful husband; there is in them a ring of sincerity that claims our compassion. It is a pitiful story, of which the end is the more tragic because it was inevitable.

Much comment has been excited by the fact that the von Bülows followed Wagner to Munich. It could not have been otherwise. They were necessary to his career, the one as his secretary,

T

the other as the only available conductor whom he could trust. And indeed all personal considerations were very soon overwhelmed in the flood of work which surrounded him. The *Flying Dutchman* was given in December; all through the winter there were concerts; and in the spring of 1865 came a magnificent performance of *Tristan* —a worthy inauguration of that superb tragedy. Besides, the King was sending for his new favourite 'two or three times a day': now to consult with Semper about plans for a new theatre; now to discuss some question of statecraft, or to talk over the shortcomings of the Ministry. It was almost a realisation of Plato's philosopher-politician, and it very soon brought about the results which that most sensible of Idealists predicted. The responsible advisers of the Crown protested against this encroachment on their prerogatives; the populace remembered Lola Montes, and grumbled at a fresh dynasty of the theatre. Before the end of 1865 Wagner had made Munich too hot for him, and retired to Switzerland, stoutly declaring that the people were on his side, and that he was only waiting 'until the King could change his counsellors.'

From 1866 to 1872 he lived at Triebschen, near Lucerne, working steadily at the *Ring*, and paying occasional visits to Munich for the performance of his other operas. *Meistersinger* was produced with great success in the summer of 1868, *Rheingold* in 1869, *Walküre* in 1870, and by the next year the last two parts of the Tetralogy were practically completed. In addition to this work, he had also returned to the arena of controversial authorship.

Beside the essay, *Ueber Staat und Religion*, written at the request of King Louis, he published during these seven years nearly all the papers which appear in the 8th and 9th volumes of his collected works, such as the monograph on Beethoven, the little tract on conducting, and the articles on German Art and German Politics. The last-named were published as a series in the *Süddeutsche Presse*, of which one of the editors—August Roeckel—had good reason to know Wagner's opinions on both subjects.

Of his minor writings at this time little need be said. There are a few poems of no great merit, a letter on the proposed Conservatorium at Munich, some scraps of biography or criticism, and an exceedingly foolish extravaganza on the siege of Paris, entitled *Eine Kapitulation*. The blaze of indignation which this work excited in Paris has somewhat blinded us to its real demerits. It is not malicious enough to be an act of revenge; it is not coherent enough to be a satire; from beginning to end it contains nothing except some tolerable gibes at Victor Hugo, and some music-hall songs of more than usual insipidity. If anyone wishes to see 'a burlesque of the siege,' he has only to consult the Parisian comic papers of 1870: he will assuredly not find it in this so-called comedy.

Meantime an important change was taking place in Wagner's domestic life. In 1866 his wife Minna died at Dresden; in 1870 he married Cosima von Bülow, the divorced wife of his friend and pupil. By imperceptible degrees they had passed from sympathy to comradeship, from comradeship to passion; at last the brink was reached, and it was impossible to stop. While Minna was alive Wagner had kept faith with her; after her death he allowed himself to drift into a companionship which was becoming more and more a necessity of his nature. There is no need to enter here into the ethical aspect of the question, but it should be added that the marriage was almost ideally happy. Husband and wife were sincerely attached to each other, and before long their union was enriched by the birth of Wagner's only child—his son Siegfried. 'Think what I must feel,' he writes to his friend Praeger, 'that this has at last fallen to my share.' His joy found expression in the 'Siegfried Idyll,' which was composed as a surprise for Madame Wagner, and first performed as an *aubade* on her birthday. It is not difficult to trace the influence of the new home in this sweetest and most serene of musical poems. Its delicate strains are like some melodious verse of Shelley, written in his sea-washed balcony, with Mary Wollstonecraft at his side.

In 1872 Wagner was recalled to Bavaria. The proposals for a new theatre at Munich had fallen through, and the King would authorise no alternative plan without the presence of his adviser. After some consideration Wagner decided on Bayreuth, held two or three preliminary discussions at Lucerne with Neumann the architect, wrote an elaborate scheme, in which every detail of construction was included, and finally set 'off to superintend matters in person. The sum required was £45,000 of which a large amount was subscribed at once, and the rest collected gradually by Wagner societies and Wagner concerts in every quarter of the globe. On May 22d the foundation stone was laid, and by August 13, 1876, the gigantic theatre was ready for use. It was opened with three complete performances of the *Ring*, under the conductorship of Dr Richter; Wilhelmj led the orchestra, and almost every great operatic artist in Germany took part in the performance. Indeed, nothing in the whole history of the Bayreuth festival is more remarkable than the generous enthusiasm with which musicians of all classes have offered themselves for the cause. It is only of recent years that the scheme has succeeded in paying its expenses; yet there has never been any show of hesitation or discontent. Services have been given as a labour of love, and that not only by friends, but by many to whom the Master was personally unknown. Holidays have been sacrificed, and engagements cancelled that a little provincial town might hear the best possible interpretation of works at which the majority of the public was still inclined to scoff. Now the reward has come, and the Wagner Theatre may almost be described in Dr Praeger's phrase as the Mecca of musicians.

Success, however, came slowly. The first festival ended with a deficit of over £7000, and Wagner was once more driven to the uncongenial expedient of giving concerts. At the beginning of 1877 he came over to London, where the famous series took place at the Albert Hall. It included selections out of all his operas, from *Rienzi* to *Götterdämmerung*, performed by an orchestra of 170, and directed partly by Dr Richter, partly by the Composer himself. But age and illness were beginning to tell upon Wagner's power as a conductor. Throughout the London visit he was below his mark;

irritable at rehearsals, nervous and restless during performance, and prostrated with weariness as soon as the concert was ended. Still, in spite of all disappointments, the experiment enabled him to forward a little over £700 to Bayreuth, and the rest of the debt was defrayed shortly afterwards by a brilliant season of the *Ring* at Munich.

It is characteristic of Wagner that his last and finest work should be religious in treatment. 'Every great man,' says Dr Parry, 'is serious at bottom'; and none can better stand the test than the artist whose very earnestness and sincerity of purpose had driven him for so many years into revolt and exile. Hitherto he had accomplished but little in the form of sacred music: the miracle-play *Jesus von Nazareth* had never advanced beyond the first sketch; the cantata *Das Liebesmahl der Apostel* had been given once at a choral festival in Dresden and then laid aside. Now, after a lapse of thirty years, he resumed the broken threads, and wove into one noble story the legend of the Holy Grail, the message of the Redeemer, and the solemnities of the Sacramental service. Shakespeare has no figure more pathetic than that of Kundry: Goethe no scene of more tremendous import than that in which Parsifal uplifts the cup of blessing over the worship of the assembled knights. The Hymn of Adoration which closes the drama is the *Nunc Dimittis* of a long and faithful ministry.

The poem was written before Wagner's visit to London, and first read to a party of his friends at Mr Dannreuther's house in Orme Square. Shortly after his return to Bayreuth he began the music, and continued it, with intervals of severe illness, until its completion in the winter of 1881. He advanced more slowly than usual, but it was with the certain tread of mature thought, not the vacillation of weakness or senility. *Parsifal* is to him what the Ninth symphony is to Beethoven, a crown and climax in which Art transcends the limits of song and approaches those of prophecy.

There is little else to chronicle. While his health permitted he remained in his Bavarian home, receiving friends at Wahnfried, contributing detached essays and papers to the *Bayreuther Blätter*, and superintending such performances as his eccentric patron chose to demand. The winters of 1879-1881 were spent in southern Italy, where it was hoped that a milder climate would give him strength to resist the gathering and increasing attacks of disease. But his work was nearly over. He was sixty-eight years of age; his career as a Composer had lasted for half a century; he had fought single-handed against the most implacable opposition that ever obstructed the path of genius. Now, on the quiet shores of Palermo, he could close the volume and say, 'I will write no more.'

At the beginning of 1882 he returned to Bayreuth, and at once began preparations for the great festival production of *Parsifal*, which took place in the summer. Sixteen performances were given between July 28th and August 28th. The little Franconian town was full to overflowing; pilgrims more diverse than those of the Tabard arrived from every part of Europe; even hostile criticism was for once put to silence by the intense enthusiasm with which the work was received. From that time forward there has been no question of Wagner's success. He has made his mark indelibly on the world, and not all the labour of malice or pedantry can obliterate it.

But the excitement of victory overstrained a frame already enfeebled by strife and weariness. At one of the rehearsals Wagner was taken suddenly ill, and although he persevered courageously to the end of the festival, and even conducted part of the last performance, it soon became evident that his health was seriously impaired by his exertions. At his doctor's advice he went to Venice for the winter, occupying the Comte de Chambord's palace on the Grand Canal. There for a short time he rallied. On Christmas eve, his wife's birthday, he was well enough to conduct his boyish symphony in C major at the Liceo Marcello; and as late as the beginning of 1883 he was working at the series of papers on Art and Religion which had been suggested to him by the composition of *Parsifal*. But then came the end. On the afternoon of February 13th he fainted in his gondola; a few hours afterwards he died, quietly and painlessly, with his son Siegfried's name upon his lips. His body was carried back to Bayreuth and buried, amid a vast concourse of people, in the ivy-covered tomb at Wahnfried: the home of which he had written that 'there his wanderings found rest.' No oration was delivered at the graveside: only the simple prayers and benedictions of the Protestant liturgy. The loss was too great, too sudden, to be solaced by the phrases of courtly compliment or official panegyric. Nor was there need of such 'weak witness.' Wagner's true monument is in the work that he has wrought: his true praise in the feelings of love and veneration that, year by year, are gathering about his name.

III

THE IMPORT OF THE MUSIC DRAMA

THERE is no longer any need to combat the strange misconception that Wagner's operas were deliberately constructed in support of a pre-existing theory. Such a position could only have been maintained at a time when his work was little known, when his doctrines were little understood, when it was still considered possible to deny in him the possession of true artistic gifts. For the first and most essential characteristic of Art is spontaneity. In it synthesis is logically prior to analysis, conception to discussion, and the office of criticism is not to prescribe the path of genius but to record and interpret its achievements. Since, then, there are few at the present day who would have the hardihood to refuse Wagner the title of artist, we may be content to take his works on their own merits, and to recognise that in their creation he was finding the natural expression of his character, not sustaining a thesis with painstaking illustration and elaborate example. Whatever the estimate in which we hold the two great Masters of German opera, we shall not sum them up in the deplorable sentence of M. Fétis: 'Weber se livre à l'inspiration, Wagner médite et calcule.'

Still more unjust is the attack on Wagner's sincerity, which has unfortunately been revived in recent times by Mr Statham. To assert that the ten volumes are simply ingenious advertisements, that they were designed 'not to advance Art but to push Wagner,' and that their author is a 'remarkable charlatan,' who has hoodwinked us into believing that he was in earnest, all this is not criticism but invective. No doubt Mr Statham is holding a brief for Absolute as opposed to Romantic Music, no doubt he is misled by the erroneous minor premise that the work of Wagner comes into competition with that of Bach or Mozart, still it is one thing to disallow a Composer's methods, another to doubt his honesty. All authentic record of Wagner's life is unanimous in declaring that he was absolutely genuine in his devotion to his ideal; that he fought for his faith because he believed it to be true, not because he believed that it would improve his prospects. And even if this were not so, even if we had no testimony but that of inference, still the accusation would refute itself. At the time when his chief essays were written he had not composed one note of the *Ring*, or of *Tristan*, or of *Parsifal*, nor any of *Meistersinger* except a few sketches. It is to these operas that his doctrines principally apply, and we are asked to believe that he issued his polemic for no better reason than to browbeat managers into accepting his works—when they arrived, and the public into applauding them—when they were accepted.

As usual the simplest explanation is the most probable. Wagner's whole artistic personality manifested itself in two separate and independent streams.

He was at once a creator and a teacher, who embodied his ideal directly in his operas, and in his writings expressed it indirectly by reducing it to principles. It is true that he identified himself with his message: every prophet, every hero, every pioneer has done the same. For a man who is overpowered by his convictions it is impossible to keep silence, and equally impossible to content himself with cautious platitudes or impersonal compromises. He has no choice but to speak out, no alternative but to 'cry aloud and spare not,' and his very vehemence is often a sure indication of his earnestness. If this be egotism, then most of our great men have been egotists. If it be imposture, then 'Athanasius contra mundum' is the symbol of charlatanism and hypocrisy.

But the two streams though independent are parallel, and one is nearer to our comprehension than the other. It is easier to understand and estimate the value of the ideas embodied in Wagner's music after we have considered the formulæ through which they are stated in his manifestoes. Gluck's *Alceste* is made clearer to us by its introduction, Victor Hugo's *Cromwell* by its preface, and in like manner we shall find *Siegfried* and *Tristan* more intelligible by some preliminary acquaintance with *Das Kunstwerk der Zukunft* and with *Oper und Drama*. We cannot possibly judge of an artist's success or failure unless we know what are the objects which he endeavours to attain.

The main principles of Wagner's work may be expressed in two general statements. The first, which is to be found in *Die Kunst und die Revolution*, in the first book of *Das Kunstwerk der Zukunft*, and negatively in *Das Judenthum in der Musik*, runs briefly as follows. True Art is not a matter which can be determined by idle fashion or instigated by princely patronage: it is the satisfaction of a genuine need felt by the nation at large. Hence its basis is popular, social, democratic: it is the outcome of a national sentiment, the correlative of a national language. It requires life for its impulse, freedom for its atmosphere: it is stifled by luxury, by æstheticism, and by every form of artifice or conventionality. When Athens was in her prime she gave birth to Æschylus and Sophocles: when the pulse of the city ran low came Euripides and the decadence of the drama. Italy free could find utterance in the voice of Palestrina, Italy enslaved, and careless of her slavery, has no better melody than the tinkling of Rossini's guitar. It is the people that creates: it is the people that has invented speech, developed religion, and established laws and cities. From the people alone can come any hopes of an Art that has blood in its veins and sincerity in its soul.

The second principle is foreshadowed in *Eine Pilgerfahrt zu Beethoven*, stated in the later books of *Das Kunstwerk der Zukunft*, and developed at great length in *Oper und Drama*. A National Art will find its fittest embodiment in a Reformed Theatre. The drama is the most natural centre of popular culture, the readiest source from which the people can satisfy its artistic needs. It gives the simplest and most direct expression to that mimetic instinct from which, according to Aristotle, all Art is ultimately derived. It comprises within itself every form of artistic effect: the strength of poetry, the sweetness of music, the rhythmic movements of the dance, the beauty of gracious shape and glowing colour. Indeed, the separate forms have long reached maturity. There is no sculpture to set beside the Greek, no painting to set beside that of Florence and Venice; no poet has equalled Shakespeare, no musician has rivalled Beethoven: what is left for the artist of the future than that he should fuse into one complex whole the elements that have already attained their individual perfection? But the elements must be fused, not aggregated. The libretto must not be a string of empty verses, on which the Composer shall construct incongruous melodies and meaningless roulades; the spectacle must not be clogged with useless shows or tedious processions; the dance must poetise every movement and ennoble every gesture in place of interrupting the drama with the otiose episode of the ballet. In short, the whole work must be a single organic unity, in which no part is superfluous or accidental. Then follow certain prescriptions of detail. The subject should be taken, as far as possible, from national myth or popular legend; the verse should be alliterative rather than rhymed, on the ground of greater effectiveness in singing; the old conventions of grand aria, of ensemble, and of final chorus are to be discarded altogether. Even Gluck's reforms were not sufficiently far-reaching: for Gluck is as much overweighted by his aria as Racine by his tirade. In the opera of the future Music and Poetry are to be the soul and body of the same thought, clothed in a befitting garb of scenic beauty and spectacular display. It is no Utopian dream. Athens had a theatre in which her whole national life was reflected: let Germany be free and earnest and she may have the same.

With the first of these two propositions we may entirely concur. It is no doubt possible to take exception to certain phrases — Wagner forgets, for instance, that the origin of society is monarchical, not democratic, but when these are answered the main contention is still untouched. The one absolutely certain truth about Art is that it is not artificial. We may find pleasure in clever workmanship, but not the highest pleasure: the very soul of Art is inspiration, and inspiration implies genuineness of purpose. Music especially is based on the natural instincts of the race. It is not relative to this or that section, to the Barbarian or the Philistine or the Populace. No class, however low, has a right to call itself 'the people,' and it is to the people at large that Music makes its appeal. 'That which is called "the public," says Mendelssohn, 'is exactly the same here as elsewhere and everywhere: the simple public assembled together for an instant, so fluctuating, so full of curiosity, so devoid of taste, so dependent on the judgment of the musician—the so-called connoisseur. But against this we must set the great public, assembling together year after year, wiser and more just than connoisseur and musician, and judging so truly and feeling so delicately.'[1]

The second principle is curiously analogous to that of Browning's 'Cleon.' We can almost imagine Wagner saying,—

> I have not chanted verse like Homer, no—
> Nor swept string like Terpander, no—nor carved
> And painted men like Phidias and his friend :
> I am not great as they are, point by point.

[1] Letter to Jenny Lind, Leipsic, March 18, 1846.

> But I have entered into sympathy
> With these four, running these into one soul,
> Who, separate, ignored each other's arts.

Indeed the doctrine of combination was by no means a new thing. Rather it was the recovery of a lost secret, the return to an ideal that had been embodied in Greek tragedy, copied to some extent on the Roman stage, and revived in later times by Peri and Gluck. No doubt Wagner overshoots his mark when he asserts that the supreme Art of the future must consist in this fusion of pre-existing elements. We cannot believe that Absolute Music has said its last word when we have Brahms and Dvořák to convince us of the contrary. We cannot believe that poetry has fulfilled its individual function when every age is adding new contributions to the list of great poets. But though the two Arts will go on existing independently they will still have a common ground ; and that ground will be laid out on the lines which Wagner has indicated.

It is worth while quoting on this point the testimony of a poet. 'Le vers,' says M. de Banville,[1] 'est la parole humaine rhythmée de façon à pouvoir être chantée et, à proprement parler, il n'y a pas de poésie et de vers en dehors du chant. Tous les vers sont destinés à être chantés et n'existent qu'à cette condition. . . . Les vers qui ne pourraient pas être chantés si nous retrouvions, comme cela est possible, l'art perdu de la Musique Lyrique, ne sont pas en realité des vers. Je dis si nous retrouvions, car les compositions dramatiques nommées Opéras n'ont proprement rien à démêler avec ce qui fut le chant aux âges poétiques. On

[1] *Petit Traité de Poésie Française*, pp. 3-4.

y prononce il est vrai sur des airs accompagnés par une symphonie des paroles mal rhythmées et coupées, çà et la, par des assonances, mais ces paroles ne sont pas des vers, et si elles étaient des vers la musique bruyante sur laquelle on les attache ne pourrait servir à en exprimer l'accent et l'âme, puisque d'ailleurs cette musique existe par elle-même et indépendemment de toute poésie.' Here we have the same over-statement, the same representation of part as whole, but for all that the words contain a truth of the utmost value. The 'art perdu de la Musique Lyrique' is not a chimera but a reality. It may not be the only art, or the highest art; there is no necessity to compare it with the epic, or the string quartett, or the symphony; but it is the expression of a true ideal, the satisfaction of a true need. And herein is Wagner's chief claim to immortality, that he has discovered this lost art, that he has established it in his own work, and that by so doing he has transformed opera from an ingenious toy into a living organism.

There is another aspect of the case which requires careful consideration. If the different Arts are to be combined into one complex result they must make certain mutual concessions. The fusion implied in Wagner's music-drama necessarily involves some sacrifice of those individual characteristics which we should expect to find in the elements taken separately. We have no right to judge the libretto of *Tristan* by the same laws which we should apply to a poem of Goethe: to Goethe the words represent the whole medium employed; to Wagner they are only part of the medium.

We have no right to judge the music of *Parsifal* by the same laws which we should apply to a Beethoven quartett; in the quartett the music is everything, in the opera it is only a factor in the general effect. It would be almost as unreasonable to transfer the scenery of the Bayreuth theatre to a picture gallery and to estimate it by the standard of Titian or Bellini. Hence it is not fair criticism to decry Wagner's libretti after reading them in an arm-chair, or his melodies after hearing them in a concert room. The whole of his mature work was intended for the stage, and for the stage alone; it stands in relation to no other conditions; it can be estimated from no other standpoint. Grant that he occasionally permitted the concert-performance of excerpts from his operas: he did so under pressure of poverty, with extreme reluctance, and in the certain conviction that they would miss their aim. Again, the stage has its own laws and its own exigencies. Even such a literary dramatist as Racine looses immeasurably if we take him from the footlights; even such a supreme genius as Shakespeare has more power to impress us if we see the action and hear the eloquent cadences of the player's voice. And this is still more true of Wagner. The piecemeal analysis of the ingredients in his work is as uncritical as an inquiry into the different scraps of metal which Cellini melted down when he cast his Perseus.

It follows therefore that, if we hear in a concert room the 'Walkürenritt' or the 'Schmiedelied,' or the death song of Isolde, we have a right to praise, but we have not a right to blame. If we can enjoy them so much the better for us, if we cannot we must reserve judgment until we hear them under their proper conditions. It is only at the theatre that we are in a position to criticise; only when we see the drama as a whole that we can judge of the effect that it was intended to produce. The principle of 'ex pede Herculem' is a very insecure basis for an adverse decision.

But the arias of Mozart and Beethoven and Weber bear transplantation to the platform. No doubt they do; Mozart may even be said sometimes to gain by the absence of a theatrical background. But this only shows that the art of these three Composers is different from that of Wagner. His is a 'nuova musica,' a new type which differs almost as widely from Mozart as Peri from Palestrina. In one word the creator of *Zauberflöte* is to be judged as a musician; the creator of *Siegfried* is to be judged not as a musician but as a dramatist.

This distinction becomes even more apparent if we consider Wagner's attitude to those forms of composition which are not primarily intended for the theatre. Of chamber music he never produced a single note, except the boyish sonata which he wrote as a student exercise for Weinlig. His only symphony belongs to the same period and possesses the same value. Of his concert overtures one alone survives, and that is so essentially dramatic in character that we can well imagine it enriched, like the *entr'acte* of Berlioz's greatest opera, with the accessories of scenery and action. The most striking feature in his one cantata is the anticipation of a device which he afterwards employed in *Parsifal*. The themes of his *Siegfried Idyll* are,

with one exception, borrowed note for note from
the third drama of his Tetralogy, and are arranged in
a form which is only explicable on dramatic grounds.
His three marches are mere *pièces d'occasion* of no
lasting merit; and, when all these are enumerated,
there only remain a few songs and 'albumblätter,'
the chips and shavings of a great workshop. In
one word the *Siegfried Idyll* and the *Faust* overture belong in spirit to the opera house, and of
the other works some may be brought under the
same category and the rest dismissed from consideration. Wagner is no more represented by his
essays in Absolute Music than Calderon by his
'Exhortation to Silence' or Racine by his Hymns.

It must not be supposed that these preliminaries
are treacherously designed to prepare the way for
an unqualified encomium of the eleven operas.
They are simply intended to clear the ground, and
to show the real issue on which judgment can be
delivered. They leave entirely open the question
whether we approve or disapprove of the 'Art work
of the future,' and only venture to suggest that
before we do either we must ascertain what it is
that we are called upon to decide. To deny that
Wagner's ideal has a legitimate place in Art is to
disallow Greek tragedy: to appraise his result on
any other principles than those implied in his ideal
is to bid farewell at once to all methods of logical
criticism. Further, it may be argued that we have
no concern with such pre-Wagnerian productions
as *Die Feen* and *Das Liebesverbot*. They belong
essentially to the *ancien régime*, not to the Revolution; throughout their career they have only attained
to one performance apiece, and they will be left out

of court as witnesses which the counsels have agreed not to call. For all practical purposes the work which we have to appraise begins with *Rienzi* and ends with *Parsifal*.

Even within these limits the first point that presents itself to our regard is the enormous advance shown by the later operas over the earlier. As a rule Absolute Music is a gift which is born almost at full growth. The first works of Beethoven and Brahms show all the firmness and certainty of a Master: Mendelssohn wrote the octett at eighteen, Schubert and Mozart were great Composers at even an earlier age. This may be explained partly on the ground that the inspiration of Absolute Music is less related to experience than that of any other Art in the world, partly on the ground that its expression in each composer begins by adopting the phraseology of the past generation, and so enters on an inheritance of ready-made and predetermined methods. Wagner, however, like Mirabeau, had to be his own ancestor. Since Gluck the line of succession had become so broken and confused that to trace it would overtax all the resources of the Heralds' College. Beethoven found the world full of a musical system from which he could take his own point of departure. Wagner had to build on a forgotten plan with an entirely new set of materials. Hence it is only natural that his early work should be tentative, uncertain, often erroneous. But the line of development is unbroken. In *Rienzi* we have an attempt to reconcile the new ideal with the incompatible method of the grand opera; in the *Flying Dutchman* the balance begins to incline; in *Tannhäuser* and *Lohengrin* it is gradually determined in favour of drama; and finally in *Rheingold* the musical conventions are discarded altogether and the principle of dramatic unity established without reserve.

Thus the first four operas exhibit incongruities of structure which prevent them from being regarded as supremely great works of Art. They are like the intermediate forms of which biologists tell us, bridging over the gulf between two distinct genera by participating to some extent in the characteristics of both. At the same time they possess magnificent qualities: a keen sense of theatrical effect, a clearly marked power of characterisation, and, after *Rienzi* at any rate, a strength and fervour of passion which alone will account for their success. The thought is right, but the style is not yet maturely formed. The true dramatic instinct is there, but it is obscured and thwarted by the want of its own proper method of expression. Indeed, with all its inequalities, the *Flying Dutchman* was the best opera that had appeared in Germany since the death of Weber, and its two successors, if they sometimes sink lower, yet in their noblest scenes rise to a level which it never attained. Whatever verdict we may pass on them as achievements, we cannot deny that they are full of rich promise, and that their triumphs, even if intermittent, are unquestionable whenever they occur.

It is interesting to notice some details of phraseology and treatment in which Wagner's maturer manner of composition is here anticipated. The strange tonality of Senta's ballad, and still more of the introduction to Erik's cavatina, is the sign-manual of an artist who was afterwards to stretch tonality to the utmost limits that it could bear. The new systems of key-relationship exhibited in Tannhäuser's first song and in the cathedral music of *Lohengrin* marks the natural development of a mind to which key-relationship itself was to be no longer a distinctive term. The use of the two 'keyless chords'—the diminished seventh and the augmented fifth—is already apparent, not only as a ready means of modulation but as a characteristic effect of colour. The treatment of the chorus already foreshadows the dramatic polyphony of *Walküre* and *Meistersinger*. The *leit-motif* is as yet tentative and half-hearted, but it has begun its work of making the orchestra a commentary upon the action of the play. There are still traces of the old recitative, but they are gradually overborne by the monologue and the *aria parlante* of the later works. And, finally, we have the gigantic orchestra, with the unusual instruments and the unaccustomed combinations, which have made Wagner's scoring a proverb for boldness and ingenuity. There is no need to multiply examples. The third act of *Lohengrin* may be taken at once as the summary of the old method and as the point of transition to the new.

The music of *Lohengrin* was finished in the early part of 1848; that of *Rheingold* was begun in the autumn of 1858. During the interval Wagner wrote all his most important theoretical works, and the formulation of his ideas had a natural though unconscious effect on the character of his composition. Hence with *Rheingold* we take a new departure. The first four contributions to the stage were operas, the last seven are music-dramas, and it is by these especially that Wagner's aim and attainment are to be estimated. His five years' withdrawal from the theatre had given him leisure for free growth and development; the experience of an active career had already brought him complete mastery over his materials; even the isolation of his exile was in some measure compensated by the sense of liberty and the absence of restraint. From *Rheingold* onward we have the complete, unfettered expression of Wagner's ideal so far as he had power to give it embodiment.

Now, from the principle that the musical aspect is to be entirely subordinated to the dramatic, there follow logically two applications of practice: first, the repression of the chorus; second, the fusion of aria and recitative into the homogeneous *aria parlante*. About the first there cannot be two opinions. In a drama quâ drama we want actors, not chorus. It is through the former that the action is developed, and the latter can only legitimately appear when some point in the plot requires for its presentation the united voice of a multitude. Thus it is appropriate in the first scene of *Coriolanus* or the funeral scene of *Julius Cæsar*, just as it is appropriate where Tristan and Isolde land at the palace of King Mark, or Siegfried brings his captive to submit to her baleful marriage with Gunther. But to expect Wagner to cut his work into symmetrical lengths because such was the practice of Mozart is as unreasonable as to expect that Shakespeare should interrupt his action with lyric hymns, like those of the Œdipus Coloneus or the Antigone. The second point, though equally necessary, requires rather more consideration, and it will therefore be worth while to examine at greater length the nature of Wagner's monologue and the reasons which led to its adoption. It is, in fact, the keystone of the whole arch, and with it the system of music-drama, as a possibility, may be said to stand or fall.

Readers of Peacock's delightful extravaganza *Maid Marian* will remember a scene in which the heroine, abetted by the friar, defies her father's prohibitions, and announces an intention of spending her day in the forest. After a few pages of altercation in good prose the dialogue suddenly frisks into the most incongruous lyrics and duets, introduced by such artless artifices as 'Matilda and the Friar then sang together,' and the like. In an extravaganza the absurdity is of little or no account, but we feel instinctively that it would be impossible in a serious novel. Fancy Balzac putting Madame Marneffe's confession into stanzas or Tolstoi rhyming the social theories of Levine. In the same way the distinction of recitative and aria is defencible enough in *Zauberflöte* because we do not regard *Zauberflöte* as a serious drama. If we did we should at once feel the conventionality of the musical stanza. In short, any truly dramatic work, whether a novel or a play, must exhibit some homogeneity of style, and must only introduce an extraneous lyric element in cases where song forms an incident in the plot, as for instance the dirge in *Cymbeline* or the serenade in the *Two Gentlemen of Verona*. Of course the distinction is sharpest in a novel, because of the vivid contrast between prose and lyric poetry; it is less sharp in a blank verse play, less still in a so-called 'lyric drama,' where the difference mainly turns on a question of stanza. But even in the lyric drama it exists. Wagner's *aria parlante* often approximates to 'set aria,' for instance, in the song where Siegfried bids farewell to Mime, or in the glorious love duets of Walküre and Tristan, but it never breaks the continuity of style by detached stanzas unless an actual lyric is demanded as a feature in the story. The above example bears much the same relation to an operatic aria of Mozart as the Queen Mab speech in *Romeo and Juliet* does to Shelley's 'Skylark.' Mercutio's words have something of the lyric spirit, but by no possibility could Shakespeare have clothed them in a lyric form.

Aria parlante therefore follows as a necessary conclusion from the essential conception of the music-drama. In its more intense moments, as has been already said, it approximates very closely to aria, differing mainly in that the stanza is not brought to completion, but is either left on an imperfect cadence, or more frequently threaded continuously into the general texture of the verse. There remains then to consider in what should consist the musical counterpart of this 'general texture.' It cannot be the old *recitativo secco*, for that has too little beauty and too little dramatic force to bear the weight of a whole scene. Still less can we abandon music altogether and have the words spoken: for if they are spoken without accompaniment we again lose all homogeneity of style, and if they are spoken with accompaniment we not only commit the same blunder but add to it a form of expression which is intolerable to any musical ear. The only alternative is to intensify the tones of ordinary speech until they reach the minimum of tonality which is compatible with their being embodied in musical notation and accompanied by the melodies of the orchestra. This is precisely what Wagner has done. In general his *aria parlante* is a marvellously devised system of musical equivalents for the actual tones and cadences of the speaking voice. It is the same idea as that of Peri, but it is carried out by a dramatist of far greater genius, who has inherited all the experience of the two most fruitful centuries in the history of Music.

Properly speaking, then, Wagner's *aria parlante* is an intermediary—a sort of relative mean—between speech and song, approaching now one extreme, now the other, according to the dramatic exigencies of the situation. Take for example Wotan's address to Brünnhilde in the third act of *Walküre*.[1] Here the feeling of the words is stern, grave, and sombre, and the vehicle employed is therefore the barest possible analogue of ordinary declamation. There is no melody, no key, hardly anything that can be called a system of tonality; the rise and fall of the voice is just capable of being represented in notes and no more. Contrast with this the love duet at the end of *Siegfried*, rich in melodic phrases and gorgeous with orchestral colouring. Both are entirely appropriate to the occasions by which they are evoked, and though one may give more pleasure than the other it would be hard to say which is the truer Art.

There is no need to repeat in Wagner's case the rather foolish sentence first uttered by Grétry about Mozart: 'that he placed his pedestal on the stage and his statue in the orchestra.' Nor can we agree with the more subtle though not less erroneous criticism of Amiel that Wagner's is 'music de-

[1] *Pianoforte Score*, p. 245.

personalised,' in which 'man is deposed from his superior position and the centre of gravity passes into the bâton of the conductor.' But in these music-dramas, although the action on the stage is the very core and centre of the whole work, yet the orchestra is the most important of the accessories, serving not only as a support to the voice, but as a continuous commentary on the development of the plot. This function it fulfils by means of the system of *leit-motif;* the second of the two main points of detail with which Wagner's name is essentially connected. By a *leit-motif* is meant a musical phrase, short, striking, and easily recognised, which expresses either some aspect in one of the characters or some incident in the story. It thus serves to explain motives, to illustrate actions, to elucidate situations in the play, and generally to render the whole dramatic movement clear and intelligible by suggesting its proper impulse and its proper associations. There is hardly any need to give instances of a device which may be found on almost every page of every drama, but a few examples may be cited at random. When Isolde gives as she thinks the poisoned cup to Tristan, the orchestra tells us, with Sophoclean irony, that the hero is drinking not death but passion. When Fafner kills Fasolt for possession of the magic gold we know from the *leit-motif* that the victor has, together with the treasure, won the fatal curse which Alberic laid upon it. Brünnhilde, sitting widowed amid her lonely rocks, turns for solace to the ring upon her finger, and there rises faintly, as in a dream, the memory of her lover and the far-off echo of his vows. Klingsor utters the words of enchantment that are to call Kundry to his service, and we hear her despairing cry come before she rises to obey the summons. Of course the device is not new; the idea may be traced in germ as far back as Monteverde's *Orfeo*, but none of Wagner's predecessors have employed it with such consummate ability or such conspicuous success. And not only does he turn it to the utmost dramatic use of which it is capable, he also makes of it a means of furthering the purely musical value and interest of his work. For, in the first place, the 'motives' are always ingenious, and, when occasion requires, exceedingly beautiful in addition; and, in the second, they are often developed with the same fulness of thematic treatment which marks the advance of Beethoven's sonata over that of Mozart and Haydn. The first scene of *Tristan*, for instance, opens with a 'free fantasia' on the theme of the sailor's song; the first scene of *Siegfried* is held together, musically speaking, by the rhythm of Mime's hammer; and numberless other examples could be adduced. It is impossible to deny that here, even apart from the play, we have a distinct artistic gain. The elaboration of phases with various forms of rhythm and harmony is one of the most important elements in musical expression, and by no Composer, except perhaps Beethoven and Brahms, has it been adopted with more entire mastery than by the supposed 'enemy of Music.'

Moritz Hauptmann in one of his letters quotes a current epigram to the effect that Wagner was 'a better poet than Beethoven, and a better Composer than Goethe.' The arrow falls a little wide of the mark, since in Wagner, as we have seen, the functions of poet and composer are merged into that of dramatist, and cannot legitimately be considered apart from one another. Tried by the standard of *Faust*, the verse is not great verse, though it in no way merits the disastrous fate which it has usually met at the hands of its English translators. Tried by the standard of *Fidelio*, the music is often lacking in purity and repression, though it does not deserve to be estimated by the inadequate performance of casual selections. But with all imperfections it is still sufficiently wonderful that a single man should have combined in his own person so many divers gifts and capacities. A performance at Bayreuth is a complex whole of which every element has been determined by the genius of one mind, and it is surely asking too much of human nature that we should expect absolute perfection in each individually. Further, Wagner's faults are essentially those of a pioneer: occasional roughness or exuberance, experiment in untried methods, bold adventure along an untrodden path. The direction is true and right, but there may sometimes be errors of judgment in the manner in which it is followed. Hence in examining the separate music-dramas we must remember that criticism itself has its necessary limitations. If, on the whole, they fail to impress us, we may conclude that Wagner's ideal is, at any rate for the present, unattainable. If, on the whole, they succeed in their object we may justly condone imperfections of detail and rest satisfied with Horace's verdict—

Ubi plura nitent in carmine non ego paucis
Offendar maculis.

Now in the *Ring* there is one serious defect which

may be noticed at the outset. Dramatically speaking, it is too long, the action sometimes drags heavily, the work contains passages which are redundant and superfluous. An audience which has already seen *Rheingold* and *Walküre* has no need of the elaborate dialogue between Mime and the Wanderer; Siegfried's account of his boyhood in the second act of *Götterdämmerung* tells us nothing that we did not know before, and merely delays the crisis which it is intended to prepare. No doubt these and similar passages are often of great musical beauty, but to advance that plea is to surrender Wagner's whole position. His work is to be judged not as music but as drama: and in our breathless nineteenth century one of the conditions of drama is prompt sequence of incident and unbroken continuity of plot. The cause of this redundancy may be found in the peculiar circumstances under which the libretto was written. It has already been stated that the book of *Götterdämmerung* was written before that of *Siegfried* was contemplated, and that *Rheingold* and *Walküre* were only added afterwards. Thus when the superfluities were conceived they were not superfluous; and we may readily understand that when the four poems were finished Wagner allowed them to remain untouched, remembering that in his favourite ideal of Greek tragedy the movement is not always rapid, and recalling the fondness of his countrymen for vastness of scale and thoroughness of treatment.

The story is admirably suited for dramatic purposes. It is strong, vigorous, tragic; its characters forcibly conceived and clearly contrasted; its climax sheer and overwhelming. If a weak point could be found it would be the facile *deus ex machinâ* of Gutrune's love potion, which not only introduces an artificial element where the event could easily have been caused by natural means but somewhat diverts the intense personal sympathy which we feel at the spectacle of Brünnhilde's wrongs. Yet even here is a fine irony in Siegfried's pledging the cup to his absent mistress, unwitting that its enchantment will make him forget her altogether. And in any case, apart from this single detail, the story is of high poetic value throughout, striking in incident, heroic in spirit, and centred round one of the noblest heroines in all Art. In these present days when anyone can gain credit for 'subtle analysis of a woman's soul,' if he possesses some dabbling acquaintance with its morbid anatomy, it is as bracing as a breath of sea air to turn to the figure of Brünnhilde. Wagner has left us many dreams of fair women: Senta the devoted, Elizabeth the saintly, Eva the bewitching, but above them all towers his warrior-maiden, constant, fearless, and invincible.

Of the four dramas *Rheingold* is undoubtedly the weakest, *Siegfried* undoubtedly the finest. The latter, indeed, is the strongest in construction and the most vigorous in workmanship of all Wagner's creations, and its gold is studded with such gems as the 'Schmiedelied,' the 'Waldwebung,' and the magnificent duet on which the 'Siegfried Idyll' was subsequently founded. *Walküre* is a very unequal work. It contains, perhaps, as many supremely fine numbers as *Siegfried* itself; but, except for the closing scene, the second act is rather tedious, and some of the other monologues stand in need of a judicious curtailment. *Götterdämmerung* gives a little the impression that its first two acts were written for the sake of the third. But the whole scene of Siegfried's death, the superb funeral march, in which *motif* after *motif* tells the story of the murdered hero, the blazing pyre upon which Brünnhilde dies amid the wreck of Walhalla, and the overthrow of the very gods themselves, these form a climax of epic grandeur, presented with a vividness of reality which no epic can ever attain. We may well concede the blemishes of the great Tetralogy. It is no table-land of monotonous uniformity: it is a mountain range in which, though the valleys sometimes sink to our common level, the peaks rise upward into a pure and cloudless heaven.

If *Siegfried* is the strongest of the music-dramas *Tristan* is the most musical. Here again we may notice some slowness of dramatic movement; Wagner is so anxious to express the full psychological significance of every scene that he sometimes unduly prolongs the situation until the orchestra has had its say; but for intensity of passion and charm of melodic phrase the work is unrivalled in the whole record of opera. From the fascinating theme with which the overture opens, a theme, by the way, which no man could have written who had not thrown off allegiance to our normal scale, there is scarcely a page which does not contain some imperious appeal to the artistic sense. The whole composition is as full of melody as *Romeo and Juliet.* It is all set in one mood—the love of man for woman; it leaves out of sight the sterner, graver aspects of life; its lesson may even be 'dangerous' for those weak souls who persist in regarding every work of Art as a guide to conduct. Yet even on the emotional side there is nothing poor or sensual or vulgar : it is passion if you will, but passion idealised—the love of Shelley and Shakespeare, not that of Davenant and Byron. And in its purely artistic aspect *Tristan* is simply irresistible. As we listen we forget to criticise ; we forget the conventions of the stage, the material surroundings, the lapse of time, everything except the delight of the clinging melodies and the warm, rich colouring of the orchestra.

There are two reasons why *Parsifal* has a claim to be considered Wagner's masterpiece. In the first place its emotional level is more sublime than that of its predecessors. The central conception of the *Ring* is strength, that of *Tristan* is passion, that of *Parsifal* is goodness, and it would require some audacity of paradox to deny that the first two only acquire their real value when they are elements in the last. Parsifal, through sheer purity and innocence of heart, triumphs in that noblest of all victories which turns an enemy into a disciple. Kundry, enslaved to the vile service of the enchanter, is ransomed and redeemed by the man whose ruin she was forced to attempt. A story of such spiritual beauty, touched and glorified with the mystic halo of religion, may well be ranked among the few immortalities of Art. Its significance, at any rate, raises it above the aim of all other operatic work. In the second place, it is the most homogeneous of the music-dramas : that in which the different elements are most completely fused into unity. 'Taken by itself,' says Dr Parry, 'the music is not so powerful nor so rich as in others of Wagner's work ; and the drama, read by itself, is not so striking, nor are the characters so distinct as in *Tristan* or the *Nibelung* series. But all the elements of Art help one another. The music throws light upon the drama and intensifies it, and the situations and actions on the stage react upon the music and give it a significance which is otherwise overlooked.'[1] In other words, it is the most complete embodiment of Wagner's dramatic theory, and so may be regarded as in a sense the climax of his work. No doubt much of its tremendous impressiveness is due to its choice of subject; but it should be added that the treatment is on the whole worthy and adequate. The music may be less rich than that of *Tristan*, but it is more dignified and restrained. The characters may be less distinct than those of *Siegfried*, but they are more significant and suggestive. Perhaps its highest praise is that on first hearing we leave the theatre with no clear discrimination of detail—overwhelmed with a great experience which we cannot analyse. It is only afterwards that we begin to notice the beauty of the overture, the fascination of the garden scene, and the stately march movement which ushers in the Grail.

Meistersinger has purposely been kept to the end, since, among Wagner's artistic products, it stands on a special footing of its own. It may be said to belong to both his creative periods, for the first sketches were written in 1845, about the time of *Lohengrin*, and the work was finished twenty-two years later, between the composition of *Tristan* and the completion of *Siegfried*. Again, there are certain details of workmanship which are implied in its character as a comedy. Just as humorous verse makes a point of ingenious stanzas, of fantastic

[1] *Studies of the Great Composers*, p. 353.

metres, and of burlesque rhymes, so a comic opera will naturally permit itself to lay more stress on musical forms and musical devices. Hence *Meistersinger* is full of more or less detachable melodies: Walther's three songs, Hans Sach's ballad, Beckmesser's absurd serenade, and the like. They do not in the least interfere with the continuity of the story, but a comic story allows more room for them than a tragic. The more conventional form of the music is in no sense a recantation: it is entirely consistent with Wagner's principles, and forms the natural outcome of his plot. But the drama is too well known and too popular to need any defence. From first to last it is a thoroughly genial work, with plenty of sound comedy, plenty of good-humoured satire, plenty of tune, and an astonishing display of recondite rhythm and ingenious polyphony.

If the foregoing considerations are accepted there will be no great difficulty in determining Wagner's place in the history of Art. He no more comes into competition with other Composers than with other dramatists. He no more professes to supersede Mozart than to supersede Shakespeare. He is the virtual creator of a new form, in which his only predecessors are too remote to afford him more than the outlined suggestion of an ideal. This view of the case receives additional testimony from his criticisms. Nothing can be further from the truth than to represent him as a mere iconoclast, laying about the musical Pantheon with an undiscriminating sledge-hammer. Of Palestrina, of Bach, of Mozart, of Weber, and, above all, of Beethoven he speaks with the highest admiration and reverence; Berlioz he discusses with great sympathy and insight;[1] of Mendelssohn he says, 'he was a landscape painter of the first order.' With Schubert and Schumann he was a little less in touch, and Meyerbeer, of course, he detested. But in whatever estimation we hold his judgment we must at least admit that he was glad to recognise good work when he saw it, and that he often saw it in systems which were entirely alien to his own. No doubt he was not in all respects a great critic, but he was great enough to acknowledge that Art admits fundamental differences of method, and that the artist's work must be tested in reference to the method which he adopts.

If he be tried by that law there is little doubt of the verdict. We may not regard his work as final—to do so would be to despair of human progress—but we shall assuredly admit that his ideal is a true and valuable contribution to the Art of the world, and that his approximations to it in practice show a continuous and steady advance. It is inconceivable that opera should ever return to the untenable position from which it has been dislodged. Whatever be the fate of his music-dramas, the theory of Art which animated him will also animate his successors. Whether his work has entered or not into the promised land, it has at least led us out of the house of bondage.

It is neither likely nor advisable that he should exercise any permanent influence on Composers of other musical forms. The symphony, the quartett, and the sonata are better without him, for they were not of his world. But if opera is to be something more than an idle amusement, if it is to em-

[1] See the essay printed in M. Camille Benoit's *Wagner*, pp. 187-200.

body a national character and to fulfil a national aspiration, if, in one word, it is to take rank as serious Art, then in the whole range of its record will be found no greater name than that of Wagner. He has clothed it with new life, he has taught it to deliver a new message, and the echoes of his voice will last, not only in his own work but in that of the days to come.

INDEX

A

A Travers Chants, 55, 138.
Abt Vogler, 10.
Académie de Musique, 77, 85, 252.
Addison, 67, 229, 237.
Agnes von Hohenstaufen, 266.
Ah ! che la morte, 47.
Alceste, 78, 300.
Allgemeine Musikalische Zeitung, 161.
L'Allegro, 48.
Ambros, 112.
Amiel, 316.
Amusat, 77.
Ancient Mariner, 30.
Andersen, Hans, 32.
Andrea del Sarto, 166.
Anti-Jacobin, 182.
Arabeske, 169.
Arbuthnot, 162.
Architecture, relation to music, 8.
Aristotle, 8, 301.
Arnal, 102, 136.
Arnold, Matthew, 53.
Art, popular basis of, 4 ; aim, 6 ; classical and romantic, 17-18.
Artôt, 131.
Arts, Representative, distinguished from Music, 6-12 (see 199-201).
Athalie, 87.
Athenæum, 58.
Auber, 247, 252, 254.
Ausonius, 25.
Austria, Berlioz's tour in, 110-112.

B

Bach, Schumann influenced by, 155-6, 210-211.
Bach, illustrations from, 19, 27, 49, 67.
Baillot, 254.
Balfe, 115, 182.
Banville, 19, 304, 305.
Barbara Allen, 43.
Barbier, 254.
Bargiel, 195.
Bayreuth, 151, 157 ; Wagner at, 292, 273, 295.

Bayreuther Blätter, 295.
Béatrice et Bénédict, 51, 122.
Beethoven, criticised in the 'Quarterly Review and Magazine,' 57-58 ; corrected by editors and critics, 85 ; symphonies in Paris, 87-8, 109 ; influence on Berlioz, 126 ; orchestration, 141 ; influence on Schumann, 210 ; method contrasted with Schumann's, 212, 213-215 ; influence on Wagner, 242, 243, 245, 251, 257.
Beethoven, eine Pilgerfahrt zu, 259, 301.
Beethoven (Wagner's), 291.
Beethoven, illustrations from, 12, 13, 19, 20, 22, 27-29, 34, 37, 40, 41, 43, 48, 51, 62, 127, 131, 307, 309, 317.
Bellini, Giovanni, 48, 306.
Bellini, Vincenzo, 98, 247, 251.
Bennett, Sterndale, 44, 65, 199, 228.
Benvenuto, Cellini, 241, 306.
Benvenuto Cellini (Berlioz's), 103, 105, 106, 118.
Beranger, 103, 254.
Beriot, De, 112.
Berlin, 108, 112, 178, 186, 228, 250, 261, 268.
Berlioz (Hector), birth and early life, 73-74 ; first compositions, 75 ; sent to the medical school at Paris, 77 ; determines on a musical career, 78 ; studies with Lesueur, 79 ; writes a mass for St Roch, 80 ; fails in the Conservatoire examination, 81 ; recalled by Dr Berlioz, 81 ; thrown on his own resources, 83 ; Prix de Rome, first failure, 84 ; second, 86 ; sees Miss Smithson at the Odéon, 87 ; begins journalism, 88 ; Prix de Rome, second prize, 88 ; Symphonie Fantastique and Tempest Fantasie, 89 ; Prix de Rome not awarded, 90 ; meets Mdlle. Mooke, 91 ; wins the Prix de Rome, 72, 92 ; first performance of Symphonie Fantastique, 92 ; meets Mendelssohn, 94 ; King Lear Overture, 96 ; Lélio and the Rob Roy Overture, 97 ; La Captive, 98 ; marries Miss Smithson, 99 ; Paganini and the Childe Harold Symphony, 100-101 ; birth of Louis Berlioz, 102 ; journalism and controversy, 102-103 ; Benvenuto Cellini, 103 ; Requiem, 104 ; applies for Pro-

fessorship at Conservatoire, 104; failure of Benvenuto Cellini, 105; Paganini gives him 20,000 francs for the Childe Harold Symphony, 106; leaves Paris, 107; Mdlle. Recio, 107; tour in Germany, 108; Freischütz, 109; tour in Austria, 110-112; Damnation de Faust, 112; tour in Russia, 112-114; Roqueplan and the Opera. 114; visits to England, 115-116; death of Dr Berlioz, 116; Treatise on Instrumentation, 117; Chœur des Bergers, 117; death of his wife, 119; marries Mdlle. Recio, 119; Te Deum, 120; elected into the Academy, 120; made librarian of the Conservatoire. 120; Les Troyens, 121-122; Béatrice et Bénédict, 122; last Russian visit, 122; death, 123.
Berlioz as a composer. Theory of Composition, 125; imaginative power, 125-128; treatment of terror, 128; of love, 129; humour, 130; spectacular music, 131; 'programme music,' 131-136; melody, 137-8; harmony, 139; form, 140; orchestration, 141-143; conclusion, 143.
Berlioz as a critic, 144-146, 156, 177.
Berlioz and Schumann, 149, 156, 163, 177, 179.
Berlioz and Wagner, 121, 141, 283-284, 286.
Berlioz, illustrations from, 5, 21, 33, 51, 55, 56, 62, 307.
Berlioz (Dr Louis), 73, 75, 76, 78, 81, 83, 93, 114, 116.
Bernard, 109.
Bertin, 106.
Berton, 88.
Beverley, 79, 80.
Bienaimé, 105.
Birmingham Festival, 55.
Bishop, Sir H., 182.
Blake, 4, 9, 22.
Bloc, 87.
Blumenstück, 169, 218.
Böhme, 195, 215.
Bohemia, 176, 268.
Boieldieu, 90, 91.
Botticelli, 241.
Boulogne, 253.
Bourget, 133.
Brahms and Schumann, 196-197.
Brahms, illustrations from, 16, 27, 28, 29. 34, 56, 59, 63, 67, 127, 129, 175, 217, 219, 222, 304, 317.
Brazil, Emperor of, 285.
Brendel, Dr, 277.
Breslau, 112, 167.
Browning, 18, 25.
Bruschini, I due, 109.
Brussells, Berlioz's visit to, 107.
Bülow, Von, 278; Madame. 289, 291.
Byron, 72, 150, 152, 183, 224.

C

C Major Symphony (Schubert's), 169-171.
Calderon, 308.
Callot, 207.
Candide, 49.
Captive. La, 98, 130, 137.
Caran d'Ache, 53.
Caricature, La, 102.
Carlyle, 259.
Carnaval, 164. 214.
Carnaval Romain, 107, 113, 130, 141.
Carus, Dr, 154.
Carvalho, 120, 285, 287.
Cassel, 265, 280.
Castilblaize, 85, 109.
Catel, 75, 91.
Cham, 122, 286.
Cherubini, 78, 81, 87-8, 91, 105.
Chœur des Bergers, 117, 137.
Chœur des Ombres, 138.
Chopin, Berlioz and, 145; Schumann and, 156, 159, 162, 203, 228.
Chopin, illustrations from, 21, 26, 28 41, 43, 129, 132.
Choral Symphony, 98, 242, 268.
Chorley, 58. 59, 180, 281.
Cinq Mars, 71.
'Classical' music, 9, 14, 18, 38, 41.
Cleon (Browning's), 303.
Coleridge, 28, 30, 239.
Cologne, 165, 191, 192.
Colombus Overture, 251, 259.
Comte, 275.
Conservatoire, Leipsic, 177, 190; Paris, 56, 78, 80, 87, 92, 101, 104, 106, 118, 120, 159; Vienna, 190.
Corneille, 87, 126.
Corsair (Berlioz's), 141, 143; Byron's, 183.
Costa, 280. 281.
Côte St André, La, 73. 80, 81, 93, 114, 116.
Counterpoint, 12; and Polyphony, 19-20; Berlioz's, 139-140.
Cour d'Orleans, George Sand's salon, 255.
Creation, 201.
Cromwell, Victor Hugo's, 71, 300.
Cuzzoni, 238.

D

Dafne, 237.
Damnation de Faust, 89, 112, 116, 125, 127-9, 137, 138, 140, 143.
Damrémont, 104.
Danaïdes (Salieri's), 77.
Dannreuther, Mr, 245, 274.
Dante, 28, 48.
David, 177, 179.
Davidsbund, 163, 203.
Davidsbündlertänze, 206, 217.
Davidson, 281.
De Profundis, 67.
Deak, 111.
Débats, 86, 102, 106, 259, 273.
Delaroche, 255.
Diabelli variations, 164, 219.
Dichterliebe, 173.
Dietrich, 195.

Dietsch, 258, 259, 285.
Donizetti, 33, 110, 111, 115, 256.
Donna Serpente, 247.
Dorn, 159, 160, 163, 205, 243, 245, 251, 252.
Dostoieffsky, 72.
Dresden, Berlioz's visit to, 108, 284; Weber at, 151; Schumann at, 184, 190; Wagner at, 185, 190, 240-242, 263-273.
Dresdener Abendzeitung, 259.
Drouet, 76.
Duc, 117.
Ducré, Pierre, 117.
Dumas, 72, 86, 254.
Dumersan, 255.
Duponchel, 104.
Duprez, 105.
Düsseldorf, Schumann director at, 191-195.
Dvorák, illustrations from, 21, 25, 55, 62, 67 141 175, 304.

E

EDDAS, 278.
Egmont, 242.
Eichendorf, 202.
Elégie (Berlioz's), 126, 129.
Elégie impromptu, 85.
Eliot, George, 31.
Empress Eudocia, 25.
Enfance du Christ, 117, 125, 128, 137, 139.
England, Berlioz's visits to, 115, 118; Wagner's first visit to, 280-283; second, 293-294.
English music, decadence, 65-66; present outlook, 66-68; as estimated by Berlioz, 116; in the time of Schumann, 182.
English musical criticism, 55-61.
English Symphony, 67.
Erba, 30.
Erinnerung, 31, 187.
Erlkönig, 145.
Eroica, 27, 43, 58.
Estelle, 75, 79, 80.
Études Symphoniques, 164, 166, 217, 219.
Euryanthe, 201, 225.
Euridice, 237.
Eusebius, 163, 164, 171.

F

FANTASIESTÜCKE, 205.
Faschingsschwank aus Wien, 169. 175.
Faust, 88, 183, 187, 225.
Faust (Berlioz's) (See Damnation de Faust.)
Faust overture. 257-8, 308.
Favorita, La, 111, 256.
Feen, Die, 247, 248, 308.
Felix Meritis, 162, 165.
Ferrand, 88, 103, 115, 118, 133.
Fétis (elder), 14, 15, 55, 72, 85, 101, 117.
Fétis (younger), 102.

Feuillets d'Album, 137.
Fidelio, 51, 145, 183, 230, 239.
Figaro, 97.
Fink, 161.
Fischer, 263.
Fitness, Principle of, general statement, 48; sacred and secular, 48-9; Rossini's Stabat Mater, 49; theatrical church music, 51; Parsifal, 52; further distinctions, 52-3.
Flegeljahre, 162, 203.
Florence, 65, 95.
Florestan, 162, 163, 164, 171, 203, 205, 207, 229.
Florian, 75, 79.
Flying Dutchman, the, 258, 259, 260, 261, 264, 265, 290, 309, 310.
France, 71, 98, 110, 112, 120, 122, 125, 149, 150, 163, 165, 180, 183.
Frankfort, 108, 158, 271.
Frankh, 73.
Franz, 180.
Frauenliebe, 173.
Frauenlob, 289.
Freigedank, K., 275.
Fricken, Ernestine von, 166.
Frühlingsnacht, 220.

G

GADE, 177.
Galilei Vincenzio, 255.
Gautier, 146.
Gay-Lussac, 77.
Gazette Musicale, 102, 259.
Genoveva, 187, 188, 189, 191, 224.
Gérard, 85, 89, 100.
Géricault, 71.
Germany, 64, 66, 84, 108, 149, 150, 154, 162, 165, 178, 181, 183, 190, 211.
Gerono, 79.
Geyer, 240, 241.
Gluck, influence on Berlioz, 75, 77-79; on Schumann, 211; position in the history of Opera, 238, 302, 304, 309.
Gluck, illustrations from, 12, 19, 85, 117, 125, 139, 145.
Goethe, 22, 88, 89, 112, 153, 183, 187, 193, 202, 229, 305, 317.
Götterdämmerung, 270, 278, 319, 320, 321.
Goldoni, 238, 247.
Golo, 187, 224.
Gounod, 29, 114, 123.
Gozzi, 247.
Grand-Cartaret, M., 286.
Grétry, 85, 315.
Grieg, 67.
Grillparzer, 160.
Grisar, 114.
Grotesques de la Musique, 110, 144.

H

HABENECK, 85, 104, 105, 108.
Hainberger, 272.

Härtel, 179, 190.
Halévy, 114, 254, 256, 276.
Hallé, Sir Charles, 143.
Hamburg, 108, 176, 190, 196.
Handel, illustrations from, 16, 19, 28, 30, 31, 33, 35, 73, 85, 145, 211, 217.
Hanover, 197.
Hardy, 86.
Harmonicon, the, 57.
Harold en Italie, 106, 126, 127, 128, 135, 137, 138, 139, 140, 143, 179.
Haslinger, 85.
Hasse, 126, 237.
Hauptmann Moritz, 317.
Haydn, illustrations from, 13, 15, 58, 73, 127, 138, 155, 179, 199, 210, 212, 217, 219, 228.
Hebbel, 186, 206.
Hebrides, 164.
Heidelberg, 156, 157, 158, 202.
Heine, 18, 91, 97, 108, 128, 135, 150, 153, 157, 164, 173, 179, 193, 202, 204, 217, 220, 255.
Heller, 108.
Henselt, 151.
Hermann and Dorothea, 193.
Hernani, 71.
Hesperus, 154.
Hiller, 91, 156, 190, 191.
Hochzeit, Die, 245.
Hoffmann, 206-208, 243.
Holland, 197.
Homer, 25.
Horace, 32. 43, 76, 318.
Hottin, 78.
Hueffer. Dr. 227.
Hugo, Victor, 18, 71, 98. 291.
Huguenots, Les, 229, 230.
Hullah, 40, 59.
Humoreske, 169, 218.
Hymne à la France, 130.

I

ILIAD, 202.
Inferno, 48, 127.
Invitation à la Valse, 109, 142.
Iphigénie en Aulide, 268.
Iphigénie en Tauride, 115, 145.
Israel in Egypt, 9, 30·31, 193.
Italian Symphony, 165.
Italy, Berlioz in, 94-98; Schumann's visit, 157; Wagner in, 280.

J

JESSONDA, 183.
Joachim, 191, 196. 197.
Jockey-Club (Paris), 287.
Johnson, Dr, 244.
Joli, 255.
Jonson, Ben, 128.
Jubilee Cantata, 50.
Judas Maccabæus, 31.
Judenthum in der Musik, Das, 253, 275-278.
Judith, 34, 60.
Juive, La, 278.
Julius Cæsar Overture, 192.
Jullien, 115, 252.

K

KAHLERT, 167.
Kant, 47, 193.
Kapitulation, Eine, 291.
Keats, 18, 25, 31, 56.
Keferstein, 171.
Kemble, Charles, 86.
Kerl, 30.
Kinderscenen, 169.
King Arthur, 65.
King's Son, the, 192.
King Lear Overture, 33, 96, 138, 141, 143.
Klopstock, 153.
Knorr, Julius, 161.
König, 251.
Königsberg, 165, 193; Wagner at, 250-251.
Königswart, 176.
Kossmaly, 176, 211.
Krebs, 190.
Kreischa, 190.
Kreisleriana, 169, 206-209, 218.
Kreuzer, 85, 88, 91.
Krüger, 178. 184.
Kunst und die Revolution, die, 273, 300.
Kunst und Religion, über. 296.
Kunstwerk der Zukumft, das, 300, 301.
Kuntzsch, 151, 184.

L

LA FONTAINE, 247.
Labour, principle of, general statement, 32-3; examples of carelessness, 33; contrasts, 34; true and false simplicity, 34-6.
La ci darem, 15, 28.
Lacnith, 85.
Lamentations (Palestrina), 49.
Larochefoucault, 87.
Laube, 243, 244. 247, 248, 251, 265.
Leipsic, Berlioz at, 108, 177; Schumann at, 153-6, 158-183, 188, 194; Mendelssohn at, 108, 164-166, 169, 174; Wagner at, 160, 240, 242-246.
Leipsic, 177, 190, 191, 192, 196, 207. 228.
Lélio, 97, 101, 111, 138.
Lenore (Raff's), 140.
Lesueur, 79. 80, 81, 88, 244.
Lessing, 53, 54.
Letourneur, 86.
Liebesfrühling, 173.
Liebesmahl der Apostel, das, 265.
Liebesverbot, Das, 248, 249-250, 253 255-256, 308.
Lieder ohne Wörte, 187.
Lippo Lippi, Fra, 46.
Liston, 86.
Liszt, 21, 92, 100, 104, 108, 112, 201, 229, 255, 258, 272-275.
Litanei, 220.

Index

Literary Gazette, 56.
Lohengrin, 59, 143, 268, 270, 274, 288, 309, 311.
London, 181, 253; Wagner in, 280-283, 293.
Louis XIV., 18, 34, 237.
Louis Philippe, 252.
Louis II., 288, 291.
Louvre, 72.
Lubbert, 89.
Lucerne, 285.
Lucia di Lammermoor, 115.
Luck of Edenhall, 195.
Lutèce, 128.
Lüttichau, Von, 259, 267, 269.
Lwoff, 112, 145.

M

MAGDEBURG, Wagner at, 249-251.
Malibran, 182.
Manfred, 189, 194, 215, 222, 225.
Manfred von Hohenstaufen, 260.
Marenzio, 67.
Marschner, 154, 239.
Marx, 89.
Masaniello, 110, 247.
Massart, Mdme., 121.
Masson, 79.
Matthäus-Passion, 49.
Meistersinger, 27, 239, 288, 311, 323-324.
Menace des Francs, 130.
Mendelssohn, relation to Berlioz, 94, 108; to Schumann, 162, 164, 174-182, 185, 211, 228; to Wagner, 108, 245, 246, 276, 325.
Mendelssohn, illustrations from, 16, 26, 29, 31, 75, 145, 303.
Messiah, the, 27, 31, 127, 217.
Metastasio, 238.
Metternich, Prince, 111, 176; Princess, 286.
Meudon, 259.
Meyerbeer, 59, 122, 229, 230, 252, 253, 255, 258, 276-278, 325.
Milton, 28, 48, 67, 153.
Missa Papæ Marcelli, 127.
Missolonghi, 72.
Molière, 241.
Monde Dramatique, 102.
Montégut, 33.
Monteverde, 12, 19, 317.
Montgomery, 135.
Mooke, Mdlle., 91, 95.
Moore, 98, 226.
Morlacchi, 185, 264.
Morley, 67.
Moscheles, 152, 177, 181.
Moscow, 113.
Moré in Egitto, 110.
Mozart, illustrations from, 15, 27, 29, 43, 51, 85, 90, 126, 142, 155, 156, 160, 163, 183, 199, 204, 209, 210, 215, 217, 219, 222, 224, 228, 239, 245, 307, 312, 315, 324.
Müller, 242.
Munich, 157, 248, 288, 289.
Music, popular basis of, 4-6; distinguished from representative arts, 6-12; classical and romantic, 9, 19; reason for false taste, 36-8; sensuous and spiritual aspects, 45-7.
Musical criticism, difficulty, 10; standpoints, 13; want of method, 53; English, 57-61; suggestions, 61-64; outline, 124.
Musical Form, Berlioz's, 140; Schumann's, 215-7.
Musical Judgment, principles of, general statement, 13, 17, 21; vitality, 22-32; labour, 32-36; proportion, 39-47; fitness, 48-53.
'Musical Standard,' 60.
'Musical Times,' 60.
'Musical World,' 282.
Musico-Poetical Club, 208.
Musset, 129, 202, 254.
Myrthen, 173.
Mystères d'Isis, 85.

N

NACHTLIED, 189.
Nachtmusik (Mozart's), 43.
Nägeli, 85.
Napoleon III., 103, 284, 286.
Nerval Gérard, 112.
Neue Zeitschrift, 108, 161-162, 165, 169, 170, 177, 181, 182, 183, 196, 203, 207, 227, 250, 259, 275, 277.
Nibelungenlied, 270, 278.
Nice, 96, 101.
Nice, la tour de, 109.
Nicolai, 111.
Nicolaischule, 242.
Niederrheinische Musikfeste, 191.
Nonne Sanglante, 108, 114.
Nottebohm, 190.
Nourrit, 254.
Noveletten, 168, 206, 214, 218.
Nuits d'Eté, 138.

O

OBERON, 145.
Odéon, 85, 86.
Odyssey, 202, 204, 241.
Offenbach, 53.
Old Philharmonic, 280, 281.
Oldenburg, Prince of, 181.
Olympic, 266.
Onslow, 145.
Oper und Drama, 248, 253, 275, 300, 301.
Opera, sketch of, before Wagner, 235-239.
Opera in England, 85, 115, 182.
Opera in France, 85, 109, 120-122, 237, 238.
Opera in Germany, 182, 237-239, 249.
Opera in Italy, 97, 235-7.
(*See* Berlioz, Schumann, Wagner.)
Opéra Comique, 103.
Ophelia, 86, 99, 119.
Orchestration, Berlioz's, 83, 141-143; Schumann's, 222.
Orestes, 238.
Orfeo, 75, 77, 145, 239.
Orpheus (Death of), 84, 87.

P

Paer, 88.
Paganini, 98, 100, 101, 106, 158.
Painting, in relation to music, 6, 7, 8, 18, 166.
Paisiello, 237.
Palermo, 295.
Palestrina, 49, 124, 145, 201, 228, 235, 307.
Papillons, 157, 160, 203, 204, 214, 218.
Paradise and the Peri, 178-180, 182, 183, 197, 212.
Paris, Berlioz at, 71, 77, 82-91, 95, 98, 101, 106-108, 114, 116-118, 120, 123, 145, 159; Wagner at, 254-262, 273, 285-287.
Parry Dr, 34, 294.
Parsifal, 52, 67, 226, 260, 267, 274, 294-295, 306, 307, 309, 322-323.
Pastoral Symphony, 9, 58, 131.
Pathétique, 41, 48, 100, 213.
Peacock, 313.
Pergolesi, 237.
Peri, 235, 236, 237, 239, 304, 307.
Pesth, 111.
Petrarch, 202.
Pierson, 66.
Pilgrimage of the Rose, 192, 194, 226.
Pillet, 109, 255, 258, 285.
Planer Wilhelmina, 251.
Plato, 7, 23, 39, 197, 290.
Pleyel, 76.
Poetry, relation to music, 6, 8, 9, 28.
Pohl, Dr, 192, 193, 194.
Pons, 80, 82, 83.
Praeger, 280, 283, 289.
Prague, 112, 186, 246.
Principles of musical judgment. (*See* Musical Judgment).
'Programme music,' 131-136. (*See* 204-210).
Prometheus, 60, 179.
Proportion, principle of, general statement, 39-40; illustration from Sonata, 40; examples, 41; law of climax, 42; examples, 43; recurrent phrases, 44-5; sensuous and spiritual aspects of music, 45-7.
Prussia, 112, 114.
Punch, 285.
Purcell, 65, 67.

Q

Quarterly Review, 56.
Quarterly Review and Magazine, 57, 58.

R

Racine, 72, 150, 302, 306, 308.
Raff, 140.
Rakoczky, 5, 111, 142.
Rameau, 19, 75.
Raro, 163, 203.
Rasoumoffsky Quartettes, 27, 216.
Recio, Mdlle., 107, 119.

Redemption, 29.
Reinich, 186.
Reissiger, 263, 264.
Rénovateur, 102.
Requiem (Mozart's), 27; Dvorák's, 55; Berlioz's, 104, 126, 128, 130, 142, 143; Schumann's, 194, 217.
Requiem for Mignon, 189, 226.
Rheingold, 132, 279, 280, 311, 312, 319, 320.
Richter, Dr Hans, 293.
Richter, Jean Paul, 150, 153, 154, 161, 170, 202, 203, 207, 211.
Rienzi, 252, 253, 258, 260-261, 263, 265, 266, 268, 278, 309, 310.
Rietz, 188, 189, 191.
Riga, Wagner at, 252.
Ring, The, 288, 318.
Ringelhardt, 248, 250.
Rinuccini, 235, 236.
Rio, 285.
Rob Roy, 98.
Robin des Bois, 85, 109.
Rockstro, Mr, 239.
Roeckel, August, 269-272, 291; Edward, 272.
Roger, 254.
'Romantic' ideal in music, general statement, 17-19; illustrated by Berlioz, 125-131; discussion of, 200-210.
Romantic movement in literature, 18-19, 71, 149-151.
Romberg, 112, 181.
Rome, 84, 96, 127.
Romeo, 88, 97, 248, 314.
Romeo and Juliet Symphony, 106, 116, 129, 133, 137, 143, 179, 254.
Roqueplan, 114.
Rosamund (Addison's), 237.
Rosen, 154, 156, 202.
Rossetti, 204.
Rossini, illustrations from, 33, 49, 59, 85, 106, 109, 145, 229, 255, 276.
Rousseau, 275.
Rubini, 252.
Rubinstein, Joseph, 55.
Rudel, 153, 158.
Rückert, 173, 189, 202.
Rule Britannia Overture, 251.
Ruskin, 25.
Russia, 72, 112, 116, 180.

S

Sacred Music, 48-52, 226.
Sainte Beuve, 53-54.
Sainton, 280, 283.
Salieri, 77.
Sand, George, 137. (*See* 255).
Sardanapalus, 91, 92, 94.
Sartor Resartus, 259.
Saurin, 79.
Saxony, 71, 190, 191, 261, 270, 281.
Scarlatti, A., 236.
Scarlatti, D., 19.
Scheveningen, 195.
Schicksalslied, 127.

Schiller, 153.
Schlegel, A., 150.
Schlesinger, 255, 259.
Schnabel, Dr, 181.
Schneeberg, 156, 160, 181.
Schöne Wiege, 174, 220.
Schönefeld, 172.
Schopenhauer, 6, 9.
Schröder, Devrient, Mdlle., 248, 261, 263, 265, 266.
Schubert and Schumann, 156, 169, 205, 217, 220.
Schubert, illustrations from, 22, 33, 34, 37, 40, 41, 48, 51, 62, 85, 94, 132, 137, 145, 154, 160, 162, 164, 170, 176, 199, 211, 212, 215, 221, 227.
Schumann (Robert), birth, 150; early days, 151; enters the Zwickau Gymnasium, 152; Leipsic University, 153; influence of Richter, 153-4; takes lessons from Wieck, 154-5; Clara Wieck, 155; influence of J. S. Bach, 155-6; early compositions, 156; goes to Heidelberg, 156; Abegg Variations and Papillors, 157; travels in Italy, 157; decides on a musical career, 158; accident to his hand, 159; studies composition with Dorn, 159-160; compositions of 1833, 160; the Neue Zeitschrift, 161-163; the Davidsbund, 163; the Etudes Symphoniques, 164; meets Mendelssohn, 165; Ernestine von Fricken, 166; betrothal to Clara Wieck, 167; further pianoforte compositions, 168; moves to Vienna, 169; Schubert's C Major Symphony, 169-171; doctor's degree, 171; marriage, 172; songs, 173; symphonies, 174; chamber music, 175; preparations for Vienna, 176; the Leipsic conservatorium, 177; reconciliation with Wieck, 178; Paradise and the Peri, 178-9; visit to Russia, 179-180; German Opera, 182-3; first attack of illness, 183; moves to Dresden, 184; Symphony in C Major, 184; Wagner, 185-6; Genoveva, 186-7; death of Mendelssohn, 187; Faust's Salvation, 187-8; production of Genoveva, 189; compositions of 1849, 189; applies for directorship at Dresden, 190; obtains that at Dusseldorf, 191; further attacks of illness, 192; compositions at Dusseldorf, 192-3; 'Schumann week' at Leipsic, 194; last compositions, 194-5; Brahms, 196; tour in Holland, 197; last illness, 197; death, 198.
Schumann as composer, the poetic ideal, 201-210; influence of Bach, 210-211; method of composition, 212; melody, 213-5; form, 215-7; revision, 217; pianoforte works, 217-9; songs, 220; orchestral works, 220-3; chamber music, 223-4; dramatic works, 224-6; cantatas, 226; Mass and Requiem, 227.
Schumann as critic, 'subjectivity,' 227-8; breadth of range, 228; discrimination, 229; Meyerbeer, 229-30; critical method, 230.

Schumann and Beethoven contrasted, 212, 213-215, 217.
Schumann and Berlioz, 149, 156, 163, 177, 179.
Schumann and Mendelssohn, 165, 177, 185, 187, 211, 228.
Schumann and Schubert, 156, 169, 205, 217, 220.
Schumann and Wagner, 185, 190, 250.
Schumann, illustrations from, 16, 19, 21, 25, 26, 27, 28, 29, 31, 34, 45, 55, 58, 62, 63, 67, 73, 129.
Schumann, August, 150-152.
Schumann, Madame, 177-180. (See Wieck, Clara.)
Schunke, 161, 215.
Scott, Walter, 85, 150, 202.
Scribe, 114, 251.
Scudo, 118.
Sculpture, relation to music, 6-8, 18.
Semper, 290.
Senesino, 238.
Shakespeare, 6, 9, 19, 86, 87, 89, 90, 111, 150, 171, 192, 202, 228, 241, 242, 248, 302, 306, 312, 314, 324.
Shelley, 9, 18, 22, 56, 72, 231, 314.
Siegfried, 59, 132, 247, 267, 278-280, 284, 307, 314, 315, 319-325.
Siegfried Idyll, 292, 307, 308.
Simonin de Sire, 203.
Smart, Sir George, 251.
Smithson, Miss, 86, 87, 98, 99.
Socrates, 22, 23.
Soirées d'Orchestre, 144.
Songs, popular, 5, 26, 35; narrative, 37; Berlioz's, 137-8; Schumann's 173, 228.
Spanisches Liederspiel, 189.
Spectator, 67.
Spenser, 75.
Spezia, 280.
Spohr, 28, 46, 145, 182, 188, 229, 265, 280.
Spontini, 126, 265, 266.
Stabat Mater (Rossini's), 49.
Stanford, Dr. 35.
Staudigl, 111.
Stevenson, Mr, 49.
Stern, Daniel, 255.
Sterne, 153.
Strauss, 26, 111.
Süddeutsche Presse, 291.
Sullivan, Sir Arthur, 178.
Sumer is i-cumen in, 65.
'Sunday Times,' 282.
Swift, 195.
Symphonie Funèbre et Triomphale, 107, 123.
Symphonie Fantastique, 75, 76, 89, 92, 94, 97, 102, 127, 129, 133, 135, 137, 140, 143, 165, 215, 217, 229.

T

TALLIS, 65.
Tannhäuser, 14, 15, 59, 108, 121, 122, 185, 186, 229, 260, 261, 263, 265-267, 272, 275, 281, 283, 284, 286, 287, 309

Tasso, 88, 195.
Tausch, 195.
Te Deum (Berlioz's), 120, 123, 137, 142, 143.
Tempest, 89, 142.
Tennyson, 28.
Teplitz, 263, 288.
Thackeray, 34, 229.
Thalberg, 254.
Théâtre de la Renaissance, 255, 256.
Théâtre de Nouveautés, 83, 89.
Théâtre Italien, 85, 89.
Thénaud, 77.
Thibaut, 157, 158.
Thiers, 104.
Thomas, A., 123.
Thomas, M., 112.
Thomaschule, 242.
Tichatschek, 261, 263, 266.
Tieck, 185.
'Times,' The, 281.
Tintoret, 27, 34
Titian, 85. 306.
Titurel, 260.
Toccata (Schumann's), 157, 160.
Töpken, 159.
Torquato Tasso (Goethe's), 22.
Tourguénieff, 71.
Traumerei, 218.
Treatise on Instrumentation, 117.
Trial of Mr Handel, 162.
Tristan und Isolde, 59, 129, 145, 239, 274, 284, 285, 288, 290, 305, 317, 321-322.
Triumphs of Oriana, 65.
Troubadours and Trouvères, 5.
Troyens, les, 121, 122, 129, 130, 137, 188, 234.
Turner, 7.
Tver, 181.

U

UHLAND, 193, 194, 217.
Urio, 30.
Ursulines, Convent of the, 74.

V

VAISSEAU Fantôme, 259, 263.
Valentino, 80.
Vampyr, Der, 183.
Vanderdecken, 253.
Velasquez, 34.
Venice, 157.
Verdi, 47, 59, 114.
Verhulst, 178, 184, 195.
Vernet, Horace, 93, 96, 255.
'Verzweifle nicht im Schmerzensthal,' 189.
Vestale, La, 266.
Vienna, 110, 169, 176, 177, 186, 190, 196, 197, 239, 242.
Vigny, Alfred de, 71.
Villanelle, 138.
Vinet, 53.
Vita Nuova, 43.

Vitality, principle of, meaning, 22; test, 24; want of genuineness in bad art, 25-6; coincidence, quotation and plagiarism, 26-32; conclusion, 32.
Voigt, Henrietta, 164, 203.
Volksblatte, Die, 271.
Volkslieder, 5, 26, 35, 222.
'Vom Pagen und der Königstochter,' 194.
Voss, 150, 202.

W

WÄCHTER, 263.
Wagner, Richard, birth, 240; education in Dresden, 241; returns to Leipsic, 242; studies Beethoven, 243; friendship with Laube, 243-244; studies with Weinlig, 244-245; visit to Vienna, 246; chorus master at Würzburg, 246; Die Feen, 247; Das Liebesverbot, 248-250; Madgeburg, 249; marriage, 251; director at Königsberg, 251; Rienzi, 252; departure for Paris, 252; meets Meyerbeer, 253; failure in Paris, 255-259; Faust Overture, 257; Flying Dutchman, 258-259; Rienzi accepted at Dresden, 260; return to Dresden, 261; production of Rienzi, 263; of the Flying Dutchman, 264; Spontini, 265-266; production of Tannhäuser, 266-267; Rienzi at Dresden, 268; politics, 269; Lohengrin, 270; revolution at Dresden, 271-272; second visit to Paris, 273; settles at Zurich, 273; Lohengrin at Weimar, 274; friendship with Liszt, 274-5; Das Judenthum in der Musik, 275-278; Libretto of the Ring, 278-279; Rheingold and Walküre, 280; first visit to London, 280-284; Tristan, 284; third visit to Paris, 285; failure of Tannhäuser at Paris, 287; return to Germany, 287; Meistersinger, 288; summoned to Bavaria, 288; Cosima von Bülow, 289; retires to Lucerne, 290; Eine Kapitulation, 291; death of his wife, 291; marries Cosima von Bülow, 291; birth of his son, 292; Siegfried Idyll, 292; Theatre at Bayreuth, 292-293; second visit to London, 293; Parsifal, 294; visit to Palermo, 295; production of Parsifal, 295; visit to Venice, 296; death, 296.
Wagner as a dramatist, theory of the Music Drama, 300-307; indifference to absolute music, 307-308; gradual advance, 309; early operas, 310-311; aria parlante, 312-315; leit-motif, 315-317; the Ring, 318-321; Tristan, 321-322; Parsifal, 322-323; Meistersinger, 323-324; conclusion, 324-326.
Wagner as a critic, principles, 301-304; estimate of preceding composers, 324-325.
Wagner and Berlioz, 121, 141, 283-284, 286.
Wagner and Schumann, 185, 190, 250.
Wagner, illustrations from, 6, 12, 25, 31, 44, 52, 55, 59, 63, 71, 75, 85, 129, 141, 212.
Wagner, Albert, 246.

Index

Wagner, Frau, 257, 261, 288-289, 291.
Wagner, Joanna, 266.
Wagner, Rosalie, 242.
Wahnfried, 295.
Waldscenen, 206.
Waldstein, 41, 48, 58, 100.
Walküre, 59, 279, 280, 283, 284, 311, 315, 319, 320.
Walpurgisnacht, 165
Walt, 204.
Walt Whitman, 19.
Warum, 43, 205, 218.
Wasielewski, 152, 191, 193.
Waverley overture, 83, 141.
Weber, 50, 97, 145, 151, 185, 201, 211, 225, 239, 242, 257, 266, 267, 293, 307 310.
Weihnachtsalbum, 205.
Weimar, 108, 151, 188, 191, 256. 272, 274, 275.
Weinlig, 244, 245, 307.
Wesley, S. S., 65.
Widmung, 35, 220.
Wieck, 154, 158, 159, 161, 165, 167, 168, 171, 178.

Wieck, Clara, 154, 159, 160, 162, 166, 167, 168, 172, 217.
Wieland der Schmied, 284.
Wielhorsky, 181.
Wiener Musikalische Zeitung, 160.
Winckelmann, 53.
Wohltemperirte Klavier, 27.
Wolfram von Eschenbach, 260.
Wordsworth, 30, 231.
Wult, 204.
Würzburg, 246, 248.

Z

Zampa, 246
Zauberflöte, 35, 88, 239, 313.
Zeitschrift für die Elegante Welt, Die, 244.
Zeitz, 152.
Ziska, 192
Zuccalmaglio, 183, 239.
Zurich, 108, 273, 278, 279, 280, 284.
Zwickau, 150 151, 152, 160, 184.

THE END

COLSTON AND COMPANY, PRINTERS, EDINBURGH.

www.ingramcontent.com/pod-product-compliance
Lightning Source LLC
Chambersburg PA
CBHW020247240426
43672CB00006B/661